# POETRY IN GENERAL

LITERATURE NOW

LITERATURE NOW

Matthew Hart, David James, and Rebecca L. Walkowitz, Series Editors

Literature Now offers a distinct vision of late-twentieth- and early-twenty-first-century literary culture. Addressing contemporary literature and the ways we understand its meaning, the series includes books that are comparative and transnational in scope as well as those that focus on national and regional literary cultures.

Keegan Cook Finberg, *Poetry in General: How a Literary Form Became Public*

Jennifer Scappetone, *Poetry After Barbarism: The Invention of Motherless Tongues and Resistance to Fascism*

Alexander Manshel, *Writing Backwards: Historical Fiction and the Reshaping of the American Canon*

Glenda Carpio, *Migrant Aesthetics: Contemporary Fiction, Global Migration, and the Limits of Empathy*

John Brooks, *The Racial Unfamiliar: Illegibility in Black Literature and Culture*

Vidyan Ravinthiran, *Worlds Woven Together: Essays on Poetry and Poetics*

Ellen Jones, *Literature in Motion: Translating Multilingualism Across the Americas*

Thomas Heise, *The Gentrification Plot: New York and the Postindustrial Crime Novel*

Sunny Xiang, *Tonal Intelligence: The Aesthetics of Asian Inscrutability During the Long Cold War*

Jessica Pressman, *Bookishness: Loving Books in a Digital Age*

Heather Houser, *Infowhelm: Environmental Art and Literature in an Age of Data*

Christy Wampole, *Degenerative Realism: Novel and Nation in Twenty-First-Century France*

Sarah Chihaya, Merve Emre, Katherine Hill, and Jill Richards, *The Ferrante Letters: An Experiment in Collective Criticism*

Peter Morey, *Islamophobia and the Novel*

Gloria Fisk, *Orhan Pamuk and the Good of World Literature*

For a complete list of books in the series, please see the Columbia University Press website.

# POETRY IN GENERAL

## HOW A LITERARY FORM BECAME PUBLIC

KEEGAN COOK FINBERG

Columbia University Press
*New York*

Columbia University Press
*Publishers Since 1893*
New York   Chichester, West Sussex

Copyright © 2025 Columbia University Press
All rights reserved

Library of Congress Cataloging-in-Publication Data
Names: Finberg, Keegan Cook, author.
Title: Poetry in general : how a literary form became public / Keegan Cook Finberg.
Description: New York : Columbia University Press, [2025] | Series: Literature now | Includes bibliographical references and index. |
Identifiers: LCCN 2025013076 | ISBN 9780231219211 (hardback) | ISBN 9780231219228 (trade paperback) | ISBN 9780231562584 (ebook)
Subjects: LCSH: Political poetry, American—History and criticism. | American poetry—20th century—History and criticism. | American poetry—21st century—History and criticism. | Poetry—Social aspects—United States.
Classification: LCC PS310.P6 F57 2025 | DDC 811/.54093581—dc23/eng/20250531

Cover design: Julia Kushnirsky

GPSR Authorized Representative: Easy Access System Europe, Mustamäe tee 50, 10621 Tallinn, Estonia, gpsr.requests@easproject.com

FOR ANDY

# CONTENTS

INTRODUCTION
1

1. ASSIMILATING THE ARTS: POETRY AND DIFFERENCE
IN YOKO ONO'S INSTRUCTIONS
20

2. FLUXUS SCORES AND THE BUREAUCRATIZATION
OF EVERYDAY LIFE
39

3. "I DO THIS I DO THAT": COLD WAR SPATIAL POETICS
AND THE NEW YORK SCHOOL
67

4. FEMINIST PROCEDURE AND DURATIONAL CONSTRAINT:
REPRODUCTION, WELFARE, AND "LOSING MYSELF"
95

5. DOCUMENTAL POETRY AND THE PRIVATIZATION
OF INTERPRETATION
126

CODA
151

*Acknowledgments 169*
*Notes 175*
*Bibliography 217*
*Index 239*

# POETRY IN GENERAL

# INTRODUCTION

Letters, narratives, and instructions about U.S. wars in the Middle East that employ vocabulary created by the Department of Defense; a family archival project that also reprints botanical illustrations from museums and manuals about Indigenous and colonial Guam; oral histories, photos, and government descriptions of the Korean Demilitarized Zone; an explanation of the official guidelines for how people should conduct themselves at the Standing Rock protest camp alongside a rewriting of a congressional resolution.[1] The previous list contains four brief descriptions of books that are all considered poetry. In fact, it describes exemplary, even dominant contemporary poetry in the United States; each of these books has been a finalist for the National Book Award for Poetry since 2016. They are archetypal models of poetry, and they are also interdisciplinary books. Each of the poetry projects in my list performs distinct functions, but their technique is similar: they all enter bureaucratic, archival, and governmental systems to usurp their tools, ultimately refracting and critiquing U.S. public forms.

*Poetry in General* will trace the history of these types of poetic entanglements with institutions and government apparatuses to suggest that the category of poetry expanded in the second half of the twentieth century to respond to changes in notions of the public. This is a simple assertion that nevertheless animates a way of thinking about poetry and public life that diverges from recent trends in poetry studies. Instead of focusing on how poets engage a public audience or on how contemporary deviations in engagement might differ from previous types or theories of poetry, I claim that poetry becomes "general" as the category takes structures that are bound to state facilitation of capitalism, policy, and rationality as its subject and its fodder. The term "general" here serves a twofold purpose. First, it refers to the interdisciplinary turn in poetry as art reached a phase of dematerialization and could no longer be assumed to fall within categories like "painting" or "sculpture." And second, "general" pertains to the common, as constitutive of a public, where a public is in flux and shaped by state power.

This double sense of "general" characterizes the aesthetic and political stakes of my argument; I am discussing interdisciplinary poetry that is preoccupied with the public and interacts and intervenes with its various forms. For example, take Jena Osman's *Public Figures* (2014), a record of the many points of view of the public statues of Philadelphia.[2] Osman begins by photographing and writing about what the statues see or what scenes they gaze upon. Most of these figural statues are carrying weapons—explorers with swords and war heroes with muskets—and Osman's book ultimately documents state violence that is otherwise unnoticed or eclipsed. The book reprints drone transcripts found on YouTube, and by transforming public records of events to poetry, *Public Figures* exposes and interrogates privatization and privatizing technologies, including military and police violence, figurations of the nuclear family, property of wealthy estates, and even education as a dwindling common good. *Public Figures* was part of a wave of poetry that illuminated mechanisms of privatization through the use of multiple types of media. Documental poems, or poems about, in, or made of the public, were not new, but they became ubiquitous around 2014; conversations about them sped up and took on new urgency in the postrecession context in the United States.[3]

Issues of the public—what it is made of, how it signifies, and where it is—were in the air in the early 2010s. In the University of California (UC) system, where I was studying at that time, tuition had skyrocketed because of state disinvestment. In the fall of 2009, in response to the latest round of fee increases, enrollment cuts, layoffs, furloughs, and increased class sizes, students waged a series of protests across the UC system, including the occupation of a graduate space called "the commons" at UC Santa Cruz. This tactic of occupying privately owned "public" property became commonplace a couple of years later with the international Occupy Movement, which brought attention to ever-more privatized wealth. Most meetings that I went to were using various forms of consensus-based decision making. It felt like publicness meant something different—people were changing private spaces in its name—and communal life was transforming. Experimental literature was taking on these subjects widely, in genres and media that were not immediately recognizable but would be categorized as poetry. Poets like Osman were writing about and talking about public spaces and ways of belonging in very explicit ways and were also restructuring their own relation to any conception of a literary public sphere. In *Ursula or University*, a memoir-manifesto-poem about poetry institutions and what activities count as labor, Stephanie Young writes about this preoccupation with publicness as a material fact of the poetry community, not only the subject of the poems: "And then something about the house, how the readings, what felt like the most exciting readings, and the friendliest, increasingly moved into private, into the semi-private house. . . . How the reading went from being terrifyingly public to terrifyingly private, but documented in a kind of semi-public of the Internet."[4] This interest took place within poetry publics and communities and also in poets' assessment of how poems relate to the social contexts that produce them. Some poets were reproducing whole public archives for a small readership, others were reproducing private archives for a larger poetry institution, and many were mixing these forms.[5] Conversations about publicness, surveillance, personhood, and the problems with official records or monuments were urgent at this moment, and what counted as poetry was transforming on a large scale to pictures of statues, transcripts, captions, and instructions, first in experimental circles and then beyond.

Was twenty-first-century poetry becoming more public or more private? In the context of the hyperprivatization of the early twenty-first century, "public" was no longer a clear political or aesthetic category. What do the longer histories of multiple processes of privatization do to the category of poetry, and how might these shifts signal a way to periodize poetry? Certainly, poetry has always taken in aspects beyond its supposed and sometimes narrowly conceived literary purview, but from the 1960s to the present, it has done so in ways that question its relevance and place as a public form.

I argue that the interdisciplinary capaciousness of contemporary poetry has its antecedents in poetic responses to transformations in the state's relationship to a public, from the height of the hierarchized welfare state to the privatization and hypersegmentation of neoliberalism. As Craig Dworkin succinctly describes the phenomenon, "Something I find very interesting about the category of poetry in the 20th and 21st century is that it's so generously capacious. It takes things in."[6] For some time, the category of poetry has been "taking in," or comprehending worlds outside aesthetic confines.[7] Poetry's capacity for "taking in"—implicating publics through interdisciplinary means—began about 1960, at the height of the welfare state. Over the next sixty years, through multiple degradations of and changes to what constitutes the public in the United States, poetry has become voracious, incorporating more and different types of material. This heterogeneous body of interdisciplinary poetry that responds to notions of the public from the 1960s to the present is the subject of this book.

The term "public" will do some heavy lifting in these pages, where I employ it at the convergence of several discourses. It is a slippery concept, with a necessarily rich definition, and a term that has brought confusion. I use "public" to signify both the aesthetic and materialist concerns of the commons and how the commons interact with state support. As Nancy Fraser notes, the phrase "the public sphere" often conflates at least three analytically distinct things: the state, the official economy of paid employment, and multiple arenas of public discourse.[8] Fraser proposes that the description of multiple networked public spheres would be a more appropriate model of critique for existing democracy—she is writing in 1990—and that these publics would need to include the interests that masculinist ideology has labeled "private." Writing about our contemporary moment, Kathi Weeks illustrates that "public" categories like work are simultaneously privatized, individualized, and subordinated to property rights, even if work is a public liberal social relation and an ultimate site for the exercise of political power.[9] Weeks, Fraser, and other scholars will animate specific instances of "public" in the chapters that follow, but my key term, "public forms," attempts to fathom this moving target throughout. By "public forms," I mean structures that are bound to the state facilitation of capitalism, policy, and rationality; public forms are also methods by which poets contend with language that has been privatized by modes of specialization, mystification, and barred access. For example, some of the varied public forms this book will examine include instructions, memos, courtroom transcripts, banking statements, and diets. The term "forms" brings together the aesthetic and political concerns of these structures as they are used in poems.[10] In this sense public forms include multimedia projects that are bound to and speak to the public.

Poetry as a public form brings together a large range of interdisciplinary material. For example, without this frame, it might not be clear how Ken Friedman's "Mandatory Happening" (1966) is related to Jena Osman's *Public Figures*, or even how it is a poem. Yet I will argue that poetry of the 2000s resonates with interdisciplinary writing from as early as the 1960s that is also preoccupied with notions of a public, and that it is helpful to put them in the same category. On May 1, 1966, around midnight, Friedman went around knocking on doors at Shimer College in Mt. Carol, Illinois.[11] When someone answered the door, Friedman handed them a small paper that read:

> You will, having looked at this page,
> either decide to read it or you will not.
> Having made your decision, the happening
> is now over.[12]

Later that year, after Friedman left Shimer to collaborate on interdisciplinary Fluxus endeavors in New York City, the Fluxus impresario George Maciunas designed a card for the event with the name "Mandatory Happening." The card was placed inside a box with a picture of Uncle Sam who wants you "for a mandatory happening."[13] "Mandatory Happening" engages notions of the public as only poetry can do; even though it is a "happening," its "event" is reading. It captures a crucial aspect of reading and discovery: The reader has already read the word "mandatory" when they find out that what they are doing is mandatory. Furthermore, they have no chance to decide because, by the time the reader has read that there is a decision to be made, the decision has been made. In other words, the joke of the happening is that it is only meant to be read.

Through this immediacy of address so present that it is suddenly past, "Mandatory Happening" takes notions of the public as its subject and, like Osman's work, it presses on what is and is not evident in any given instant. If Friedman knocked on your door around midnight, you might think about the military draft; you might think about racial and sexual violence. The knock on your door is occurring within the context of U.S. ascendancy and expanded social welfare in spite of—because of—ongoing global violence and the sedimentation of assimilative immigration policies. The war in Vietnam was escalating, and the United States was announcing record casualty numbers each week. If you are sleeping at midnight or perhaps doing homework, you might not be thinking about global violence through a U.S.-sponsored agenda for freedom. You were probably aware, however, that all around you raged what Christine Hong has called the "covert domestic wars" of racial profiling and racial discrimination.[14] The American suburbs were growing wealthier as a modern American middle class was fashioned by increasingly disadvantaging Black people and other people of color through various local and state zoning laws.[15] By donning benefits based on the category of employment status, the federal government held up a social welfare system that privileged a white, male subject and disadvantaged most everyone else.[16] As manufacturing increased around the world, the United States was deindustrializing and turning to an economy more reliant on white-collar labor.[17] And this was a peaceful era of increased satisfaction, wealth, and growing availability of commodities for some.

Friedman's and Osman's poems undertake poetry as a public form, and both point to the centrality of state violence to the public. Yet their varying poetics also highlight separate historical formations of the public. "Mandatory Happening" spoofs the bureaucracy of its moment. It does not bring its reader directly into history, just further into their own "now," their situated identity and geographical coordinates, the public of the instruction. Friedman's public forms are index cards and the administrative imperative, and his poem somewhat playfully mimics an administrative resistance to the myriad structures of Uncle Sam. Much later, Osman illuminates what might be otherwise unseen, interpreting and holding space for what has been eclipsed entirely by privatization. She inserts histories—even reiterating and recycling historical texts—that otherwise have no place in the smoothly segmented sectors of the present. Her postrecession poetics respond to the academicized enclosure of intellectual and artistic life.

The question of why and how the category of poetry became so capacious shapes the contours of this book because the process is tactical, changing in historical instance and with shifts in policy and rationality. I argue most broadly that this expansion of poetry into the arenas of work, property, and politics runs in tandem with shifts in the government's relationship to the economy. I show how poetry transforms its function in response to the degradation of the social democratic notion of the public in the United States after the midcentury, an era often regarded as the apex of the U.S. social welfare state. During this period of institutional and governmental change—first toward an age of "affirmative action for whites" that further transferred wealth and privileges to white cis-male Americans, and eventually toward privatization and public austerity for all as a means to augment and maintain this previous transfer—poetry became a capacious force in the arts because it could speak directly to the category of the public.[18] The book tracks interdisciplinary poetic forms in relationship with changes in government policies about scientific management, health care, housing, and corporations. These changes tell the story of an evolving consensus about work and leisure that make up the state's facilitation of capitalism, which intensifies and sediments racial and gender inequity in the second half of the twentieth century.

### INTERDISCIPLINARITY AND GENERALITY

To tell both the aesthetic story of the expansion of the category of poetry and the political story with which it is in conversation, I look to how interdisciplinarity, or disciplinary expansion, is theorized across multiple fields. In addition to a description of the poetry that I have been discussing, "interdisciplinarity" refers to knowledge-producing practices that are a signature intellectual trend of the Cold War period. This trend is closely tied with the military-industrial-university complex and recently has been shown to live a rich existence beyond the 1960s.[19] The poetry that I discuss is an epistemological project that is in conversation with knowledge-producing academic disciplines such as history, law, geography, and economics, domains that are shaped by this interdisciplinary trend and that explicitly study public forms.

One explanation of interdisciplinarity trends speaks directly to epistemological projects like the poems that I study here and their relation to political economy. Critics across philosophy, literature, and the arts have theorized the midcentury shift to white-collar labor in the United States— or the move to administration rather than production of commodities— and the corresponding turn to aesthetic abstraction or bureaucratization in arts and culture.[20] One suggestion is that, due to dematerialization in both an aesthetic and economic sense, works of art no longer adhered to disciplinary boundaries like sculpture, poetry, or painting. The hallmark of dematerialization for plastic and visual arts is "the linguistic turn," or the trend toward works of art that consist of language. And yet, abstraction is not the whole story. While cultural categories like art dematerialize as capitalism bureaucratizes in the West, all forms of material life continue here and elsewhere. As Gayatri Spivak puts it simply, "To buy a self-contained version of the West is to ignore its production by the imperialist project."[21] In more recent writings, Spivak speaks to Western abstraction in all forms: "Finance capital, the abstract as such, cannot operate without interruption by the empirical."[22] As I think through the movement of poetry to "take in" in the United States (the focus of this book), I am vigilant of the fact that much of the material being transformed into poetry is produced via hyperexploitation.[23] For example, in the pages of *Poetry in General*, I discuss transcripts made by unnamed gig workers (chapter 5), dehumanizing work and welfare practices (chapters 2 and 4), and various modes of displacement and disinvestment (chapters 1 and 3) as part of the process that this poetry engages and illuminates. I draw from postcolonial and ethnic studies scholarship to keep these processes in view through the smooth maneuverings of American administration, the liberal discourse of rights and wealth, and the systems of white supremacist value that obscure them.

Within literary studies, the label "poetry" has become a catchall for abstract works in language that also reach across media and disciplines. As disciplinary and media boundaries degraded and transformed, sometimes this work is also called "experimental literature" or "avant-garde poetry," but those terms as not as useful for my purposes because they explicitly exclude what might be already canonized, traditional, or normative. Instead, the category of poetry is widening, and in its voracious capacity, it is a cipher for my complex questions about abstraction, materiality, and social life. I consider the expanding nature of what we deem poetry, what is sometimes studied as the site of formal excess or artistic extremity, to bring together political and aesthetic concerns.

The short title of this book, *Poetry in General*, captures these interests. In part, the phrase "in general" comes from an art historical theory of the turn toward dematerialization and disintegration of disciplinary boundaries: what is called a period of "art in general." This concept and its stakes are clearly illustrated in a published conversation between art critics as they discuss the reception history of Marcel Duchamp's readymade in the West in the 1960s.[24] In this conversation, Thierry de Duve suggests that the debate about media autonomy in the art world led to a "general" category of the arts shortly after, just as Duchamp's work was more widely celebrated. He explains, "Art in general became possible. Most people take that for granted. To me it is still startling that you could be an artist without being either a painter or a sculptor or a musician or a poet or an architect or a playwright or whatever. An artist in general. 'What is your profession?' 'Oh, I'm an artist.'"[25] De Duve theorizes the model of "art in general" in this conversation and somewhat in *Kant After Duchamp*, and then expands it in a series of essays for *Art Forum International* in 2013 and 2014.[26] However, he does not explore what this "generalness" means for work or social belonging (both of which are clearly at stake given his initial illustration of a conversation about professions) and only briefly touches on how media capaciousness is shaped by and shapes political economy.[27] De Duve and other art historians use the term "general" in relation to aesthetic intermedia and multimedia practice (as opposed to a particular or partial practice), a sense of the word that is important to my consideration of interdisciplinarity.

To account for the complexity of the processes of interdisciplinary abstraction, I also use the term "general" in a sense that evokes its definition as pertaining to the common, as constitutive of a public, and where public is in flux and contested by state power.[28] The term "general" comes from the Latin, Anglo-Norman, and French to mean, at least in part, a reference to a class of the public or even the formation of a jurisdiction or deliberative body. My emphasis on publicness within the word "general" has a polemical aim to show how, as some public forms degraded, poetry spilled into ever more areas of public life and into multiple media and disciplines. For example, my last chapter will show how poetry can simultaneously interpret the specialized language of legal documents and create accessible spaces for this interpretation. This connection between generality and hierarchization or stratification of the public hews to the etymology of "general" more largely; *generalis* came to be used in contrast to *specialis* in Classical Latin, and so too in English and many other Romance and Germanic languages where we think through "genus" and its subset, "species." We hear this echo as we fathom all classes and groupings, from "genres" of literature to "genders" of people.[29]

In art history and studio art (where the term "genre" is not in the lexicon), the words "discipline" and "medium" are often interchangeable. In that discourse, medium signifies material. In this book, when I discuss poetry moving between media, I also mean a process of moving between disciplines. However, I do not wish to claim that medium and discipline are synonyms here because this book does not discuss either as isolated, static phenomena.[30] For me, the term "interdisciplinarity" signifies this very attention to the process of multiple-media activity. The works I study here take forms from one discipline and pull them into or onto another. The term "poetry in general" captures the process of poetry's interdisciplinary formation while also thinking with scholars who have productively mapped poetry as a genre.[31] Here, I will trace poetry (genre, generally) through instructions, lists, diet regimens, and particular legal and financial records (media).[32] Yoko Ono calls one version of the refraction of the genre of poetry through various forms of media "assimilating the arts." Bernadette Mayer calls another version of it an intention "to record special states of consciousness," where "special" means "change, sudden change, high, low, food, levels of attention." M. NourbeSe Philip calls it a "recombinant antinarrative" of "the story that can't ever be told." Each poet that I will discuss employs language as an activity that moves between and through disciplines to fathom a public. One of the things I like about poetry as "general" rather than poetry as "genre," per se, is that it so completely signifies the discourse, both as it is and as it does.

---

Poetry in general is a process and a formal category—works in language that also incorporate other disciplines and move through media—that responds to the state facilitation of capital in the postwar era in the United

States to variously resist, neutralize, and interpret polarized and punitive conditions. By naming and charting the category, *Poetry in General* exposes how theories and activities of interdisciplinarity are politically charged and impact our understanding of "public" and "private" arenas like work, leisure, race, and gender.

To clarify how poetry in general is related to these categories and to political economy, I use the term "racial capitalism," which comes from an expansive, multidisciplinary body of scholarship that limns how racism, war, and liberalism are imbricated in capitalist accumulation.[33] In brief, "racial capitalism" points to structures of capitalism that privilege certain forms of life and labor by imposing various forms of death on others.[34] This modality is elaborated by my first chapter, in my discussion of Yoko Ono's instructions that thematize the effects of post–World War II imperialism on work and identity formation. In this chapter and throughout the book, along with "racial capitalism," I use the term "neoliberalism" to indicate "a form of governmental reasoning" that develops and intensifies this racializing philosophy as an economic theory characterized by "strong private property rights, free markets, and free trade."[35] As Candice Amich describes, neoliberalism is not just a mechanism of upward wealth distribution, privatization, and a mode of rationality but also a "redistribution of the sensible" that is registered in our bodies as it criminalizes mutual caretaking and social welfare.[36] Amich's extension of both David Harvey's and Wendy Brown's account of neoliberalism—blending Marxist and Foucauldian approaches—clarifies the stakes of embodied practices as a site of poetry that I discuss here. For example, in chapter 4, I analyze the documentation of Bernadette Mayer, Eleanor Antin, and Adrian Piper's bodies undergoing hunger regimes in response to the criminalization of abortion and welfare services. Poetry's generalness grapples with forms of partiality, precarity, and publicness under racial capitalism and neoliberalism, attempting to speak directly to both the moment of "uneasy peace" following World War II and the post-Keynesian response to a crisis of accumulation that governs state's policy involvement in capitalism and shapes daily experience.[37]

The story of the U.S. state's facilitation of capitalism moves with the category of poetry that I trace: the 1960s brought a suite of Keynesian policies and trends that supported an uneven—racialized, Westernized—notion of "the public" through ongoing and morphing urban renewal, white flight, and suburbanization. The degradation of this perforated public sphere brought workfare and corporatism of the late 1960s and 1970s, during and after which the U.S. economy restructured to favor finance. In my attempt to chart poetry's expansion, which includes its interdisciplinarity and abstraction, as in part an imperialist phenomenon, the book travels from versions of global capitalism that require violence (chapter 1) to the burgeoning American suburbs (chapter 2), to the spaces of the churning metropole (chapter 3), to projects that attempt to materialize state processes that manage food assistance and education, forms that are sometimes thought to serve the common good (chapters 4 and 5). In sketching these moves through poetry in general, my book does not purport to be an exhaustive or chronologically complete tale of the second half of the twentieth century. Rather, by exploring particular contours of public life (labor practices and immigration aimed at productivity, suburbanization and commodification, urban renewal and privatizing architecture, welfare and abortion regulation, corporatizing education policy) *Poetry in General* offers an examination of how poetry usurped the tools of a key set of policies that shape the period. Unlike many books that tell a story of neoliberalism and the development of racial capitalism in the twentieth century by looking to the 1970s and 1980s as key moments, my book lingers on the long 1960s, disentangling the tendrils of liberalism and following their reach up to the bust-and-boom fiscal crisis that marked the end of the century.

The 1960s process of deindustrialization, deskilling, administration, and neoliberal versions of "human capital" that obscure and abstract labor do not make work disappear. Rather, the shift to white-collar work and bureaucratization that occurred after World War II intensifies work for most people as it seamlessly disguises the machinations of capitalism. Leigh Claire La Berge calls this truth—the fact that people must work longer and harder as wages are diminished—"decommodification," which she argues, becomes dominant in the 1970s.[38] La Berge examines artwork that is socially engaged after the early 1970s to contend with how art operates within and against the need to be paid for work. Likewise, Shannon Jackson, Helen Anne Molesworth, and Julia Bryan-Wilson examine the preoccupation with work in the 1970s and after; Bryan-Wilson dubs this type of art "occupational realism," a contemporary category of art in which artists perform unpaid work to think through systems of precarity.[39] I begin my study earlier than theirs, noting that it was the 1960s that brought art and work together in forms so similar that they have been called the "administrative aesthetic," dematerialized, indexical, and managerial. In other words, in the 1960s, language-based art and work began to mirror each other and indeed borrow from each other's conceptual framework. At this moment, in a newly deindustrializing economy, poetry takes in the scientific management systems of Taylorism and post-Taylorism: the memos, bullets, and lists of the office. The poetry of this archive works within and against the systems of racial capitalism that lead to decommodification of the 1970s and sowed the seeds for a crisis in welfare of the 1990s and beyond.

In addition to sketching a history of work, the book tracks other throughlines and fissures in the story of U.S. state policy affecting welfare. For example, another current running through the book is reproductive rights and abortion care. Abortion providing and receiving is rendered clearly in these works as central to liberation, autonomy, and the public good. Just as with questions of immigration (chapter 1), suburbanization and urban renewal (chapters 2 and 3), state politics of abortion are tied to patriarchal notions of family and care that serve the aims of capital accumulation.[40] Chapter 4 focuses on three poems written on the precipice of *Roe v. Wade* (1973) that consider the lack of access to abortion alongside dehumanizing aspects of Aid to Families with Dependent Children (AFDC) and food assistance programming. Chapter 5 examines an act of legislative and extralegislative protest against antiabortion bills on the precipice of *Dobbs v. Jackson* (2022), as reproductive care became increasingly restricted at the state level. Situating Counterpath's abortion rights poem, which reproduces a filibuster using the hypergigified work of a "human intelligence task" program, in this current allows a consideration of abortion care alongside privatization of education through debt and bureaucratic forms of racial capitalism in the early 2000s.

Taking into account these fissures and unevenness in the history of state policy affecting health care, welfare, and work, the poetry I study here still tells a somewhat chronological story. Fluxus poets (Yoko Ono, George Brecht, and others) and the New York School poets (Frank O'Hara, Kenneth Koch, Amiri Baraka, and others) illustrate techniques of corporatization by utilizing spaces—for example, privately owned "public" spaces and the organizational methods of bureaucracy—as their poetics.

Fluxus scores tell us "to do" things on index-sized cards; Fluxus contracts and lists grapple with burgeoning scientific management theories of work, immigration policy, and even new landscapes of suburbia. Similarly, New York School poet Frank O'Hara's poetics catalogued "I do this I do that" against the backdrop of urban renewal and within privatizing architectural spaces. Putting together techniques of abstraction, confession, and instruction, this expanded category of poetry makes space for exchange and coalition building within poetic production.

After the optimism of 1960s coalition building had dampened, and expansionist politics were tempered by inflation and rising neoconservatism, poetry paradoxically embodied attempts at direct resistance. The second part of the book continues to trace poetry as the category that makes legible otherwise unseen political movements and political failures as they relate to notions of a public. In the 1970s, as forms of privatization affected women in particular, resistance to diminishing welfare and restrictive health services was central to feminist discourse emerging at that time. Widening the category of procedure and constraint to include an array of feminist works—from body art to procedural poetry—that use constraint-based processes to probe sociopolitical conditions, the category of poetry in general suggests a single site of resistance to interrogate several types of government regulation of bodies. Duration-based constraints like the documentation of hunger within a timed physical diet (Eleanor Antin, Adrian Piper) and recording of states of consciousness about food (Bernadette Mayer), critique restricted abortion access and stigmatized welfare services simultaneously through remaking the cisgender feminine body.

The last part of the book focuses on poetry in general that illustrates and critiques the academicization of poetry and criticism in a growing higher education economy. Responding to the solidification of neoliberalism by the 1980s, this poetry directly interprets, by way of absorption, public and semipublic documents of atrocities and failures. In the early 2000s and 2010s, degree-granting programs were sold as a ticket into both the world of creation and interpretation of poetry. Techniques of conceptual poetry and documentary poetics are embedded in this paradigm, a vision that interpretive models have been increasingly rarefied outside universities. The projects I examine revise debates about art's autonomy by explicitly commenting on the privatization of interpretation, showing how it occurs within and outside academic and digitized spaces. The poetry of an important legal case for abolition retold (M. NourbeSe Philip), the dialogue of an eleven-hour filibuster to thwart antichoice legislation (Wendy Davis), and credit documents from the 2008 recession (Mathew Timmons) reveal public ways to read, interpret, and mourn ongoing racial capitalism in the afterlives of slavery, antiabortion legislation, and mass debt.

---

Along with this introduction, chapter 1, "Assimilating the Arts: Poetry and Difference in Yoko Ono's Instructions," illustrates the theoretical concepts behind "poetry in general" by connecting debates about media autonomy and interdisciplinary art to theories about the work of the nation-state. This dialectical relationship of art to politics is poetry in general, and naming the category helps to identify shifts in liberal rationality with a model of resistance in mind. I take the poetry of Fluxus member Yoko Ono to provide a crucial but previously ignored theory of how interdisciplinary art intervenes in philosophies of immigration, labor, and renewed forms of racial capitalism after World War II. I focus on Ono's "instructions" written between the United States and Japan, and her book *Grapefruit* (Tokyo, 1964), which has previously confounded literary and arts genres but is most often read as a performance log. When read as a work of poetry, *Grapefruit* critiques global capitalism, parodies emerging neoliberal labor practices, and creates reading structures to resist capitalist market logics. Considering her references to the bombings of Hiroshima and Nagasaki and the Americanizing of postwar Japan in light of Keynesian liberalism, my argument suggests that Ono's instructions forge a connection between media philosophy and theories of difference. *Grapefruit* illustrates not only the limits of arguments about "pure" media but also the assimilationist politics inherent in notions of media blending or "arts in general," which was central to Ono's Fluxus milieu. Ono's philosophy of overlapping arts rather than intermixing arts—her contention that intermedial poetry is not a "fusion" of media but a "gathering" of it, "like as many flowers"—indicates that coalition building against racial liberalism relies on a nuanced philosophy of difference.[41] This antiassimilationist art and political theory suggests honoring difference through interdisciplinarity and coalition building, a philosophy that illustrates how art and racialization are tied to theories of labor and the state.

Chapter 2, "Fluxus Scores and the Bureaucratization of Everyday Life" draws out the theory that instructions are a unique category for establishing "poetry in general" by examining the Fluxus score. These instruction-based texts produced en masse and globally from 1959 to 1966 are rarely read outside the disciplines of art history, music, or performance studies, but when they are read as poetry, they provide a means to explore interdisciplinary enactment that becomes crucial to the category. These scores are meant to be read, but their realization or performance is implied, which gives them a complicated ontological status. This status, and the attention it requires, I argue, mirrors the logic of corporatization and the separation of office work from domestic life. Focusing primarily on a box of event cards, *Water Yam* by George Brecht (1963), "Fluxus Scores" illustrates how the infiltration of corporate tools like physical handbooks, manuals, memos, catalogs, to-do lists, and mandated affective rituals suggest vibrant spaces outside white-collar and pink-collar logic and reason. I show how *Water Yam* probes the space between the simultaneous rise of office work and suburbanization. *Water Yam*'s fodder is the commodity cultures that furnish commutes, homes, and corporations, and its scores—and whether and how to perform them—expose these cultures' ties to racial capitalist policies.

Like the Fluxus scores that implore their reader to "do" something, which I examine in my first two chapters, early New York School poetry chronicles a poet narrating, "I do this I do that." Traveling from the suburb back to the city, the poems I examine in chapter 3, "'I do this I do that': Cold War Spatial Poetics and the New York School," use forms of several key architectural sites in New York City (including its suburbs) and the romantic imaginary of Paris to unravel dominant structures of nationalism, racial liberalism, and homophobic urban practices. I discuss *Locus Solus*, a short-lived journal that represents the most unified voice of the New York School of poets. My reading of *Locus Solus* shows how the magazine itself (1) enacts the creation of an active, plural, and participatory space in print and (2) shows how play with real space (New York and Paris sites) participates in philosophies of geopolitical containment, expansion, penetration, and renewal with Cold War conceptions of cultural ascendency. The chapter continues with an examination of Frank

O'Hara's poetry about modernist skyscrapers—the Seagram Building, in particular—to provide an extensive example of the characteristic of New York School poetry to figure codes, designs, and real spaces of the city not only as a depiction of a sensorium but a guide for political and aesthetic engagement.

Chapter 4, "Feminist Procedure and Durational Constraint: Reproduction, Welfare, and 'Losing Myself,'" examines the relationship between legal constraints on bodies and the legacy of procedural feminist form. Speaking directly to the tightening of welfare and health services in the United States, especially those affecting women, literature and art that uses constraint as a public form exposes alternatives to capitalist and patriarchal notions of gender. The chapter explores techniques of procedure and constraint in writing by Adrian Piper, Bernadette Mayer, and Eleanor Antin from 1971 and 1972 that centers hunger as resistance. As scholars of neoliberalism have shown, in feminist liberation discourse emerging at that time, "the public sphere" came to denote anything outside the domestic sphere, and the female cisgender body was often the site of discussions about state censorship, indenture, or commodification. Constraints like the documentation of starvation or dieting (Adrian Piper, Eleanor Antin) and mapping states of consciousness surrounding food and hunger (Bernadette Mayer) illustrate and critique restricted mobility as the debate to legalize abortion took center stage. Each of these projects are interdisciplinary in their own way, incorporating photography and performance as well as historical records and lists made public. My focus on constraint as public resistance shows that poetry in general remakes how we think of the relationship between bodies, language, and spaces. Forms of procedure and constraint map out material spaces that illustrate how bodies are shaped by multiple social constraints that are not otherwise in conversation.

I then turn to the early 2000s, a moment that some consider near total saturation of the U.S. neoliberal project, and explore poetry that employs interdisciplinary public forms to neutralize the work of the state. Chapter 5, "Documental Poetry and the Privatization of Interpretation," examines poetry that reframes and interprets public and semipublic materials. Techniques of rewriting and repurposing documents, which have become ubiquitous in twenty-first-century poetry, furthered the post-1960s rematerialization of forms and expanded what counts as poetry to a vast array of material. Following Michael Leong, I call this work, which cuts across multiple taxonomies in contemporary poetry, "documental poetry," and I closely examine three book-length examples from the early financial recession: M. NourbeSe Philip's *Zong!* (2008), a rewriting of the 1783 English legal case involving the murder of 150 enslaved people onboard the *Zong* ship; *Let Her Speak: Transcript of Texas State Senator Wendy Davis's June 25, 2013, Filibuster of the Texas State Senate*, a script of the dialogue of an eleven-hour filibuster to thwart antichoice legislation (2013); and Mathew Timmons's *CREDIT*, which documents credit offers from the 2007 economic bubble and rejections from the 2008 crash (2009).[42] By reinscribing atrocities and failures through moving texts between public and private boundaries created by academic and semiacademic institutions, these poems offer a close look at the privatization of poetry and its interpretation. I argue that, by posing questions of livelihood through material and genre concerns, documental poetry rehashes debates about art's autonomy. However, instead of enacting a total absorption of the art object into representations of capital (as documental poetry's critics claim), these projects comment on how arts funding and government policies affecting higher education have reoriented the relationship between interpretation and the public. This poetry is seemingly more privatized, and yet the poetry maintains the space of public archiving and parsing, an offering of a general, albeit small, public good.

In the coda, I consider the role of institutions in poetry in general in our moment, examining several projects that partake in institutional critique of academia and academic culture but also gesture more widely to the relationship and practice of poetry to public life. Recently, scholars have focused their attention on the institutions that create and sustain poetry—academia and alternative academic and public intellectual spaces—with a pointed lack of attention to experimental practices like constraint, collage, and multimedia poems, focusing instead on the institution of the lyric or on the rise of "lyric theory." Even when attending to the avant-garde, there persists a critical blind spot about poetry that engages public forms. Far from trying to redeem documental or conceptual writing as such, I attempt to use helpful conclusions from recent scholarship about literature and institutionalization—and the way that poetry has created certain forms of criticism and interpretation within and outside academia—to illustrate that the ongoing world of documental poetics is one place where particularly useful types of institutional expression emerge. Current documental poetry critiques the insular, dehistoricized rise of debt-accumulating MFA programs to bring poetry into intellectual, social, and material life of the university and beyond. I end by briefly examining poetry by Lena Chen, Holly Melgard, and Vanessa Jimenez Gabb that looks like public criticism as it performs critique and repair.

By positing that poetry is uniquely positioned to speak to the state's facilitation of capital, *Poetry in General* provides a politically charged and versatile definition of the form. My attempt to theorize the role of poetry in the political landscape and in everyday life comes from my love for and awe at its workings. Far from a transcendent medium that will lift us out of poisoned systems—and even further from the actions or action plans that will recover those systems—the material that I study here attempts to figure the general, open, collective, and public. In sputtering fits and starts, and in ways that I hope this book will illuminate, it sometimes does just that. With wholeness and heart, poetry in general aesthetically renders social and political life as possible, as an interdisciplinary public form.

# 1

## ASSIMILATING THE ARTS

Poetry and Difference in Yoko Ono's Instructions

In what she called a "footnote" to a lecture and performance at Wesleyan University in 1966, Yoko Ono addressed the philosophical issues of overlapping arts media and identities. Differentiating her work from "Happenings," which were long nonlinear performances becoming popular in Tokyo and New York, she offers an artist's statement as a philosophy of difference:

> People talk about happening. They say that art is headed towards that direction, that happening is assimilating the arts. I don't believe in collectivism of art nor in having only one direction in anything. I think it is nice to return to having many different arts, including happening, just as having many flowers. In fact, we could have more arts "smell," "weight," "taste," "cry," "anger" (competition of anger, that sort of thing), etc. People might say, that we never experience things separately, they are always in fusion, and that is why "the happening," which is a fusion of all sensory perceptions. Yes, I agree, but if that is so, it is all the more reason and challenge to create a sensory experience isolated from other sensory experiences, which is something rare in daily life. Art is not merely a duplication of life. To assimilate art in life, is different from art duplicating life.[1]

Ono's repeated use of the word "assimilate" for the growing together of the arts is loaded: Ono's background made her interested in issues of cultural assimilation in both the United States and Japan.[2] The daughter of a wealthy banking family, Ono lived between the two countries her whole life. At the start of World War II, the family moved back to Japan because of growing anti-Japanese sentiment in the United States. First, they lived in Tokyo during the firebombing, and then Ono moved to the countryside for the duration of the war, where villagers made fun of her for being Americanized. Shortly after the war, Ono settled in the United States permanently, although her adult life in the 1960s was punctuated by trips to Tokyo.

Several years before her Wesleyan lecture, as Ono was creating instruction art that bridges artistic media categories, the question of which immigrants could achieve cultural assimilation was a preoccupation of sociological public discourse in the United States.[3] When Ono gave her Wesleyan lecture in January 1966, the 1965 Hart-Celler Act, an immigration act that abolished the national origins quota system that favored northern Europeans, had recently been signed into law. This national origins system was repealed based on reports that concluded that all ethnicities were equally "assimilable," despite previous suggestions that people from Asian and African countries were less likely to assimilate, or, as the U.S. President's Commission on Immigration and Naturalization put it, less likely to make "satisfactory adjustment to the American scene" and therefore should be limited in number.[4] The 1965 law repealed overtly racist exclusions to instead instate a system that privileged certain classes and occupations based on the supposed needs of the U.S. labor force. A preference for scientists, engineers, and doctors brought an influx of Asian immigrants to the United States, beginning what many argue was a new manifestation of anti-Asian racism.[5]

When Ono critiques a conversation about assimilation, I suggest that readers recall not only interdisciplinary blending in the art world but also the cultural project that seeks to homogenize racial and ethnic difference in favor of capitalist forms that obscure and exploit them. This valence of "assimilation" invokes issues central to Ono's work: relations between the United States and Japan as they were shaped by policies built on the management of difference through economic and labor-based modes. The word "assimilate" echoes Ono's experience as an immigrant and nods toward American racism against Japanese people in particular during and after World War II. In this light, a political theory of identity becomes visible; this passage from Ono's footnote to her lecture-performance suggests that it is most possible to honor the strengths of singularity by a practice of intermixing but not fusing culture.

Encapsulating Ono's aesthetic theory in addition to her art's political possibility, this passage also enters a robust contemporaneous conversation in the art world: debates about artistic autonomy and absorption. Arguing that a turn to interdisciplinarity may be "assimilating the arts" and that this process is related to the act of "assimil[ation] of art in life," Ono speaks against the arguments of critics like Michael Fried and Clement Greenberg that interdisciplinary artwork degrades individual media specificity.[6] She is against any program that would flatten her notion of various hybrid identities, which exist "like many flowers" inasmuch as they have togetherness but never "one direction." "Happenings," interdisciplinary public performances, that Fried or Greenberg would argue damage the arts that they incorporate, like painting or theater, are, for Ono, actually the artworks most suited to isolating and deepening those very independent media.[7] She continues, "But returning to having various divisions of art, does not mean, for instance, that one must only use sounds as a means to create music. One may give instructions to watch the fire for 10 days in order to create a vision in ones mind."[8] In this last argumentative turn, Ono makes reading central to her artwork: the process of combining art practices that also respects discrete identities—or sensations—happens best through reading instructions.

Interpreting Ono's work this way highlights a political and aesthetic philosophy that intervenes in previous debates about modernist media autonomy, illustrating not only the limits of arguments about "pure" media but also the assimilationist politics inherent in notions of media blending or "intermedia," which was central to Ono's Fluxus milieu.[9] Ono's philosophy of isolating identity through overlapping arts illustrates the potential of refusing both approaches and instead insists on a dialectical relationship to politics through reading instructions.

My interpretation of Ono's assertion in this lecture-performance footnote—and the expanded philosophy of her instructions—carves one path for the category of poetry in the rest of the century and beyond. Although Ono's instructions have previously confounded literary and arts genres, here I suggest that Ono's emphasis on a particular type of reading allows for a fruitful categorization of her instructions as poetry.

And when her instructions are read as poetry, they engage capitalist fictions about race and immigration through an attention to changing labor practices and changing publics in the United States and Japan. *Poetry in General* begins with an extended examination of the work of Yoko Ono to illustrate how debates about media autonomy and intermedial art are tied to the nation-state's strategies for managing capital. Her instructions provide a crucial but previously ignored theory of how interdisciplinary art intervenes uniquely in philosophies of immigration, labor, and renewed forms of racial capitalism after World War II.

This chapter attends to Ono's book *Grapefruit* (Tokyo, 1964) and works written between the United States and Japan in the 1950s and 1960s. I illustrate how, while setting a path for the category of poetry, *Grapefruit* critiques global capitalism, parodies emerging neoliberal labor practices, and creates reading structures to resist capitalist market logics. As Ono scholars have noted, many of her instructions reference the bombings of Hiroshima and Nagasaki and the Americanizing of postwar Japan under a U.S. constitution. Instead of putting these instructions within a framework of trauma or destruction art, however, I use "poetry in general," which offers a theory of how racialized and gendered bodies remake the public through usurping its tools. This frame affords Ono's instructions the imperative to differ from Ono's verbal declaration of her political commitments, which have been various, ambivalent, or vague over the years.[10] I draw a throughline between *Grapefruit*'s attention to neocolonialism, labor management systems in postwar Japan, and burgeoning global neoliberal rationality as part of the matrix of racial capitalism.[11] Ono's work offers a critique of genre and a theory of difference that anticipates later approaches to coalition building in feminist and ethnic studies. For example, her instructions are in conversation with models of difference and interdisciplinarity that have been picked up in the last decade by scholars who see minority social movements in the 1960s and 1970s as central to shifting institutional technologies of power.[12]

Within these pages, I animate the definition of "poetry in general" and limn its theoretical stakes via a reading of Ono's instructions. *Grapefruit* begins a lineage of material that will include other Fluxus artists writing in the imperative mode, but also, for example, Frank O'Hara chronicling his day, Adrian Piper making contact with her physical appearance in the mirror, and Mathew Timmons redacting his bills and advertisements. Each of these works are poetry in general because they identify shifts in liberal rationality with a model of public engagement as resistance in mind.

## POETRY IN GENERAL AND *GRAPEFRUIT*

What sort of poetry is telling someone to "watch the fire for 10 days"? Ono called work of this kind that makes up *Grapefruit*, "instructions," "events," "scores," or "pieces." In the same "footnote" I quoted above, she writes, "Event, to me, is not an assimilation of all the other arts as Happening seems to be, but an extrication from the various sensory perceptions. It is not a getting togetherness as most happenings are, but a dealing with oneself."[13] Art like this probes models of aesthetic interdisciplinarity to explore how national projects to reimagine race through capitalist fictions are central to "dealing with oneself" or to considering identity. Although this process of considering identity centers the comprehension of texts, it is active and public.

To illustrate what I mean by "public" in this instance, I must periodize the 1964 edition of *Grapefruit* with an attention to genre. Coming at a moment when interdisciplinary works were challenging conventions in the arts, Ono's book *Grapefruit* offers an opportunity to bridge current academic disciplinary divides. As a text from a gallery artist and musician, it invites the methodology of literary scholarship to politicize debates about media autonomy in art history. At the same time, it brings notions of action into the realm of poetry, which is still often imagined to be a singular, private activity. Ono has borne the brunt of racist misogyny both in the popular eye and in art historical and literary studies scholarship. Working between and beyond nation and genre as well as between and beyond accepted gender expectations, Ono hit a sensitive nerve. When she was taken seriously by the art world—even if her reception in popular culture was wildly unfair—her work from the 1960s was frequently studied as protofeminist or protoconceptual art. These readings often ignore the racial, cultural, and linguistic aspects of her instructions to focus on performance. Recently, critics have been readier to connect her early artwork to the violence of both the Vietnam

War and World War II, and in the last twenty years or so, Ono's art of the 1960s has gained warmer popular and scholarly attention.[14] However, the difficulty of balancing Ono's life story, her aesthetic contribution, and her politics has created siloed areas of study in the arts; until some very recent scholarship, *Grapefruit* was frequently neglected by both the poetry world and the art world.[15]

The 1964 edition of *Grapefruit* is a book of instructions mostly in English that also uses the Japanese language. The instructions are divided into the sections "Music," "Painting," "Event," "Poetry," and "Object." It is substantially different from the 1970 version in English, which was published by Simon and Schuster, despite the fact that they are often conflated.[16] Putting the 1964 edition in its proper context is important both because of its position as a piece of bilingual literature and because the years following *Grapefruit*'s publication would bring the height of the period that art critics have called the era of "arts in general" or the "dematerialization of art."[17] Ono's work fits this genre of "arts in general" because the "general" notion of artworks is most apparent in action-based, performance, and participatory art of the period, categories that a work like *Grapefruit* invokes.

It is important to note that, although the description of "arts in general" came to characterize experimental work from the 1960s New York scene—and scores like Ono's came to be emblematic of Fluxus art—Ono had been working with notions of event before the 1960s. She can be credited with the very first "event" as artwork. "Lighting Piece" ("light a match and watch till it goes out") was written and performed in 1955, and "Secret Piece," which instructs readers to play a note "with the accompaniment of the birds singing at dawn," was written in 1953. Both works were compiled in *Grapefruit*, but despite the central importance of *Grapefruit* to the zeitgeist, Ono's work is not often considered part of this philosophical turn; even within Fluxus, a group otherwise known for its inclusivity, she was often bullied or excluded.[18]

Putting *Grapefruit* at the center of this interdisciplinary moment in the 1960s illuminates it more clearly. As theorist Thierry de Duve explains about interdisciplinarity of the sixties, "To me it is still startling that you could be an artist without being either a painter or a sculptor or a musician or a poet or an architect or a playwright or whatever. An artist in general. 'What is your profession?' 'Oh, I'm an artist.'"[19]

In the introduction to this book, I pointed out that de Duve's suggestion of how "professions" are reorganized is crucial; this period of generality is intricately tied to changing labor practices and new class formation. Further explicating this quotation here, I will note that de Duve's performative interplay of overheard conversation illustrates that the trend toward interdisciplinarity of the 1960s is theatrical and participatory. What's more, his explanation, which consists of overheard conversation as performance, draws on the history of poetry. Because poetry is an intimate address meant to be overheard, as the adage about lyric claims, it has always raised questions about what constitutes the public and private spheres.[20] De Duve's illustrative artist exists within a poetic mode of address—performatively "to" someone by way of "overheard" readership—created between "the public" and "the private" in 1965, when these very categories were becoming increasingly contested. With the assimilationist project as the backdrop, U.S. conservatives began to represent the state as a coercive force against individual freedom, and Keynesian liberals and leftists began to use "the public" as shorthand for an interest in guaranteeing access to all.[21]

Linking arts "in general" to methods of reading poetry, Yoko Ono's *Grapefruit* engages changing labor practices and changing publics, an engagement that is inextricable from Ono's interdisciplinary experiments with reading. Reading *Grapefruit* allows us one lens through which to see that this larger turn toward reading and enactment was a response to anxieties about both media autonomy and changing national models of economy and identity. Ono's instructions show how "arts in general" shapes the category of poetry as well. When discussing literature—and poetry in particular—notions of midcentury reading are usually constructed around ideas of a private or even antitheatrical activity, what is considered "modernist reading" or even "good reading."[22] As many scholars have shown, modernist reading is invested in the entrenchment of the familiar liberal categories of public and private.[23] At the same time, however, reading is an integral part of experimental and participatory arts in the twentieth century; these experiences of reading are just not usually classified as poetry or thought of as literature. Keeping the valence of "general" that includes the commons and its interactions with the innerworkings of the state is important here because it seats Ono's work as socially engaged.[24]

Reading Ono's scores as poetry illustrates the multiple registers of what she calls assimilation; as the instructions move between arts media, they also acknowledge the violence undergirding national economic and racialization projects. For example, "Blood Piece," a score that appears in the painting section, meditates on the difficulty of achieving a singular art (rather than what Ono calls a "fusion") through impossibilities of bodily participation:

> Use your blood to paint.
> Keep painting until you faint. (a)
> Keep painting until you die. (b)
>
> 1960 spring[25]

Although it is impossible by normative standards of performance duration, over the course of an entire lifetime, an artist could theoretically perform the entire score. Or the lack of lettering after the first line could indicate that the second two lines are choices—a performer can choose to follow path (a) or (b). These musings on how—or if—the score should be performed are created by the verbal pun on the "pain" in "painting." By literalizing the pun, "Blood Piece" shows the futility of realizing pure (or unassimilated) painting and opens questions of readerly participation with impossible instructions. The score draws attention to bodily cycles, duration, the limits of genre or medium, and the limits of labor (should the performer faint or die from doing the work?).

It is through an extended pause with the text that we come to these conclusions. The piece almost enforces this type of attention through its difficulty as performance. It's hard to pass over it quickly, yet at the same time it troubles this familiar category of attention toward poetry in its impulse toward painting. "Blood Piece" makes a strong statement about the impossibility of realizing the work as instructed while working within a poetic mode. It also points to the difficulty of inhabiting any space or genre permanently (we must use poetry to explore the duration of painting, for example) and to the ethics of work (if I'm not willing to perform the score, then who is?). It's important to note that, in *Grapefruit*, these instructions are interspersed with other pieces that are easier to perform (hammer a nail into a mirror; light a match; count the wrinkles on a stomach). Because they sometimes call us to act, they make us think about reading as a more expansive process, using and moving beyond the categories that modernist close reading allows.

Engaging in this active process reveals *Grapefruit* to be a political text, exemplative of a theatrical element of reading that becomes increasingly definitive in experimental poetry of the period. Ono shows that dominant midcentury accounts of art and literature that pit theatricality against absorption—public against private—do not work here. Despite their clear relationship to performance, these works require reading, the very model of absorptive activity, according to polemical accounts of medium specificity in art history.[26] Likewise, the literary critical accounts of reading that separate poetry from the public sphere and from political change cannot hold up against such theatrics. Over the next four chapters, I explore works by George Brecht, Frank O'Hara, Amiri Baraka, Eleanor Antin, Adrian Piper, Bernadette Mayer, M. NourbeSe Philip, Mathew Timmons, Vanessa Jimenez Gabb, Holly Melgard, and Lena Chen that follow in the wake of Ono's work.

My commitment to reading these texts "as poetry" is partly a response to what I see as the impoverishment of that category as it has been constructed since modernist formulations. As a critical conversation about media specificity and art practices came to define modernism, experimental work became obsessed with emplaced legibility.[27] Many arguments about modernism, and about the avant-gardes specifically, attend to works like Fluxus scores as artworks or performances rather than as texts, thereby excluding them from critical conversations about reading, but my tactic takes the rise of language-based participatory work as signaling a political possibility of procedural reading. By reconfiguring arguments about the end of media specificity more broadly, this change also signals the end of a sort of closed-genre poetry, codified by various theories of experimental writing, modernism, and New Critical reading methods. Despite wanting to read Ono's work—and the other works in this book—as poetry, I am not interested in pointing out the formal similarities between these scores and more traditional poetry, although this could be done easily. I contend that, if read with the procedures that we use to read poems, Ono's instructions can activate the category in ways that serve to broaden both interdisciplinary modernist studies and theories of modern poetics. This requires attending to these works as written documents, although we know that event scores on the page should not be thought as fixed complete texts.

Circulation and reading practice are inextricable—performative and public "events" of the time are interpersonal and quiet when they are mailed or printed as instructions in a book. Ono sometimes mailed her instructions (mail art was the main conduit of dissemination for many Fluxus members), and international small Fluxus presses like Beau Geste and Something Else Press were part of a larger trend in emergent global networks of readership.[28] In the case of *Grapefruit*, despite producing only five hundred copies in 1964, Ono sent birth announcements to an international group of artists proclaiming the arrival of the book alongside pictures of her newborn baby. *Grapefruit*'s "birth" happened to coincide roughly with Tokyo hosting the Olympics, a feat that was meant to showcase Japan's full recovery from World War II and its subsequent economic prosperity.[29] Ono was in Tokyo at this time (she lived in Tokyo from March 1962 to September 1964 before returning to New York) and, because she was interested in nationalist spectacle, she set up a small stand in the midst of promotion for this premiere global cultural event in order to peddle her book.[30] This combination of the gendered metaphor of production through the art of the birth announcement and her liminal participation in nationalist spectacle exemplifies some of the central preoccupations of *Grapefruit*.

## READING *GRAPEFRUIT*

Although Ono had been working on instructions through the 1950s, she did not previously publish them. She had been corresponding with George Maciunas, the founder and self-elected chair of Fluxus, about a publication of her complete works, but when Maciunas's disorganization and lack of funds made it seem like it might not happen in a timely fashion, Ono published it herself in 1964 in Tokyo by means of a small press she called Wunternaum. During the phase before publication, *Grapefruit* underwent several modes of presentation and circulated through multiple media in addition to meditating on fusion and isolation within the work itself.

Although they were written in the English language, Ono's texts from this period were often first created within a Japanese context.[31] The Japanese context for the scores is crucial not only because of Ono's personal experiences during the war, experiences that directly inspired her scores but also because the scores reflect the larger political climate in Japan. The Allied occupation lasted from 1945 to 1952, the later part of which violently imposed an agenda of antiliberal and antileft ideals.[32] The Cold War Americanized Japan—when the occupation was over, the Japanese were left with a U.S. constitution and a security treaty that kept a large number of U.S. troops on Japanese soil—and it brought rapid economic growth. The period coinciding with the Cold War was later referred to as the "economic miracle," or Japan's "miracle economy," and 1964 was the acme. Tokyo hosted the Olympics to demonstrate this wealth (for example, with the display of the Shinkansen high-speed train) and also to demonstrate to the world how westernization shaped Japanese culture. Writing about the arts festival at the Olympics, Noriko Aso explains that "the vision of Japan represented [in the ancient arts exhibition]—homogenizing, purportedly inclusive yet elite centered, asserting an independent stance that was nevertheless tilted toward the United States and away from Asia—served at once to strengthen mechanisms of domestic mobilization and to reaffirm the position of Japan in the international order born of the Cold War."[33]

Japanese culture was affected not just by increased Americanization and wealth accumulation but also by major changes in the ideology of labor, manufacturing, and production. After Japan's defeat, General Douglas MacArthur's headquarters, which oversaw the occupation of Japan, created several methods for overhauling industry, including training programs in scientific management run by the Civil Communications Section and the Japanese Productivity Center. These programs, created by American managers and adopted for Japanese workplace propaganda, emphasize small changes to improve efficiency and productivity at group and individual levels rather than as part of a totalizing plan based on innovation or on worker skill development.[34] Systems like lean production and Kaizen—a business term that can be translated to mean "continuous improvement"—changed the Japanese economy through a management philosophy based on personal responsibility from the lowest acceptable level. Built on philosophies that target the responsibility of individual workers, these types of strategies, which anticipate and later echo American neoliberal philosophy, became a standard for Japanese economic production and success.

Ono's *Grapefruit* responds to this combination of Japanese defeat, Americanization, economic boom, and change in labor. Like these scientific management programs, her book focuses on small changes and improvements, and although it ridicules notions of Kaizen as productive in a capitalist sense, *Grapefruit* also makes a link to the U.S. version of liberalism, which was moving into neoliberalism at this time. This set of concerns is apparent through a number of textual choices unique to the 1964 edition. Although most of the book is in English, every few pages opens to a spread of an English score on the left page with Japanese text on the right. Illustrating Ono's philosophy of resistance to assimilation, the scores in Japanese are not translated versions of the English scores that face them but rather different scores altogether (for example, scores in English in the "Music" section appear in Japanese in the "Event" section). In another bewildering touch, the Japanese scores are clearly translated versions of the English, but they differ substantially, often including extra lines and omitting examples or dates.[35] Ono further resists streamlined organization from the top by not numbering the book's pages. Lest one think that Ono's art performs a sort of lean production, however, she also challenges efficiency of any kind by writing the book title by hand on each copy in her initial print run of five hundred. To parody American nationalism, the book claims that it was copyrighted on the Fourth of July.[36] On its dedication page, it also cites many of the major players of the New York avant-garde as influences, marking Ono as a New Yorker within a particular milieu even while the scores in both English and Japanese reference forms of traditional Japanese culture.[37] An important part of *Grapefruit* is the going-between aspect of cultural and national identity; many accounts claim that Ono gave the book its title to show the hybridization of her cultures—at the time she believed a grapefruit to be a mixture of an orange and a lemon—and took it to be an analogy to her mixed sense of belonging. These markers heighten our awareness of the cultural moment of exchange and domination between the United States and Japan.

The textual history of *Grapefruit* further reveals its preoccupation with issues of efficiency, inclusivity, and agency. Many of these instructions began as what Ono calls "word spread scores," or instructions passed on by word of mouth. Some of them were written down for a solo exhibition in 1961 at George Maciunas's gallery, the AG Gallery, on Madison Avenue in New York City. The small show was an exhibition of paintings and drawings that ran for two weeks in the dark (Maciunas could not pay electricity bills). In a display of the mixture of cultural influences that interested Ono, the front of the gallery featured Ono's "instruction paintings," and the back showed her traditional Japanese calligraphy paintings done in sumi ink. When visitors arrived, Ono would show them around the gallery and explain the instructions behind each painting shown in the instruction area. For example, she would tell them that the oddly shaped canvas on the floor was "Painting to Be Stepped on" and that they were welcome to help make it. For "Smoke Painting," she invited visitors to burn part of the canvas on the wall and watch it smolder. Small notes with the scores written out were also affixed to these works. These pieces have been called destruction art, and if placed within the context of Ono's history—her family hid during the 1945 bombing of Tokyo, and she did indeed watch the city smolder—they meditate on how art is engaged in global political action.[38] This word-of-mouth method of conveying the work provided an auditory performance and a communal interaction; in this way, the scores are realized several times over—by concept, text, voice, or action that follows, and by the object resulting. In other words, her earliest pieces, although reliant on language, were deeply involved in questions of perception, the body, and community. A connection with her audience was crucial to the way she thought about her scores.

As Ono continued to live and exhibit her work in both the United States and Japan, her instructions would migrate between the English and Japanese languages. In her subsequent exhibitions, Ono included more written scores, a move that deemphasized the presence of the artist (once she even had her husband write the scores for her to remove herself even further from the process) and highlighted issues of unrealizability or impossibility.[39] As Thomas Kellein points out, the small innovation of unrealizability, or scores meant to be read (not performed or created in the gallery), was actually something of a boon for Maciunas and for

Fluxus.⁴⁰ It was economically helpful to all involved that, in 1962, Yoko Ono presented her work at the Sogetsu Art Center in Tokyo but replaced the paintings that had been on the wall at the AG Gallery with texts for people to read. It meant less expensive materials and no cost to move or install artworks; in sum, it meant less preparation and production time. Ono had developed a small but ingenious innovation within the Fluxus production process.

As we saw with "Blood Piece," Ono's art from this period has more to do with the impossibility of following instruction—and the possibility of creating procedural reading strategies—than expensive paintings. Scores like "Laugh Piece" (keep laughing for a week) and "Cough Piece" (keep coughing for a year) are straightforward instructions but impossible to realize. This impossibility is an important part of the object and the purpose of the art, even as it was a money-saving convenience for the Fluxus group. The oscillation between object and performance is an integral part of Ono's work throughout the 1960s, and the first edition of *Grapefruit* begins with a note to George Maciunas that explains, "Most of my pieces are meant to be spread by word of mouth, therefore, do not have scores ... word-spread pieces are not included in this text."⁴¹ Ono's scores can work like a game of "Telephone" to morph and change with personalities and misunderstandings. By hinting that there is something that readers cannot access, this letter deems the word-spread scores impossible to reify and therefore uncommodifiable (to Maciunas's chagrin). It also exposes a paradox of participation: readers should know that there is work they can never access.

By leaving the question open about whether or how we are to perform these works, *Grapefruit* asks more broadly whether participation or action is possible through reading, which echoes its major political inquiry about participation in a changing public sphere. We can see the action of arts media circulating or switching as a way of addressing these questions. The fact that there is no subject in the scores except the reading subject persuades readers into action.⁴² In this way, Ono is maintaining her own sense of community outside the community of the audience-reader that Maciunas has set for her. Her word-spread mode of circulation engenders an affective participatory experience of the gallery that is distinct from circulation of the market. *Grapefruit*'s revolutionary potential lives in this very multiplicity.⁴³

When *Grapefruit* circulates as a book, it is marked by these other modes of earlier and simultaneous circulation. In a Japanese context, the scores speak against efficiency, models of economic growth, and assimilation to a Western cultural landscape. Within an American context, the scores present a question of how one can participate in the public when the public is disappearing. As political theorist Wendy Brown writes, "As neoliberalism wages war on public goods and the very idea of a public, including citizenship beyond membership, it dramatically thins public life without killing politics."[44] Ono's work moves through national contexts to dramatize this conundrum of the displacement but continuation of politics, here defined as struggles over resources and values. Even Ono's earliest pieces questioned the boundaries of performance, the politics of the body, and what makes community.

In *Grapefruit*'s organization as a book, these preoccupations become even clearer. For example, the section headings of the book indicating genres do not necessarily describe differences in each section's content. A score in one section could just as easily appear in the next section; sometimes instructions do in fact appear in multiple sections in English and Japanese, respectively. Yet, despite the seemingly whimsical nature of the sections, in the midst of the coming together of all the arts or, as Ono calls it, "the fusion of all sensory perceptions," Ono, and other Fluxus artists of her milieu, organize their books by genre.[45] Writing about this trend of generic nominalism in Fluxus, Branden Joseph states the issue clearly: although Fluxus scores work to dissolve the disciplinary status of the object, they do "not imply that there [is] magically, no longer any such thing as a painting or a sculpture . . . [they do] imply . . . that the disciplinary and medium based distinctions traditionally handed down could no longer be received as ontological facts, or even mutually accepted conventions, but had to be reiterated in each instance."[46] In other words, genres still denote specific attributes. However, by reiterating the media in each instance, attention goes to the medium as much as to the "content" of the score. For Ono's work, this amplification or reiteration is about coalition, difference, and the possibilities that reading holds. In showing the impossibility of a distinct or monolithic medium or category, Ono emphasizes the centrality of reading to any art form.

In each section, Ono's scores stem from social and political contexts as well as comment upon them. Ono herself has said that her idea for instructions came from periods during the war, after the firebombing of Tokyo, when her family was starving, and she exchanged fake meal orders with her brother.⁴⁷ "Tunafish Sandwich Piece" is an illustrative example of the helpfulness of Ono's wartime story. It recalls the bombings of Hiroshima and Nagasaki by asking us to imagine the melting of "one thousand suns in the / sky at the same time" that shine for one hour and then "melt."⁴⁸ While recalling unprecedented destruction, it is also a cheery American meal order ending "make one tunafish sandwich and eat." It appears in the "Music" section in English and again in Japanese in the "Painting" section, invoking not only a plausible sandwich, or something to see, but also an impossible sound: the sound of thermonuclear threat and remembrance. Its simultaneity encapsulates what Christine Hong explains as the common American myth that the 1950s and 1960s were moneyed and cheerful, which fails to recognize "the potent imperialist concoction at the heart of military Keynesianism—the notion that U.S. war violence abroad stimulated universal prosperity, expanded social welfare, and democratization at home—within the lethality of Jim Crow."⁴⁹

I turn to one final piece from *Grapefruit* to explore a modality of racial capitalism that will echo throughout this book:

SUPPLY GOODS STORE PIECE

Open a supply goods store where you sell body supplies:

Tail
Hair
Lump
Hump
Horn
Halo
The third eye
etc.

1964 spring⁵⁰

Although it is obvious why this piece is categorized under "Object" (this one is in English only), it seems a dark take on the blazon form as the bodies of absent subjects are cut into pieces to shill. The odd diction of "supply," a word with etymological roots in plenty and abundance, illustrates that these bodily pieces are extra and to be displayed for potential supplemental use.[51] Just as the sections of the book show, in this particular piece, categorization is a generative process. Ono shows that the very losses and gains brought about by circulating through arts media, genre, and spaces are also the fluid or movement-bound aspects of identity and bodies. This consideration of bodily fusions remakes theories of media essentialism or purity, allowing distinct categories to be active singular forms while also creating combinatory identities or collectives. Here notions of reading poetry include durational quandaries, halos, and humps. By reading the scores as poems, we expose not only their localized cultural and ethical implications—the way they answer political and aesthetic concerns of the time or the way they interpret this moment of arts in general—but also the cultural and ethical concerns that surround this type of interdisciplinarity.

These notions of interdisciplinarity are often cordoned off from theories of political resistance or organizing, even if both are crucial to the category of poetry and its study. By now it should be clear that I think of interdisciplinarity and political resistance within the same paradigm. To come back to the beginning of this chapter, Ono does not "believe in collectivism" but she advocates for creation of "many different arts" coming together as "many flowers." For Audre Lorde, who delivered a speech entitled "Learning from the 60s" in 1982, the strongest coalition building in Black communities must be based in a mutual understanding of difference across race, class, and nation. Lorde explains, "In order to work together we do not have to become a mix of indistinguishable particles.... Unity implies the coming together of elements which are, to begin with, varied and diverse in their particular natures."[52] Lorde suggests strength comes from honoring difference. More recently, Grace Kyungwon Hong developed a theoretical paradigm based on an expansion of this notion. Hong uses the term "difference" to refer to a "practice that holds in suspension (without requiring resolution) contradictory, mutually exclusive, and negating impulses." She writes, "'Difference' names an epistemological position, onotological condition, and political strategy that reckons with the shift in the technologies of power that we might as well call 'neoliberal.'"[53] In 1964, Ono's hope "to assimilate art in life" by attending to difference through combination (rather than fusion) prefigures part of Hong's philosophy. Ono's poetics uses interdisciplinarity to expand notions of the public as they interchange between nations and to question what poetry can do for political action.

"Supply Goods Store Piece" is also about a store. It brings our attention to supply chains, goods, and logistics; the score creates a market category for body parts and animal parts, suggesting that they should be categorized and sold. Thus, some of the historical stakes of the political categories of "public" and "private"—the terms that scholars like Lisa Duggan argue are the master terms of neoliberalism and liberalism—emerge when we consider the way Ono handles "supplies." These terms hide stark inequalities of wealth and power and of class, race, gender, and sexuality across nation-states as well as within them. Duggan writes, "Inequalities are routinely assigned to 'private' life, understood as 'natural,' and bracketed away from consideration in the 'public' life of the state."[54] Ono brings previously naturalized as well as racialized and sexualized parts into public commerce, ultimately questioning distinctions between these categories. This move of making public and of cynically monetizing is a hallmark of the era as liberalism gives way to neoliberalism. As theorists like Wendy Brown have argued, this increasing marketization built a form of reason that configures all aspects of existence in economic terms. The score points out that we surely buy and sell our lumps and humps as part of living under capitalism, but we don't usually call it that. Furthermore, it is rare that we acknowledge our tails, horns, and halos—these magic animalized extensions, perhaps reminders of myths and exclusions based on gender and ethnic markers—while we are at the store.

These issues of the privatization of race and gender as well as increasingly marketized reason are carefully figured in Ono's "Supply Goods Store Piece," and they are important to think about in terms of the genre categories of *Grapefruit*; the genre categories are used to market and make public and also to explore and think beyond the very boundaries of marketable forms of reason. "Supply Goods Store Piece" demonstrates that dismemberment is at the center of commerce. Many instructions will not codify how to do the work or realize them; for example, "Blood Piece" exposes the inherent pain in doing work; "Tunafish Sandwich Piece" takes atomic bombing as an ingredient to an American meal. In these acts, Ono's scores evoke a central tenet of racial capitalism: that some are subjected to violence and death to add value to those granted the privilege of life. As Grace Hong explains, after World War II, "the mutually constitutive relationship between life and death—the fact that life for some must mean death for others—remains disavowed and thus unchallenged."[55] Or as Ono shows us in "Touch Poem VI," "Invite only dead people." Inviting dead people is necessary for the reproduction of those living. This relationship between value production and violence is apropos to *Grapefruit*'s position between Japan and the United States; Japan's economic and political success relied not only on a catastrophic military defeat but also on a U.S. martial order to establish economic management techniques and modes of state governance.

In *Poetry in General*, I wager that we can arrive at these conclusions through modes of reading and attention. Reading poetry in this case reveals that Ono's philosophy of difference is a practice that combats liberal logics, pointing out both overt racism and disingenuous "assimilation" in arts and culture. *Grapefruit* illustrates not only the limits of arguments about "pure" media but also the assimilationist politics inherent in notions of media blending or "arts in general." Refusing both approaches, *Grapefruit* instead insists on a relationship between politics and aesthetics that envisions coalition building and potential ways of combating the logics of racial capitalism. The other works that I examine within these pages likewise build complex systems of negotiation that reflect and manage the role of the transforming public sphere.

# 2

## FLUXUS SCORES AND THE BUREAUCRATIZATION OF EVERYDAY LIFE

This chapter illustrates how corporate tools and cultures of consumer capitalism develop in conversation with aesthetic form. In the years that the Fluxus score became a genre, the U.S. economy moved away from blue-collar production and toward an administrative, office-based version of labor. This change in political economy pushed creative production toward a new type of logic and a new look; during this period, "artwork becomes paperwork."[1]

Take George Brecht's "Word Event" (figure 2.1). Although it could be performed, like Ono's instructions, it is not merely performance, and thinking about it only as a script misses the mark. The page layout, title, and the suggestive temporality or narrative of "Word Event" would be lost in a theatrical performance of observing an exit sign, or announcing "exit," as one leaves the room, for example. (This would later become a popular score to perform at the end of Fluxus concerts to tell the audience that it was time to leave.) On the page, the card could be about the banishment of the subject, a character named Exit, even about the everyday performance of reading the word "exit." Through the title, the score points to "Exit's" inability to move, act, or create without being read—and this is the event. Brecht himself thought about the doors to and from rooms of his house in suburban New Jersey and considered himself constantly performing "Word Event." Like Ono's instructions that I discussed in my last chapter, "Word Event" holds the temporal structure of a command and

WORD EVENT

● EXIT

G.Brecht
Spring, 1961

FIGURE 2.1 George Brecht, "Word Event," *Water Yam* (notecard from box), 1963. University of California, Santa Cruz (UCSC), Special Collections. © 2024 Artists Rights Society (ARS), New York/VG Bild-Kunst, Bonn.

of an informational list. In this way, it suggests its own revision, expressing the various natures of iteration. Unlike most of Ono's instructions, however, "Word Event" recalls bureaucratic documents in its syntax and typography; bullets, the combination of handwriting and type, or different sized type, create the look and feel of a memo. Oddly, the condensed and elliptical nature of its form suggest the look of both office paperwork and poetry. This chapter will suggest that scores like this one spatialize white-collar labor by recalling the racialized process of suburbanization and cultures of office work. Here we see both the memo form and suburban doors activated in poetry. How do the spaces of the midcentury office—both the spatialization of white-collar work via suburbanization and the space afforded on the page by the memo form—activate poetry?

My last chapter examined Yoko Ono's *Grapefruit* in detail to show how interdisciplinarity is politically charged. I argued that reading *Grapefruit* as poetry in general illuminates a modality of racial capitalism and provides structures of coalition building for imagining otherwise. This chapter will zoom out to explore the role of instructions in the changing category of poetry and to put Ono's work in conversation with another book of instructions, George Brecht's *Water Yam* (1963). Instructions—or event scores, as George Brecht called this type of work—congeal and circulate moments of imperative reading, providing a method for rethinking genre to recontextualize questions of identity, political context, and aesthetic lineage. Bringing methods from literary studies to event scores shows how these writings play a role in the larger shift away from poetry as a genre removed from the public and into a "general" public currency of everyday life. Fluxus provides a method of examining interdisciplinary textual material that increasingly gets labeled as poetry in the second half of the twentieth century, due in part to shifts in capital.

*Water Yam*, like Yoko Ono's *Grapefruit*, is a text that compiled instructions, or event scores, pieces that also circulated by mail, in galleries, and through festivals or performances. While Ono's looks like a book, Brecht's, designed collaboratively with George Maciunas, is a box of cards of various sizes, none of them larger than an index card.[2] These types of instruction pieces (event scores) would become a hallmark of Fluxus, although the texts that make up the focus of this chapter—and the last—were created before Fluxus began to gain its reputation as a group.[3] Because of their publication and circulation, *Water Yam* and *Grapefruit* influenced many artists in and outside the Fluxus group to write events.[4] Fluxus artists would sometimes write their events in order to be performed, mailed, or displayed. However, in recalling the codex, these two collections assert that textuality is crucial to their projects, even if they suggest performance in the imperative mode.

As "artwork becomes paperwork" in this moment of white-collar boom, structures of work, property, and politics are forever changed. Bringing a class analysis to Benjamin Buchloh's argument about the "aesthetics of administration," Jasper Bernes concludes that 1960s artists engaged in this paperwork aesthetic were mimicking managers-in-name-only due to increasingly complex administrative structures. These manager-artists carried antagonism toward their work that sparked experimental forms that in turn shaped the workplace. *Poetry in General*'s central argument reflects my agreement that readers should recognize a reciprocal conversation between bureaucratic aesthetic form and increasingly administrative methods of labor rather than merely see white-collar office work shaping aesthetic possibilities. One of the places that Bernes and my argument diverges, however, is how to attend to language art marked by these forms. For Bernes, the language in administrative aesthetics is "information," which he suggests behaves like matter but is "not really material."[5] This notion that information acts as material because it requires a "series of techniques or processes: rearranging, sorting, cataloging, parsing, transcribing, excerpting," but is not *really* material stems from theories of conceptual art like Lucy Lippard's and Rosalind Krauss's as well as Buchloh's. Interpreting theories of "dematerialization" and "indexicality" to mean that language becomes information allows Bernes to call for less separation between art and poetry of the 1960s and 1970s as these categories become intertwined.[6] Yet adapting this art historical paradigm for examining language denies a number of literary critical questions like, "What is this text about?" or, perhaps more pedagogical and apropos, "What does this language do?"

My approach is to consider the material of these books—a familiar substance that is related but in fact separate from technological changes in flows of information—as poetry. In this light, the language of *Water Yam* becomes visible as poetry that attempts to understand the relationship between poetry and capitalism by taking cultures of capital as its subject.[7] Brecht's scores garner the category of the literary through their manipulation of form and format, and yet they end up looking like documents of white-collar capitalism. I contend that literary criticism—the work of answering questions that the scores pose about poetry's relation to cultures of capitalism—can illuminate most clearly how *Water Yam* is in conversation with postwar white suburban consumer culture and the language of bureaucracy. By hewing closely to the scores, I position their dialectical relation to information as characterized by Sianne Ngai's definition of the aesthetic of "interesting." Contrary to Bernes, Ngai argues that, although the administrative aesthetic mimics paperwork, it does not consist of information; rather, it is *about* information.[8] More precisely, it is an aesthetic about "the technologically mediated dissemination of information."[9] Ngai argues that a postwar understanding of information as difference means that the category of "interesting" is a meditation on the "tension between difference and typicality—or standardization and individuation—in capitalist modernity writ large."[10] Brecht's attention to the word "exit" on his door in suburban New Jersey versus exiting more generally—or, what I will later explain as an interest in form versus format—responds to a speedup in circulation, production, and consumption in the 1960s and also to policy and legislative changes that privilege certain types of work and infrastructure as the mark of a good life.[11]

The scores of *Water Yam* interrogate the spatial and labor politics implicated in the simultaneous boom in white-collar work and white suburban spaces. The suburb and the corporation are linked in Brecht's work as an administrative aesthetic is adapted to cultivate a particular domestic scene, probing what urban historian Kenneth T. Jackson has called the "privatization of American life" that characterized the era.[12] To illuminate Brecht's attention to forms of racial capitalism affecting the suburbs and the office, in the chapter that follows I will first sketch a history of the Fluxus score, a history that puts a preoccupation with corporate research, administrative labor, and records at its origins. Histories of Fluxus usually center on music or performance, but I argue it is more helpful to think of scores as records of—or poetry that depicts—the moments between work and life, domestic and office labor. To describe the moments between the public and domestic spheres, the scores showcase commodities and illustrate how they move.[13] This chapter's second section, "'An Endless Book': George Brecht's *Water Yam*," will illuminate how commodities relate to each other to animate both corporate and reproductive labor, and the horizons of a white, American suburban imaginary in the 1960s. In this section, I will compare Brecht's work to Gertrude Stein's *Tender Buttons* (1914).[14] These works, which both engage domestic spaces in what critics have described as abstract or even illegible language, were produced roughly fifty years apart, illustrating shifts in commodity form and relation. I will show how *Water Yam* remakes Stein's poetry of actions, lists, and events not to rid the world of nouns or objects, as Stein perhaps wanted to do, but to comprehend their movement.[15] Whereas Stein's text presses on cultures of imperialism, I will show how *Water Yam* probes the space between the historically simultaneous rise of office work and suburbanization in the United States. *Water Yam*'s fodder is the commodity cultures that furnish commutes, homes, and corporations, and its scores expose these cultures' ties to white supremacist, imperialist, and settler-colonial policies.

In comparing Brecht to Stein at the end of the chapter, I do not mean to argue that *Water Yam* is influenced by Stein's *Tender Buttons*, although it is not inaccurate to say so.[16] Rather, I contend that, by comparing a work that is more or less agreed upon to be experimental poetry to Brecht's genre-defying text, we are best able to see how *Water Yam* is imbricated in what makes up poetry in general. Brecht's repurposing of Stein reflects his interest in "what language can *do*." Brecht's event scores of the 1960s anticipate what Natalia Cecire refers to as a "white recovery project," when this idealization of action-oriented language, based on an interpretation of social-scientific knowledge that was bound to state violence and prototypical whiteness, was thought to act abstractly subversive.[17] In this case, *Water Yam* will crystalize moments of domestic and bureaucratic work together through shared commodities and the spaces between. Here, I hope to show that artwork becoming "paperwork," or even what Rosalind Krauss has called indexicality in the art world, is a topic fruitfully explored as part of poetry that develops in conversation with racial capitalism and a changing public sphere. Brecht's book mediates and abstracts both language of action and of representation to repurpose the discourse of the office and the suburbs in the service of poetry.

## HISTORICIZING FLUXUS: WHICH SCORES ARE READ WHEN AND WHY

To situate events and event scores as literary texts within their cultural and historical milieu, I must provide an abbreviated history of their beginnings. This story overlaps with the history of Fluxus because the event score has come to be its emblem for good reason. My telling differs from other historical accounts in its attempt to decenter both white avant-garde lineage and the supremacy of music.[18] As my last chapter explained, Yoko Ono was writing minimalist instructions that interrogated notions of Japanese immigrant assimilation to the United States and the effects of World War II as early as the mid-1950s. An early example is her "Lighting Piece," written and performed in 1955, which consists of the following instructions: "Light a match and watch until it goes out." She was writing what she saw as poetry meant to forge imagined possibilities or, as she would explain about a decade later, "one may give instructions to watch the fire for 10 days in order to create a vision in ones mind."[19]

George Brecht, a World War II veteran working as a chemist at Johnson & Johnson, became interested in chance-based artwork as "research" in the mid-1950s.[20] Brecht was inspired by Abstract Expressionism and Duchampian ready-mades, and he identified as either a sculptor or a painter but never as a musician.[21] He created chance paintings and other types of visual art as he developed his notion of event or event score while living in suburban New Jersey and lunching with other artist-researchers like Robert Watts and Allan Kaprow.[22] His notebooks show that his interdisciplinary art experimentation was not removed from his work developing patents as a chemist, and the New Jersey contingent of Fluxus artists moved between research and development corporations, universities, and the art world.[23]

Written by people from several geographically and philosophically diverse backgrounds, this type of short instruction poetry was developed and expanded through arts networks in New York, Tokyo, and several European cities. Brecht came up with the term "Event score," which—along with "event"—became known as a catchall genre for similar works of instructions. Like Ono's fire in the mind and Friedman's "Mandatory Happening," Brecht's works were meant to be read, and their performance was optional. As he writes in his notes, "the score is an event; so is finding an incident of it."[24] Brecht believed that the instructions he put on paper such as "Exit" were meant to happen, as he puts it, "in one's own 'now.'"[25] Tellingly, in an interview with Deiter Daniels, Brecht enigmatically avoids describing how to realize or perform particular scores, instead deferring to Daniels, sometimes asking how he would realize it.[26] This tactic situates events as part of a discursive formation that includes the language of the text and its relation to other statements, even offering the reader the privileged place of interpreter or critic.

As Fluxus developed a collective identity, Ono's and Brecht's work would be expanded and disseminated by way of performance festival. In 1962, Maciunas began to organize festivals for himself and his artist friends to perform for audiences in Europe. The first festival that was publicized under the name "Fluxus" was a month-long event in Wiesbaden, Germany, in 1962. As Fluxus member Dick Higgins recalls about that event, "the festival caused great notoriety, was on German television, and was repeated in various cities beside Wiesbaden.... If we were to be identified publicly as a group, should we become one?"[27] By 1963, artists like Allison

Knowles, Wolf Vostell, Robert Watts, Ben Patterson, and Dick Higgins had traveled and performed in many European cities—Denmark, Paris, Copenhagen, Amsterdam, The Hague, Dusseldorf, and Nice—under the name Fluxus or "Festum Fluxorum." The performances were all "event" based, although they looked like mayhem. As Higgins writes, "they were a beautiful mess."[28] Eggs were thrown, heads were shaved, pianos were chopped to pieces, pans were banged on for hours.

Although audiences may never have guessed it, these wild, seemingly spontaneous events consisted of the performers following instructions. For example, in Wiesbaden, the head shaving was part of Higgins's "Danger Music 2," which reads, "Hat. Rags, Paper. Heave. Shave." The egg-throwing score reads, "Work with butter and eggs for a time."[29] Their scores are one way that these events are distinguished from previous avant-garde events, like Dada. In the case of Cabaret Voltaire in the 1910s, where Dada began, performances were either depictions of a written piece that was not in score or instruction format, or impromptu pranks.[30] When it came to Fluxus events, the directions were often simple and minimalist, even if the performances were wild. As Brecht reflected years later in his "Origin of Events," a one-page, typed, mimeographed statement in the artist file at the Museum of Modern Art (MoMA): "Later on rather to my surprise, I learned that George Maciunas in Germany and France, Cornelius Cardew and Robin Page in England, Kosugi, Kubota, Shiomi in Japan, and others had made public realizations of pieces I had always waited to notice occurring."[31] For example, at "Neo-Dada in der Musik," a 1962 performance in Dusseldorf, artists wrote the word "exit" on a chalkboard. Brecht did not think of these performances as misuse of his event scores, but he also did not think of them as part of the work or a necessary end-goal. For him, noticing that he exited through a particular door in his house in New Jersey is just as much a realization of the score as the public chalkboard and just as much a realization of the score as the moment of reading it on a page.[32] "Drip Music (Drip Event)" (figure 2.2), was often performed with a ladder, a pitcher, and a bowl on stage. However, the "music" could just as easily be a leaky sink; an experiment with a burette, which Brecht designed as a first draft to the score; or the innerworkings of one of Brecht's tampon patents that he created for Johnson & Johnson.[33] A score like "Dresser" (figure 2.3) seems merely descriptive, but one can imagine several ways it could be performed, especially if

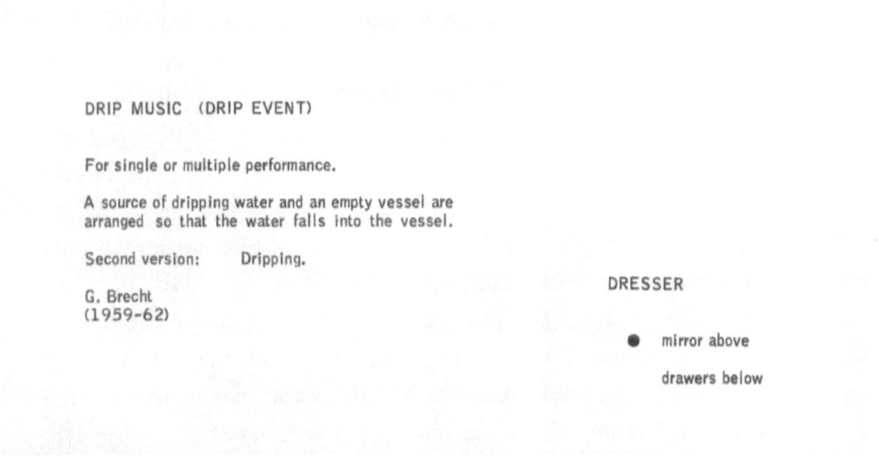

DRIP MUSIC (DRIP EVENT)

For single or multiple performance.

A source of dripping water and an empty vessel are
arranged so that the water falls into the vessel.

Second version:     Dripping.

G. Brecht
(1959-62)

DRESSER

● mirror above

  drawers below

FIGURES 2.2 AND 2.3 George Brecht, "Drip Music (Drip Event)," and "Dresser," *Water Yam* (two notecards from box), 1963. University of California, Santa Cruz (UCSC), Special Collections. © 2024 Artists Rights Society (ARS), New York/VG Bild-Kunst, Bonn.

the noun of the title could refer to either a person or a piece of furniture. Showing that the relationship between score and object could also (although more rarely) go the other way, Brecht sometimes found ordinary objects in his everyday life and called them "an object waiting to be realized."[34] The score, the object, and the object's relation to other objects would be realizations.

Stretching the notion of authorship that one might discern from Brecht's philosophy that "the event happens in one's own now," the festival artists would sometimes perform their own events and sometimes perform other artists' work. A letter from George Maciunas to La Monte Young boasts that "we [Fluxus artists] had just about performed every piece of yours in the festivals."[35] Maciunas organized each festival around this notion of collective authorship, which was in keeping with his political aims. During this period, Maciunas angered many of the Fluxus artists by asking for sole copyright authority to their work and attempting to require that they stop using their own names and instead publish exclusively as "Fluxus" with a set of codes that stood in for their identity.[36] Maciunas was against any sort of self-promotion, and he felt that in order to be a collective, the artists had to forgo personal ambition and "careerism." Disagreements about ambition and sentiment resulted. Maciunas denounced Jackson Mac Low, Nam June Paik, Carolee Schneemann, Emmett Williams, Dick Higgins, and others for "anti-collective attitude, excessive individualism, desire for personal glory, prima dona [sic] complex."[37]

Maciunas was not only the instigator of most political disagreements within Fluxus but also the orchestrator and designer of Fluxus publications, and his idiosyncratic but intense political views drove the operation. At the center of those views was a paradox. Maciunas had a strong Soviet allegiance—he wanted Fluxus to be art for the masses in a Leninist sense—and at various points, he tried to align Fluxus officially with the Communist Party in the Soviet Union.[38] He talked about revolution; wrote the famous manifesto about "[purging] the world of bourgeois sickness"; and, in an often-cited letter, he likens Fluxus to the Soviet avant-garde journal *LEF*.[39] Despite these leftist ideals, he was an entrepreneur in the capitalist sense, importing foreign goods and selling them for a markup in the United States; he urged increased productivity from Fluxus artists, telling them to work nine to five; and he modeled Fluxus on a multinational corporation complete with a brand identity.[40] I point out Maciunas's confusing political commitments because this embrace of—and simultaneous disgust with—various forms of consumer capitalism and white-collar labor characterizes much Fluxus work, albeit not as outlandishly paradoxically as Maciunas's persona. As Cuauhtémoc Medina argues, "despite its aesthetic divisions, personal animosities, philosophical misunderstandings, and political conflicts, the discourse of Fluxus is always a debate about economic development." He goes on to write that "these arguments revolve around the necessary antinomy between development and satisfaction, a tension that, despite its presence in the mere thought of work, acquires special relevance for art given the affluent society's social discovery that no matter how successfully developed an economy would be, it needed to enforce perpetual dissatisfaction."[41] It is important to keep this "tension" in mind when examining event scores. They are not a direct action—to recall the differences between Fluxus performances and Dada—but rather an indirect mode of assessment that subverts various capitalist enterprises.

The crux of the infighting about whether Fluxus is "political" is better characterized as different techniques these artists used to explore the tensions between work and nonwork. Many Fluxus artists fiercely wanted to contend with issues of consumption and white-collar labor in their work, but they did not sign on to Maciunas's convoluted ideology of Soviet administrative corporatism. Owen Smith depicts these differences as a European/American split. After Maciunas's European tour, which was organized around his principles, the artists came back to the United States and continued to work together under the name Fluxus, albeit differently. Smith explains, "Many of the artists in Europe, notably Paik, Higgins, Vostell, [Tomas] Schmit, and Maciunas, were not only aware of, but specifically interested in, the political and social implications of their work. When Maciunas tried to extend this developing identity into America in 1962, however, he came face to face with conflicting views"; Smith claims that, under Cage, artists like Brecht and Watts had no political interest or allegiance.[42] They certainly eschewed notions of a central program and refused to sign Maciunas's manifesto. Then, in May 1963, George Brecht and Robert Watts organized a New York and New Jersey event that seemed much more genteel than the European tour. The "Yam Festival" included music and performances by a variety of artists each given their own billing, many of whom were not associated with Fluxus. Yam Festival was a name thought up by Robert Watts and Brecht together in 1962 to include artworks of different genres, and it was used in correspondence for at least a year before the festival itself.[43]

The term "Yam Festival" underscores the deeply interdisciplinary nature of this work—although eschewing the model of production that interested Maciunas, Watts and Brecht found interdisciplinary, collective research central to their conception of Fluxus. Why yams? Fluxus artists and scholars explain the name "Yam Festival" by the fact that the event originally was meant to take place in the month of May, and "Yam" is "May" backward; early correspondence refers to it as "MAYTIME," which then becomes "YAM," "YAMTIME," and "YAMDAY."[44] Watt's background in pre-Columbian and non-Western art (he earned an MA at Columbia) likely made him sensitive to the importance of yams around the world and indeed attentive to the yam as a symbolic lynchpin between work and everyday life. Yams serve as the link between art and exchange in many cultures, notably in Trobriand culture, where yams serve as currency and as "both a gift and a commodity."[45] After studying with Paul Weingart, a cultural anthropologist and art historian specializing on Oceania, Watts was surely aware that, in Trobriand culture, the work put into harvesting yams is displayed as wealth in storehouses that double as gathering places for socializing in the evenings.[46] "Yam Festival" is also the name of an important yearly event celebrated around the world in early fall. This festival of the yam harvest is important, especially for Igbo and Ashanti cultures in Ghana, Nigeria, and other parts of West Africa. In addition to Watts's specialized knowledge, Brecht, Ben Patterson, and others corresponding were likely aware of the West African festival; the cultural tradition was popularized to English speakers in *Things Fall Apart* by Chinua Achebe in 1958. This reference to a variety of cultures for a mostly white experimental avant-garde festival is in line with a longer problematic history of appropriation of symbols and images of African and indigenous cultures and religions for American and European avant-garde practice.

Brecht's book *Water Yam* was published shortly after the festival, and "water yam," another name for Dioscorea alata, or greater yam, is one of the crops that would be celebrated at festivals in West Africa. Brecht's appropriation of the name is noteworthy given that the West African festivals are also displays of intermedia merriment that include dance, song, and visual arts. The water yam specifically contains economic, nutritional, and cultural value for many in West Africa, and its celebration is central to everyday life.[47] If the 1963 Yam Festival was the intermedia joyful celebration, *Water Yam* is a specimen of the important crop. This misguided attempt at homage in the naming of the festival and the book is one way that Brecht's text calls attention to labor, exchange, and art's role in satisfaction.

*Water Yam*'s publication is rooted in this history of bureaucratic copyright dispute, interdisciplinary festival, and collective research and scholarship. As with many Fluxus works, George Maciunas was the catalyst for the publication of George Brecht's *Water Yam*, which came about shortly after the Yam Festival. In fact, Maciunas took credit for both the idea of *Water Yam* and its design (figure 2.4). It is important to note, however, that the design of the cards is almost identical to Brecht's handprinted versions, which included bullet points, looked like type, and which he hectographed and mailed to friends starting in the early 1950s.[48]

FLUXUS SCORES AND THE BUREAUCRATIZATION OF EVERYDAY LIFE  51

This particular publication by Maciunas, however, was part of a plan to publish individual artist anthologies in order to gain the rights to publish all of their future works.[49] Many artists did not agree to this pact or to Maciunas's other schemes, and likewise not many "complete works" came to fruition. Brecht agreed to collaborate on the idea as long as it could be mass-produced and sold cheaply. And so, in 1963, *Water Yam* was published in Wiesbaden, where Maciunas was stationed with the U.S. Army at the time (he took the job in 1962 to avoid debt on AG Gallery), and he sold each copy for $2. Later years would bring many different editions, including wood boxes, cardboard or plastic casings, different colors and shades or weights of stock. Despite its differences from standard books—the pages are cards of different sizes, and there is no specific order to the cards—it is multiple, printed, and text based.

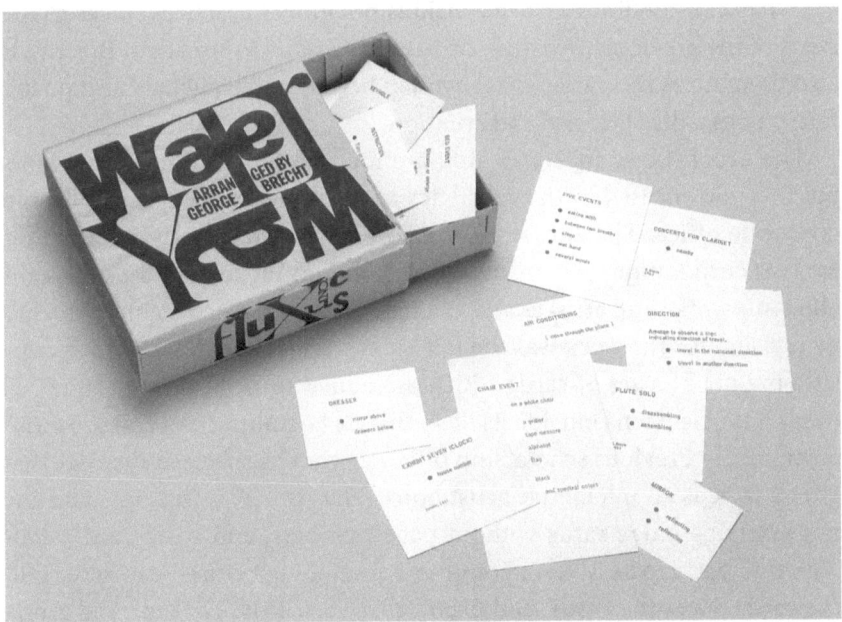

FIGURE 2.4 George Brecht, *Water Yam*, cardboard box with offset label, containing sixty-nine offset cards; overall (closed): 5⅞″ × 6 5/16″ × 1¾″, 1963. The Gilbert and Lila Silverman Fluxus Collection. Digital Image © The Museum of Modern Art/Licensed by SCALA/Art Resource, NY. © 2024 Artists Rights Society (ARS), New York/VG Bild-Kunst, Bonn.

## "AN ENDLESS BOOK":
## GEORGE BRECHT'S *WATER YAM*

The scores of George Brecht's *Water Yam* attend to the specific nature of 1960s suburbanization and white-collar labor practice in the United States. In this period, white middle- and working-class people were acquiring single-family houses and cars at a previously unseen rate, creating semi-private spheres around what Dolores Hayden calls the "sitcom suburbs."[50] This culture of consumption was marked as desirably separate from the office spaces that bankrolled it, and yet *Water Yam* brings these worlds together through address and form. Hinging on definitions of poetry that interrogate the position of multiple publics, the scores recast private relations into a broader network of records, connecting labor to infrastructure. As *Water Yam* interrogates the mobility of and relation between everyday commodities and reenvisions notational practices (ideas at the heart of the previously existing art historical scholarship about Brecht), it also thematizes the paradoxical overlap between bureaucracy and poetic form, a crucially "literary" intervention.

The event scores in *Water Yam* are focused on the domestic sphere, but they are encased in the aesthetics of the office, more specifically, the corporate office. The encasement makes sense; Brecht was a researcher for two corporations—Johnson & Johnson and Fluxus—and he thought about his work as an artist as and as a researcher interchangeably.[51] Brecht's own vision for the work was the following: "an endless book, which consists mainly of a set of cards which are added to from time to time . . . [and] has extensions outside itself so that its beginning and end are indeterminate."[52] Previous scholarship of *Water Yam* has charted theories that attend to it as an interactive artist book. The "book" is in a box, and the box contains index cards without page numbers, and so to read *Water Yam* is to participate in its ongoing and developing nature—one must pull the cards, layer the cards, and even order the cards. Liz Kotz and Anna Dezeuze have written about the resonance between *Water Yam* and contemporaneous theories of the "open work."[53] As Umberto Eco explains first in 1962, "open works" are in movement; they "continuously create their own space and the shapes to fill it."[54] In the case of *Water Yam*, the book form is set but also questioned through participatory movement or, as Eco would put it, through "the invitation to make the work together with the author."[55] Such an understanding is apropos—Kotz even goes so far as to say that these works are "absurd literalizations" of 1960s claims for readerly activity like "open work."[56] As Kotz notes, however, this claim that the reader is involved in the production or process of the artwork is often a conclusion rather than an observation that leads to fruitful interpretations. This mirrors a larger problem inherent in literary criticism about so-called experimental writing, which often ends in blanket calls for openness or contingency.[57]

Clues to interpretation might be found instead in Brecht's notion of "endlessness," or the call for continued labor contained in the work. Brecht called his works "Event scores" despite the fact that, unlike musical scores, their purpose was not notation of a composition. For Brecht, the event score was about preparation and attention: "Event scores prepare one for an event to happen in one's own 'now.'"[58] Alongside the etymological homage of "score" to music notation (referring to the practice of connecting the staves with lines or scores), and given Brecht's thoughts about how his scores were meant to "prepare one" for events in their every day, the more appropriate definition of "score" here might be keeping tally, as in a game or record.[59] Because these short instructions help us see events in our everyday life, they are the "score" of our events, the record or enumeration of these small practices. Each one is also "the essential point or crux in the matter," as though each one lets us "know the score" of daily events.[60] Event scores conjure a record.

The works for *Water Yam* look more like bureaucratic paperwork than like music. Their shape recalls the index card, an invention of the late nineteenth century that, along with the vertical file, is meant to aid internal organization. Most of the cards in the box contain small round typographical marks, easily identifiable as bullets.[61] The bullet emerged with white-collar capitalism, first associated primarily with advertising in the 1950s and then, by the 1970s, as a way to break up any type of prose into information.[62] In *Water Yam*, Brecht uses this typography to signal a bureaucratic technique for producing brevity. As John Guillory argues, in memos and other types of paperwork where brevity is prized, formatting becomes more visible; the danger being that, "if articulated structure displaces verbal connective tissue in argument, the effect of such brevity can be a kind of poverty, an overreliance on mere enumeration as a result of which logical relations fail to manifest themselves at all."⁶³ We see this danger come to fruition in the baffling content of many of the scores where the reader's object is seemingly to find the relation between the bullets.

But before we read *Water Yam* as a series of parodically bad memos, it is worth dwelling on Guillory's point about "an overreliance on enumeration." Brecht's interest in enumerating events, or scoring them, can be read as an index for the way poetry is linked to administration. As any poet might guard their formal choices, Brecht wanted to make sure that there was plenty of "empty space" around the scores when they were published and that "the format be respected."⁶⁴ By overformatting (and urging that the format be respected), Brecht's work seems especially poetry-like. As Craig Dworkin notes, an "amnesia surrounding the materiality of language" makes us think of line breaks as poetry and the prose block as the absence of any form whatsoever.⁶⁵ Dworkin goes on to estrange the prose block, but not before pointing out that many works considered poetry are printed in prose, including Stein's *Tender Buttons*. Stein's work is so obviously poetry because of its poetic language that the dense paragraph format has rarely deterred critics from calling it as such. Brecht's work, on the other hand, contains no markers of poetic language; rather, it leans on brevity and format to look like poetry. To use Guillory's phrase, there is not "connective tissue of argument" nor embellishment of poetry. *Water Yam* is entirely lacking excess where *Tender Buttons* has an abundance. It is precisely Brecht's embrace of the aesthetics of bureaucracy that also makes his cards poetry.

This is a paradox inherent to Brecht's event scores: they are overformatted, indicating a certain poetic nature, yet they point outside their form to "one's own now," as Brecht puts it. Later in his notes, he muses, "If art were not in form, it could be (life) instead of art. Or: Can art not be in form and still be art?"⁶⁶ Perhaps most illustrative of this paradox, in a letter about "Word Event" for an exhibition in 1963, Brecht writes, "It seems to be a further characteristic of my work that individual works have no definite form."⁶⁷ How can these works have so little form but so much format? In other words, these scores can be variously instantiated anywhere and anytime, but they are also singular in poetry precision. In their use of the imperative, or by insisting that the reader do something, these scores are a congealed form of labor. However, unlike commodities, which also might be described as a congealed form of labor insomuch as they seemingly embody certain forms of value under capitalism, the score's material is the stuff of poetry. Brecht's scores point out that the work of poetry is in the home, in objects, in the reader. His event scores are an internal memo telling you of all the ways you are on notice to do the work of poetry yourself. In labor terms, they are "lean"; they have no lyric excess. Conversely, Stein's *Tender Buttons* contains extraordinary surplus in its repetition, proliferation of nouns doubling as verbs, and so on. We might note that critics provide elaborate exegeses of *Tender Buttons*, but none have been seduced into believing that they have to "do" the work themselves in their own now. The excessive format and lack of form in *Water Yam* connects methods of bureaucracy (echoes of commodification and colonialism in both texts), but Brecht illustrates that this bureaucracy has directly infiltrated, indeed is instrumentalized, in the domestic spaces of the everyday, in our use of tables and chairs.

When asked about the repetition of household furniture like chairs, Brecht replied, "Yes, but that has to do with ordinariness, that doesn't have to do with a special love for chairs."[68] Brecht's interest in chronicling his "ordinary" domestic environment recalls the world of 1960s commodification (one only need to think of the famous "Kitchen debate" between Nixon and Khrushchev), but it also fits within an avant-garde tradition of animating domestic interiors, with Gertrude Stein's *Tender Buttons* as an exemplar. Both works contain an abundance of umbrellas, chairs, and tables, and both works ask questions about the relationships of ordinary household items to each other and to markets outside the home.

Helpfully for my analysis of *Water Yam*, recently Stein scholars, in fathoming Stein's chronicling of domestic objects, have turned their attention to commodity relations and social relations. Apropos to Brecht scores, Natalia Cecire has suggested that "Stein's poetics engages the public and the market, then, by centralizing feminized, typically unwaged labor, especially repetitive labor including housework and information work."[69] Sarah Blair has urged Stein's readers to consider the domestic space of Stein's texts, which mirrors the real space of 27 rue de Fleurus in Paris, where she lived and entertained, as a "social form."[70] In other words, the domestic interior space in Stein's writing of this era can be seen as the center of a cyclical consumer market, and commodity relations can be taken to create Stein's avant-garde experimentation and form. Blair writes, "Ellipses, temporal shifts, changing tonalities bespeak not only the energies of avant-garde innovation, but the uneven social relations inhering within the bourgeois home as a kind of nested space: at once sanctum sanctorum of the professional-managerial classes, laboratory for progressivist theories of domestic management, display arena for the exercise of taste, and material work-place for an expanding market of domestic laborers."[71] Tying some of these labor considerations to the global commodities they involve, Juliana Spahr argues persuasively that Stein's description of such ordinary household objects displays an awareness of—perhaps even a resistance to—empire building and colonialism of the early twentieth century.[72] By chronicling objects like a "little lingering lion and a Chinese chair," Stein, a polylingual expatriate, is calculating the stakes of an increasingly imperial world as she theorizes various forms of disorientation. For Spahr, the tables full of decentered luxuries and bourgeois objects indicate a particular domestic environment that suggests the decentering of Europe.[73] In this vein, I hope to contextualize *Water Yam*, through an interrogation of what makes a seemingly unrelated grouping of household things "ordinary" within the context of U.S. commodity history in 1963.

By thinning out descriptions of objects into their mere listing, *Water Yam* shows a portrait of what Lizabeth Cohen calls the "consumers' republic" of the 1950s. Brecht's chairs are described as "white," and they contain objects like graters, flags, and Christmas balls that one might find in increasingly suburbanized New Jersey. Brecht himself returned from his station in Germany during World War II to a country where the doubling of the median income of white households (due in part to administrative labor), mixed with the explosion of consumer credit and anticommunist sentiment, created an environment where accumulating household goods was considered patriotic. As Cohen puts it, "Faith in a mass consumption postwar economy hence came to mean much more than the ready availability of goods to buy. Rather, it stood for an elaborate, integrated ideal of economic abundance and democratic political freedom, both equitably distributed, that became almost a national civil religion from the late 1940s into the 1970s."[74]

CHAIR EVENT

    on a white chair

  a Christmas-tree ball

  flag

  can opener

black

    and spectral colors

CHAIR EVENT

    on a white chair

      a grater

      tape measure

      alphabet

      flag

      black

        and spectral colors

**FIGURES 2.5 AND 2.6** George Brecht, "Chair Event" and "Chair Event," *Water Yam* (two notecards from box), 1963. University of California, Santa Cruz (UCSC), Special Collections. © 2024 Artists Rights Society (ARS), New York/VG Bild-Kunst, Bonn.

Two versions of "Chair Event" point out what Cohen calls a "religion" by placing a flag next to a Christmas tree ball and can opener (figures 2.5 and 2.6). These parataxic lists illustrate the rapid interchange of commodities as "events." They contrast with each other ("on a white chair . . . / black / and spectral colors") in part to show their irrelevance to each other except as groups of commodities. Although Brecht himself argues that the chair here, meaning "a seat for one person (always implying more or less of comfort and ease)," is merely a referent or symbol for ordinariness, his readers must also interpret "chair" as an instance of paronomasia as well.[75] Whiteness is in the position of comfort and ease throughout *Water Yam* and it "presides" as chair of the event.[76] The presence of the French word for flesh, "chair," within this construction adds credence to the interpretation of whiteness as a social construction that depends on notions of embodiment. Allowing this type of language play opens titles to be read as "authority event" rather than "furniture event," reminding readers of the supremacy of whiteness in the suburbs along with the almost religious ideals that access to commodities were promised to grant.[77]

During this period, areas like those where Brecht lived became flourishing suburbs. In the decade from 1950 to 1960, the mostly white population of East Brunswick tripled, which mirrored a larger process of a suburbanization of New Jersey. In the postwar period, the state became 70 percent suburban and much whiter through a state government process of passing restrictive zoning laws; instating unaffordable private housing; stratifying school spending; and disallowing assembly in new "town centers," a suburban workaround to public space.[78] As Cohen argues, New Jersey paved the way for later cultural, social, and economic changes across the United States that privileged white married families with a male breadwinner and legally discriminated against every other group. Brecht's often-quoted story describes the origin of "Motor Vehicle Sundown (Event)," which is frequently credited as Brecht's first "event score": "In the Spring of 1960, standing in the woods in East Brunswick, New Jersey, where I lived at the time, waiting for my wife to come from the house, standing behind my English Ford station wagon, the motor running and the left-turn signal blinking, it occurred to me that a truly 'event' piece could be drawn from the situation."[79] The event itself contained a series of actions, none of which were unusual, but when strung together in twenty-four parts, were quite elaborate. The event illustrates the ubiquity of suburban life while also seemingly overdoing it, deadpanning these rituals to clown their seriousness or to extrapolate a "religion" of the suburbs.[80] Brecht's story illustrates the specific domestic scene of the era precisely.

If Brecht's suburban motor vehicle and his "white chair" exemplify the growing white suburbia of the 1960s that disadvantaged Black people and other minority groups, it sits comfortably next to the "Chinese chair" in Gertrude Stein's *Tender Buttons*, which illustrates a particular experience and philosophy of imperialism in the early twentieth century.[81] Both texts play intricately with relationality in domestic spaces to illustrate the cultures of capitalism that create those spaces. As Joshua Schuster shows,

TABLE

● table

TABLE

● on a white table


TABLE

● on a white table

glasses, a puzzle

and

(having to do with smoking)

FIGURES 2.7, 2.8, AND 2.9 George Brecht, "Table," "Table," "Table," *Water Yam* (three notecards from box), 1963. University of California, Santa Cruz (UCSC), Special Collections. © 2024 Artists Rights Society (ARS), New York/VG Bild-Kunst, Bonn.

Gertrude Stein's *Tender Buttons* emulates cubist paintings in an attempt to put meaning "out on the table" in a metaphorical sense.[82] *Tender Buttons*'s depiction of tables from many different angles is in dialogue with the cubist paintings that interested Stein and also with what Schuster describes as a modernist interest in nonrepresentational language that does not "center on the self or the human species" but rather on "a variety of animate and inanimate interactions."[83] *Water Yam* also takes specific stock of tables. For example, *Water Yam* contains a sequence of events called "Table" (figures 2.7, 2.8, and 2.9). The relationship between title and poem in the first card is illustrative, as though the title asks for a poem about a table and the bullet point wryly complies with something like "here is a table." However, the next two cards explore different types of relationships. The second card is a description of the title (the table is white and there is something on it). The last completes the picture; as in the cubist tradition, there are glasses, a puzzle, and a pipe on the table. The word pipe is not included but is suggested by a phrase in parentheses, seemingly further dematerializing René Magritte's "La trahison des images." The score points out that the table is elided entirely. Unlike the chairs, this is not a table event, just "table." It is the suggestion of tables where particular assemblages make events. This relation is a "puzzle" that perhaps involves glasses and smoking.

The table in *Tender Buttons* also contains glasses:

### A TABLE.

A table means does it not my dear it means a whole steadiness.
Is it likely that a change.
A table means more than a glass even a looking glass is tall.
A table means necessary places and a revision a revision of a little thing it means it does mean that there has been a stand, a stand where it did shake.[84]

The table in both Stein and Brecht's texts means "a revision." In the case of Brecht's *Water Yam*, readers witness "a revision of a little thing" as the picture becomes more exact. But in both cases, the table is a "stand," and it signifies "steadiness." In *Water Yam*, this is shown by what is on it or what makes it; in *Tender Buttons*, the work of illustration is done by definitional excurses. Both works animate the relation between everyday objects in relation to domestic life and labor. But *Water Yam*'s attention to commodity capitalism of the moment forces these objects to define each other mutually, even speak to each other.

It is not clear if Brecht or Stein had the abstract table of *Capital*'s commodity chapter in mind when they wrote, but their works certainly speak to it. In the chapter on commodities, a reoccurring table is Karl Marx's primary example of a "useful thing" that becomes abstracted, turned, and monstrous through the process of commodification under capitalism.[85]

Marx illustrates how value works under capitalism by "turning the tables" on use and exchange. When a table is a commodity in relation to other commodities, it is no longer ordinary. Instead, it is animated by social relations and it computes its own value: "it stands on its head, and evolves out of its wooden brain grotesque ideas far more wonderful than if it were to begin dancing on its own free will."[86] The figure of prosopopoeia characterizes much of this section of *Capital*, as later when commodities speak, to exclaim that in "the eyes of each other we are nothing but exchange values." But what is remarkable about Marx's standing, dancing table is that it isn't just endowed with human characteristics—if we think of doing a dance while standing on one's head as something humans can do—but it is also the source of those characteristics.[87] It grows a "wooden brain." The woodenness of the brain shows that the table has retained its substance, but because the table is a commodity, it acquires a source of thought (the brain) and grotesque ideas.

Brecht's table is also Marx's table with mysterious characteristics due to an animation projected onto it via human social relations; the table of *Water Yam* is a commodity in relation to other commodities. In this relation, the table shares its grotesque ideas with the other commodities in the ordinary environment of the text, which makes it extraordinary—it becomes an "event"—despite Brecht's interest in "ordinariness." In other words, if Marx's definition of the ordinary is that which is not animated by social relations, in Brecht's *Water Yam*, the ordinary is that which is animated by normative social relations inextricable from normative commodities.

Brecht's table speaks to words, objects, and philosophies of abstraction. It talks to mythologies of whiteness, to the double nature of language, to the standardization and individuation of itself. In Jacques Derrida's reading of this passage of Marx, Derrida imagines a séance of the table for interlocuters in "philosophy, rhetoric, poetics, from Plato to Heidegger, from Kant to Ponge, and so many others," and Brecht's table is irreducibly in attendance.[88] The card depicted in figure 2.7 reminds us that every table we encounter is an event of relationality between what Ngai calls "difference and typicality"; the other cards situate it in relation to commodities and ideas. "Table" is the source of animation and reading, and like its dancing, is an event. What distinguishes it from Stein's table, which also "shakes" at the séance of commodities under global capitalism, is the loss of connection, or connective tissue in the prose. Formatting replaces, as Stein puts it, what a table "means."

In both Stein and Brecht's work, the table "means more than a glass," or more than what is on it, because of that very juxtaposition and support. Both *Water Yam* and *Tender Buttons* ask the reader to parse relations, and often the only clues or coordinates are prepositions. Prepositions indicate linkage as event; as Chris Jennings puts it, they can be "unstable focal points where the significance of the words they link depends on an endlessly deferred question of relationship."[89] For example, take the following sequence from "Food" in *Tender Buttons*:

### POTATOES.

Real potatoes cut in between.

### POTATOES.

In the preparation of cheese, in the preparation of crackers, in the preparation of butter, in it.

### ROAST POTATOES.

Roast potatoes for.[90]

In the first "Potatoes" above, the presence of "real" potatoes suggests that the title is inauthentic. In the second "Potatoes," the title indicates the subject of the lines that follow. The last title represents a tautology and a secret—it is repeated like steps for the process of potato's preparation but the "for" shows us that there is something we are not (yet?) privy to in the scene. The introduction of "roast" as either an adjective or a verb, making the possibility of an imperative sentence as well as a descriptive title, puts even more emphasis on what is missing after the "for."[91] In *Water Yam*, there are similar sequences of poems. For example, it is unlikely that the three scores named "Stool" would be grouped together, but the repeated title would suggest linkage to any reader. The "Stool" scores read as follows: "on (or near a stool)"; "on a stool / a cane / and a package or bag of"; and last, "on a white stool / a black-and-white-striped cane / oranges in a paper bag."

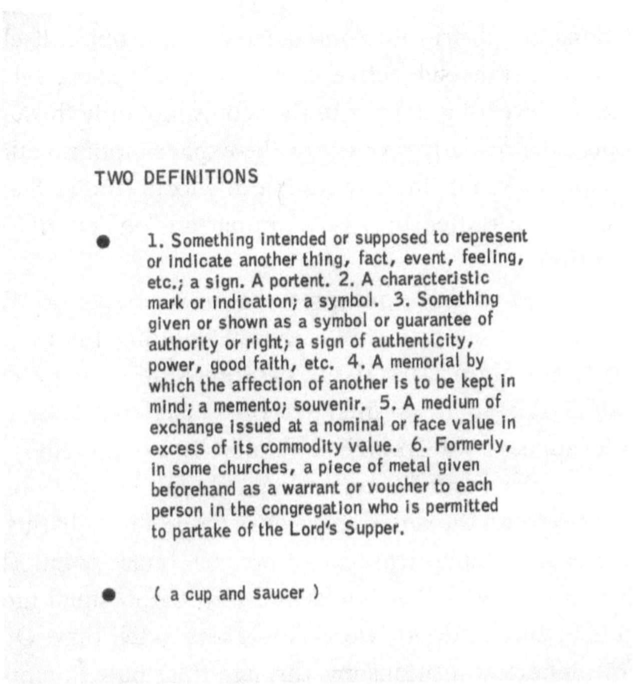

TWO DEFINITIONS

• 1. Something intended or supposed to represent or indicate another thing, fact, event, feeling, etc.; a sign. A portent. 2. A characteristic mark or indication; a symbol. 3. Something given or shown as a symbol or guarantee of authority or right; a sign of authenticity, power, good faith, etc. 4. A memorial by which the affection of another is to be kept in mind; a memento; souvenir. 5. A medium of exchange issued at a nominal or face value in excess of its commodity value. 6. Formerly, in some churches, a piece of metal given beforehand as a warrant or voucher to each person in the congregation who is permitted to partake of the Lord's Supper.

• ( a cup and saucer )

FIGURE 2.10 George Brecht, "Two Definitions," *Water Yam* (notecard from box), 1963. University of California, Santa Cruz (UCSC), Special Collections. © 2024 Artists Rights Society (ARS), New York/VG Bild-Kunst, Bonn.

(Note the absence of bullets for these scores.) The titles in the first two "Stool" poems function like "Roast Potatoes" in the Stein example above—what is important about the stool is its relation to something that is elided. As Stein ends a sentence with "for" and otherwise emphasizes "in" and "between" in the two "Potatoes," Brecht emphasizes "on" and ends a sentence with "of." In this case, if the first two cards seem like abuses of syntax, the third card is revelatory. The third card creates a scene—the object is on the stool, the object is a specific cane, and a paper bag of oranges.

Given the importance of the enigmatic prepositions, these cards are clearly not directions for sculptures (although they have been realized in galleries this way without inclusion of the score) and are not only "about" objects. Because they are flanked by prepositions suggesting new relations, the objects in question remain perpetually abstracted. As Natilee Harren writes about Fluxboxes, these stools offer "pathways to as-yet-undiscovered object-relations that deprioritize and defetishize the object itself in favor of experiences of trans-subjective identification."[92] These relations are theorized at the level of grammar in the scores, not only through invitations to touch, the readerly process, or the expansion of notation. These objects are not penetrable in their commodity form (unlike Stein, Brecht does not use "in"); rather, they take animation "on" or "of" others to become eventful.

Other examples of this nonrepresentational poetry in *Water Yam* illustrate new relations from bullet point to bullet point, eschewing even the tenuous connective tissue of prepositions. For example, in "2 Umbrellas," the poem enumerates only itself with the signals of bureaucratic language ("2 Umbrellas: • umbrella / • umbrella"). The card "Two Clocks," which reads "Two Clocks / • clothes hooks / • bird flight," also enumerates. With the verbal connective tissue absent in this list form, the title works in metaphorical relation to each bullet point. The reader must puzzle over how clothes hooks and bird flight, small moments of domestic life in and outdoors, work as markers to tell time. Other cards illustrate metaphorical relationships through their bullet points. A good example is "Two Definitions" (figure 2.10). The first bullet point is the definition of "token," which a reader may identify fairly easily. The second appears to be an illustration of "token": it is a token example of a token coin. In this case, perhaps the coin has an image of a cup and saucer on it and is meant to be used as a voucher for a cup of coffee. The parentheses signal that the bullet point works as an abstracted image similar to the pipe in "Table." As the bullets define the same object in two ways, they also illustrate individuation and standardization; any definition will be a token. The score references something like money form (tokens) to privilege language (definitions), and elide commodities completely, even in their ordinary or plain form (we don't actually get either the token with a picture of a cup and saucer or the cup of coffee itself). The score enumerates, administrates, or "scores" the marketization of objects. This word play, or new relationality, is possible because of the textual nature of the events and because of their formatting.

The examples from *Tender Buttons* that I have examined so far are from the first two sections of the book, the sections that look most like *Water Yam*. But unlike "Objects" and "Foods," Stein's third section, "Rooms," is one long prose piece that models a way of moving through enclosures; the words embody actions rather than locations or objects. This section famously begins with a strong differentiation between action and place: "Act so that there is no use in a centre. A wide action is not width."[93] The work allows certain qualities of the room to come into focus (such as the previously quoted "little lingering lion and a Chinese chair"), but it is constantly shifting; the rest of that sentence reads, "all the handsome cheese which is stone, all of it and a choice, a choice of a blotter."[94] We see a reluctance to fix things or to allow them to be static here—in the opposite mode of the object-based earlier sections, a fear that description will put rooms into stasis seems to haunt the writing. The fight against this closure or stasis is apparent in lines like "the care with which the rain is wrong and the green is wrong and the white is wrong, the care with which there is a chair and plenty of breathing. The care with which there is incredible justice and likeness, all this makes a magnificent asparagus, and also a fountain."[95] The boundary between subject and object is traversed in the movement from internal subjective truths ("care" and "wrong") into the objects ("asparagus" and "fountain"). The varying language and grammar of each of *Tender Button*'s sections create new systems: whereas the earlier sections depict cubic surfaces and lists, in "Rooms," Stein uses movement through language to create an understanding of subjectivity in space. Taken as a whole, the sections show us that a room is performed, or brought into existence, by acting in it; an object is performed by naming but not necessarily by naming the thing. Brecht's *Water Yam*, by authorizing its reader to act on or perform nouns, constitutes a transformation: it references objects and only implies truths with its format.

*Water Yam* shares many ordinary elements like tables, chairs, and umbrellas, but unlike Stein's *Tender Buttons*, it lacks the specificity to suggest opulence and the focus to indicate only one particular interior space. The images of clothes hooks and umbrellas point to homes, bird flight points to the outdoors, and lines like "Exit" and "No Vacancy" from other scores point to passing motel signs on a road trip. Brecht leaves these objects purposefully varied and blank, not only without context or connection but without detail, underscoring the importance of format for meaning making. By abstracting additional methods of abstract language, *Water Yam* paradoxically brings these methods closer to historical forms. The elimination of motion and connection mimics the highway commute, the blankness of the objects suggests an accelerated global exchange of commodities.

What are the politics of this bureaucratization of experimental literature? Is Brecht's exposure of the overlap of poetry and paperwork, the memo-ization of modernism, a liberatory gesture? Is there a horizon of possibility in this world where white tables dance off their uses and clock time is bird flight? *Water Yam* stops short of utopian promises. It does not offer alternatives to rituals of white-collar reason, but it does begin a trajectory of poetry that becomes the stuff of handbooks, to-do lists, memos, and contracts. It infiltrates corporate tools, becoming poetry in general and responding to changes in political reason and labor. The next chapter will continue my examination of subversion of corporate tools as a poetic technique as I attend to poetry that similarly asks if poetry can *do* anything. Yet unlike Brecht's scores, the poetry of the New York School that I discuss in chapter 3 uses similar tools to create spaces outside of privatized reason. Chapter 4 studies techniques of direct embodied resistance that are created by emulating records and diagrams like those that inspired Brecht. Chapter 5 will attend to poetry that interprets moments of atrocity and excess though reenacting them. These works all examine the hypothesis of Brecht's event scores: that methods for living and methods of reading are not necessarily conceived as separate in a restricted public sphere, that poetry could be the stuff of the ordinary public.

# 3

## "I DO THIS I DO THAT"

Cold War Spatial Poetics and the New York School

*With final agreement to this*
*and all that has been said*
*hithertofor and it is my*
*contention that no territorial*
*gains be garland with rosed feet—*

—GREGORY CORSO AND DWIGHT EISENHOWER, "CUT UP," *LOCUS SOLUS* II, SUMMER 1961

*The giant Norway spruce from Podunk, its lower branches bound,*
*this morning was reared into place at Rockefeller Center.*
*I thought I saw a cold blue dusty light sough in its boughs*
*the way other years the wind thrashing at the giant ornaments*
*recalled other years and Christmas trees more homey.*

—JAMES SCHUYLER, "DECEMBER," *LOCUS SOLUS* III-IV, WINTER 1962

*Let us stare out*
*at the city. It is ours*
*finally, the white spokes*
*of its will. Its sun/*
*and sea too pulling*
*at the moon.*

—LEROI JONES, "A LONG POEM FOR MYSELF," *LOCUS SOLUS* III-IV, WINTER 1962

*How often do we touch our walls?*
*A woman never knew the stairwell*
*ran behind her mirror, or her bedside*
*plaster on the neighbor's brick,*
*stares up to where she walked.*

—CARL MORSE, "ANCHOR DEMOLITION: EAST 82ND STREET," *LOCUS SOLUS* V, SPRING 1962

I begin this chapter with four quotations from poetry published in *Locus Solus*, a short-lived magazine that, despite the variousness of these examples and the journal's brief life, I will later characterize as the most unified voice of the New York School poets. Read together, these quotations merge an experiential, social, and architectural depiction of New York City with questions of urban planning, federal U.S. policy, and even global diplomacy.

This moment in New York City was marked by the experience of urban renewal and other broadly applied policies of racial liberal displacement and dispossession. In Gregory Corso's "cut-up" poem, President Dwight D. Eisenhower's martial expansionist promises for territorial gains merge with a local surrealism of feet that are pink from exertion.[1] Earlier that year, the president warned, just as he left office, against a future predication of peace on a "huge industrial and military machinery of defense."[2] This may have come as a surprise from the same president who had previously marketed Cold War nuclear power as "atoms for peace" and had positioned military expansion of vast proportions as crucial to harmony at home.[3] The syntax of Corso's poem implies that wars fought abroad will not be marked ("garland," as a verb) by fatigue at home, which amounts to an ironic recapitulation of Eisenhower's farewell or what came to be known as his "military industrial complex" speech. The poem's speaker overemphatically and ironically, or purposefully unconvincingly, suggests that Eisenhower's Cold War development of New York City—we can think of the Housing Act of 1954, which introduced "urban renewal"—is separate from violence perpetuated abroad. James Schuyler's poem considers the displacement of city residents through the metaphor of a relocated tree, which accumulates a commercial past and suggests a melancholic temporality of obsolescence at the site of

Manhattan's commercial Rockefeller Center.[4] In Amiri Baraka's (then LeRoi Jones) poem, melancholy is eclipsed with awe through the depiction of a fantasy of dominating the indefatigable force of what was referred to as "slum clearance" in the era. I will discuss Baraka's image of the city's "white spokes" and what it means in relation to anti-Black policies at length later in this chapter, but here this snippet alongside the others above, suggests a mechanized modality of displacement that is stronger than gravity's pull. Whole blocks were demolished by this modality, and Carl Morse's "Anchor Demolition" depicts collapsing tenements in Harlem and Yorkville that reveal connectivity only through loss.

Through refracting the discourse of urban planning and the capture of public spatial referents, poetry of the New York School directly engages Cold War policies of multiple scales, from issues of national security and expansion to city neighborhood associations' elitist preservationist and modernization attempts. In other words, the allocation and reallocation of public resources under urban renewal and other privatizing federal urban policy poses a central set of questions for the poetry in this chapter. I will suggest that this New York School poetry is a material, planning-historical, and political subject of interest, a proposition that departs from enduring interpretations of the city in New York School poetry as atmosphere, cultural context, or sensorial description.

Chapter 2 illustrated how the infiltration of poetry into corporate tools—physical handbooks, manuals, memos, catalogs, to-do lists, and mandated affective rituals—could scrutinize white-collar and pink-collar logic and reason. I previously argued that Fluxus scores use corporate memo form, capturing bullet points from commercialized textual culture, and skew the domestic experience of a suburb and its corporate office counterpart. This chapter considers poetry that is more accepted to be poetry, yet also participates in the work of political and aesthetic instruction. Like the Fluxus scores that implore their reader to "do" something, which I examined in my first two chapters, early New York School poetry famously chronicles a poet narrating, "I do this I do that."[5] Returning from the suburbs back to the city, here I argue that a group of mostly queer and mostly white men writing and publishing together around the same moment use corporate architectural form, capturing semipublic space for privatized activities and suggesting alternative modes of relationality and spatial practice. To attend to the project of these poems, I will discuss two contemporaneous methods of urban design: the use of urban renewal clearance strategies—which had progressed to individual site clearance by the early 1960s from the block and neighborhood clearance of renewal under Robert Moses in the mid- to late-1950s—and the privatizing impulses of corporate architecture.[6] New York School poetry considers these two methods, often simultaneously, and these methods connect New York School poetry and its attention to urban spatial practice to issues of global political change. These poems employ forms of several key architectural sites in New York City and the romantic imaginary of Paris to unravel dominant structures of nationalism, racial liberalism, and homophobic urban practices.

This chapter begins with a discussion of the short-lived magazine *Locus Solus* (1961–1962), a journal edited by John Ashbery, James Schuyler, Kenneth Koch, and Harry Mathews and published in France in the early 1960s, to illustrate that much of the work of the New York School is part of a participatory and event-oriented experimental force that broadened designations of "poetry." My reading of *Locus Solus* will show how the magazine itself enacts (1) the creation of an active, plural, and participatory space in print, and (2) how the play with real space (i.e., New York and Paris) is part of this "event" that captures philosophies of geopolitical containment, expansion, penetration, and renewal with Cold War conceptions of cultural ascendency. The chapter continues with an examination of Frank O'Hara's poetry about modernist skyscrapers and their politics to provide an extensive example of the characteristic of New York School poetry to figure codes, designs, and real spaces of the city as not only a depiction of a sensorium but also a guide for political and aesthetic engagement. I will show that the discourse of Cold War politics and nationalist ideology works as fodder for the invention of more spectacular displays of event-based identity formation and relation through the adoption of general poetic medium. These "events" stand against the pressures of forced homogeneity to interrogate the possibility of activating very real spaces. I end the chapter by reflecting on how, despite the fact that its medium is basically within the lyric tradition as we know it, New York School poetry at this moment makes space within the category of poetry in general. By attending to the politics of media in these poems that chronicle a city, it becomes clear that the

New York School poets engage American traditions of imperialism and racial capitalism. Just as Baraka's "A Long Poem" offers a glimpse of the "white spokes" spinning uneven distribution of resources and death in the city, the usually cloaked machinations of Cold War liberalism, I will show that the shiny glass curtain walls of O'Hara's skyscrapers also reveal a melancholy violence. This violence, although sheathed in notions of public interest at home and diplomacy abroad, means far-reaching displacement, dispossession, and demolition.

## WHERE IS THE NEW YORK SCHOOL?
### *LOCUS SOLUS* AS EMPLACED CURATORIAL PROJECT

There are many fascinating accounts of what makes the New York School poets a semicohesive group. Within this scholarship, much has been written about the coterie aspects of the New York School poets, emphasizing that their friendship bonds are at least one part, if not the singular factor, of what made them a "school."[7] The emplaced nature of that friendship was important—they were poets who came to New York and were writing there—but it was also full of contradictions. Three main players (Frank O'Hara, John Ashbery, and Kenneth Koch) were undergraduate students together at Harvard in the late 1940s. They met James Schuyler and Barbara Guest after they moved to New York City in the late 1950s and became close friends as well as the five central members of the school. Donald Allen's anthology, *The New American Poetry: 1945–1960*, first officially called them the New York Poets, and this was picked up in subsequent anthologies, often adding "school," to sound more like the Abstract Expressionist painting group.[8] The New York Poets grouping of Allen's anthology included Barbara Guest, Kenneth Koch, James Schuyler, Frank O'Hara, John Ashbery, and Edward Field. Field's inclusion in the section was somewhat bizarre; he later claimed he had no connection to the New York School but was included in the collection because he had a brief affair with Frank O'Hara and O'Hara persuaded Allen to include him.[9] The lives of these poets were intertwined. Ashbery, O'Hara, and Schuyler were queer poets. O'Hara and Koch had served in the military before going to Harvard for undergraduate degrees. Ashbery and Koch had been awarded Fulbright grants to study surrealism in France. O'Hara and Schuyler worked at the Museum of Modern Art (MoMA) and wrote for *Art News*. O'Hara, Ashbery, and Schuyler lived together in an apartment in Manhattan in the early 1950s.

Despite consisting of only five volumes and lasting two years, *Locus Solus* is one of the most unified examples of a voice of the New York School of poets, in part because it was a vehicle of self-definition. *Locus Solus* shows the New York School poets to be an experimental movement that enters the conversation of shifting dynamic spatial transformation of Cold War New York City—a conversation that was otherwise taking place as part of urban planning and national security—by reinserting the possibility of the role of poetry to make change or to "do" something to shape spaces. In other words, the journal includes an examination of a politics of textual spatial practice. Calling on both dynamic images of real space and on the solidified images that discourse creates about those spaces, the publication as a whole probes how spaces are defined by the geopolitics of the Cold War. In addition to "I do this I do that" poetry, the New York School is known for their occasional poems and coterie poems, works that deal with the intricacies of one unfolding event, and works that name others in their social circles, respectively.[10] O'Hara is most famous for these types of "personal poems," but other members of the school perform this practice of considering relational events in the poems published in *Locus Solus*. Like some of the other work I discuss in this book, for New York School poems, the formal boundaries of the poem on the page are insufficient to understand what it means to read. All these poems are written seemingly in the act of "doing" something, participating in an event or in an occasion, and they make us question any reading of them that is static or stationary. To be faithful to the activity of the poems, we also must *do* something. This, of course, does not mean that we ourselves must "go get a shoeshine" or arrive at "4:19 in Easthampton" upon reading "The Day That Lady Died," but it means that the poem activates our environment, or spatiality is enfolded into language as a shifting virtual space. This virtual spatiality is not simply localized to indiscriminate scenes, or places of interest to the authors of the poems. Rather, these spaces in the language of the New York School poems hinge on major global political issues of Cold War culture, and national, personal, and relational identity.

Although it was an emblem of the New York School and an engine of New York taste and style, *Locus Solus* was edited in France. Its publication story is as much about American Cold War diplomacy with France—and French influence on American experimentalism—as about friendship. John Ashbery had come to France on a Fulbright in Montpellier; when it was over, he returned to France again (this time Paris) for his dissertation research on a proto-surrealist writer of the early twentieth century, Raymond Roussel. By the late 1950s, Harry Mathews lived between his apartment in Paris and a farmhouse in Lans-en-Vercours. Ashbery introduced Mathews to the work of modern French writers, most importantly Raymond Roussel, from which they both later claimed enormous influence. Ashbery and Koch, who had been corresponding with O'Hara about a publication that might define the tenor of their work, convinced Mathews to fund the magazine with his inheritance. Mathews hadn't published much of his work at this point and felt taken advantage of at first—the New York School wanted to publish their own poetry and that of their friends—but soon he saw himself as part of the group.[11] He would later use Roussel's writing tactics and went on to be the only American included as a member of Oulipo.

The journal immediately had French avant-garde ambitions. It was named *Locus Solus* after the constraint-based novel of the same name by Raymond Roussel, and each volume begins with an untranslated French quote from Roussel. The term "locus solus" can be translated from the Latin to mean "the only place," and it is the name of the estate owned by the eccentric protagonist of Roussel's novel, which unseats structured spaces through language play, a clear ambition of the journal as well. By naming the magazine "the only place," the group charted a sovereign space and also flagged right away that this space was not exactly American, despite the fact that it was enabled by a Fulbright scholarship, American money, and programming. Each editor assumed editorial responsibility for a different issue, except Mathews who was more responsible for the "physical aspects of the magazine."[12] The central members of the school—O'Hara, Ashbery, Koch, and Schuyler—are the only poets to be published in every issue, as is Mathews. Poets that appeared in three issues include Barbara Guest, Bill Berkson, Kenward Elmslie, and Michael Benedikt, who critics sometimes consider the next ring of the inner circle of the New York School. Despite its coming from

France, including French quotations, poetry in French, translations from the French, and bearing French surrealist influences clearly, the journal included mostly New York poets and mostly circulated in New York City.[13] In addition to its Francophone allegiances, *Locus Solus*'s "squat and serious" aesthetic also set it apart from the mimeos that were just beginning to define the poetry world in Manhattan.[14]

With this anomalous French aesthetic, the editors used *Locus Solus* to create a unified New York School voice through curatorial choices and inclusions. As James Schuyler (editor of issues one and five) notes in a letter to Chester Kallman, "the unstated objective" of the "anthology magazine" was "a riposte at *The New American Poetry*, which has so thoroughly misrepresented so many of us—not completely, but the implications of context are rather overwhelming."[15] He goes on to describe the first issue as a "cheerful, serious, international, kind of Paris–New York edited contents, and that of course means you" (the Allen anthology had not included Kallman). As a manifesto, *Locus Solus* did provide some obvious correction to Allen's anthology, which had come out the year before. It showed that New York School poets also wrote prose (it would later publish criticism and nonfiction as well), and it centered the importance of collaboration. In addition to the editorship changing each issue in a sort of collaborative round robin, the entirety of volume 2 was dedicated to collaborations, putting emphasis on constraint and cut-ups, and tracing the New York School lineage in idiosyncratic ways. Schuyler's comment that the magazine is "international, kind of Paris–New York" gives a hint at the way these poets were interested in issues of America's cultural ascendance at this moment in the early 1960s, putting Paris on par with New York and centering both on the international stage.

In the notion of Schuyler's cosmopolitanism that lists "Paris–New York" as what makes *Locus Solus* international, we can hear the ring of what David Caute calls "the cultural Olympics" of the Cold War.[16] To win the game, played between the Western and Soviet countries, was to be the most modern, to show the most progress. Of course, this game was played in many fields, but in culture, it was a tussle between aesthetic abstraction from the United States (represented by New York) and forms of realism stemming from the Soviet Union and allied countries.[17] Yet Paris had a key part to play in this story as well. In the 1940s and 1950s, the United

States was invested in keeping Germany, Italy, and France within a capitalist orbit. Programs like Fulbright, which enabled *Locus Solus* (two of the editors were brought to France through the program), were exemplative of cultural diplomacy or, as historian Sam Lebovic writes, Fulbright worked as a "budget-priced megaphone to transmit American ideas to the world."[18] Even more to the point, as has been well-documented, U.S. art exhibitions abroad—and Abstract Expressionist exhibitions in particular, some of which O'Hara worked on in his job as curator of traveling exhibitions at MoMA—had a role to play in this effort toward proving cultural supremacy.[19]

Abstract Expressionism has been a relatively well-studied weapon of the Cold War. The sort of midcentury modernism, which the New York School is usually classified as, is only more recently studied as such. As Juliana Spahr puts the issue of government intervention into cultural fields during the Cold War succinctly, "The government's interest in literature should not be taken lightly."[20] She makes the case that a central story of the second half of the twentieth century is that revolutionary or resistant literature is co-opted and neutralized through its nationalist packaging. She shows that U.S. government forces amplified literature that would not contradict their politics, mostly at the expense of literature that did. Although created on the fringe of American nationalist programs like Fulbright, *Locus Solus* was not funded by the Central Intelligence Agency (CIA) or a private foundation with liberal isolationist politics. And yet it clearly engages culturally fraught images of both New York and Paris at a volatile time both in the story of experimental poetry and twentieth-century nationalism. With its yearnings for "seriousness" and with its headquarters in Paris for an American operation, one may wonder where the politics of *Locus Solus* could truly be located. It is perhaps surprising that, instead of participating in a tug of war, *Locus Solus* seems to lay New York and Paris in palimpsest, a technique that often results in revealing the deficiencies of New York City.

Volume 3–4, edited by Ashbery, shows this palimpsest formally: a section in the middle of the journal is dedicated to French poetry (translated on the left pages by Ashbery), and overlays the American poems. In the poems written in English by Americans, France and French culture plays a large part. Images of France often overset images of New York to give it romance, sophistication, and queerness. O'Hara and Bill Berkson's collaboration, "From the Memorandums of Angelicus Fobb" depicts a queer romance happening in Manhattan where France is evoked to add allure, like "after-a-French-movie-rain is over."[21] The poem lists riches of New York that seemingly add parts of France as adornment, giving Manhattan the best of both worlds. However, a sharp threat undergirds the poem when state-sanctioned homophobic violence will not let the couple be public with their love ("there are cops around"). The irony is spelled out, "Heaven is where you hang yourself / so dress up / The French will have ideas about it / if you don't."[22] Animosity toward queer people undergirds American life, even though America is depicted as "heaven." The only recourse is to "dress up" or cover the real violence that runs through American culture for an international show. In this same volume, Ashbery's "New Realism" critiques U.S. capitalism on the world stage in part through an exploration of the French art movement the *nouveaux réalisme*.[23]

The racism that this modernization and progress narrative about New York sought to cover up is also on display in *Locus Solus*. John Perrault's poem "Paris" points squarely at the hypocrisy of calling the United States more advanced at the same time that its domestic policies create disinvestment and obsolescence for most of its population. American culture is sarcastically held up as supreme through tautology. The speaker likes America better because of its "beautiful ice cold American clorinated floridated / drinking water"; the practice of shaving armpit hair, which is "so much more sanitary / It's much nicer looking when playing basketball!"; and, most of all, the "self-sufficient machinery of New York City."[24] The poem continues, "I have studied American / I know many American phrases" and then lists among these phrases benign slang like "OK" and "wise guy," alongside violent anti-Black and homophobic epithets.[25] This is a threatening America, one that seeks to establish identity on the exclusion of Blackness and sexual practices and identities considered deviant. The poem ends by probing the image of modernization and cleanliness:

> In America everyone has such nice white teeth
> How I long to run my tongue along the insides
> of those nice white teeth[26]

The French speaker, fully aware of the violence contained within an otherwise slick American image, wants to penetrate beneath its smiling, clean façade. Indeed, *Locus Solus* seems to achieve just this feat, using foreign images to probe truths of U.S. culture.

Perhaps the most famous New York School poem that overlays French and American culture is Frank O'Hara's "Adieu to Norman, Bonjour to Joan and Jean-Paul," which appears in volume 1 of *Locus Solus*. As Lytle Shaw argues, "At one level ['Adieu'] is about the movement of gesture painters (Norman Bluhm, Joan Mitchel) between Paris and New York. At a larger level, 'Adieu' deals, thematically, with establishing and maintaining both personal and national identities—French and American— within the cultural capitals of the countries. And yet these very identities were being affected by O'Hara's trips back and forth to France promoting Abstract Expressionism for the Museum of Modern Art."[27] Shaw is right to say that O'Hara participates in national identities: in this poem, putting well-known French poets' names (Pierre Reverdy, for example) next to the names of O'Hara's friends, works almost as a spell to make O'Hara's unknown friends seem famous. This literary technique mirrors some of O'Hara's other activities at the museum; in 1958, he worked on the New American Painting exhibition, which put his friends on the map in Paris. And yet the poem is emplaced in New York City; it begins "it is 12:10 in New York," and no matter how much the speaker wishes he "were reeling around Paris," he is in New York, where "everything continues to be possible."[28] The cultural supremacy of New York is maintained through fantasies and inquiries about Paris. But by inserting Paris into Manhattan as a romantic dream, this poem joins many others in *Locus Solus* that illuminate the sometimes concealed shortcomings of an increasingly hegemonic and violent Manhattan.

In other words, New York was modernizing but at what expense? Robert Moses began his decentralization plan during the boom years when New York City was the capital of modernity and culture, or as Samuel Zipp writes, "the headquarters of global capitalism, and a symbol of American power during the Cold War." Zipp continues: "Urban renewal arrived at Manhattan's moment of triumph, offering to renovate the city in line with the metropolis's mythic postwar image of itself."[29] This image was based on large-scale urban clearance, massive interstate highway development, and widespread construction of suburban housing, all of which were employed to substantially change the geographic reach and sociocultural politics of American cities and regions. The numbers are staggering; between 1955 and 1965, urban renewal displaced one third of a million U.S. urban residents from their homes, disproportionally people of color.[30] These evictions were based on racist liberal policies of what counts as a valuable part of urban life. Scholars of literature and culture, including Joshua Shannon, and Davy Knittle, have pointed out that the transformation of urban renewal brought a politics of queer melancholy that permeates art and literature of the era. Shannon illustrates that, as New York lost many of its communities, it also began to look like American corporate capitalism, a totalizing aesthetic sea change.[31] In addition to the poems featuring a Parisian comparison, *Locus Solus* contains many images of New York on its own as a contested space of urban transformation. As Knittle argues, Schuyler's poem "December," published in the double issue of *Locus Solus*, records obsolescence and disappearances within the context of renewal to account for queer and disabled experiences of temporality and urban futurity.[32] Throughout all five issues, poems by Jean Boudin, Robert Lax, Gregory Corso, Musa Guston, Carl Morse, and John Ashbery work on the edge of U.S. patriotism by setting up and then undoing images of New York City as the supreme cultural capital.[33]

This notion that the violence of white supremacy is a Cold War tool to inflict premature death on particular populations—including Black, immigrant, disabled, and queer—is clear in other poems in *Locus Solus*. Four poems by Amiri Baraka published in volume 3–4 of *Locus Solus* are otherwise uncollected and have gone unnoticed by Baraka scholars. When the double issue came out, Baraka had just published *Preface to a Twenty Volume Suicide Note*; he was editing *The Floating Bear* with Diane Di Prima; and he had already visited Cuba, a trip that scholars note, changed his politics.[34] It was three years before Baraka would radically disavow his previous life and move to Harlem, but in the *Locus Solus* poems, Baraka is considering the urban spatial nature of assimilationist politics. These poems survey the landscape of renewing Manhattan and what this transformation meant for Black life. In each poem, just underneath the abstract inclusivity of city architecture and vantage, something murderous is lurking. In a poem called "Style," perhaps referring to this very texture of the city itself, Baraka writes of the paradox of obsolescence as new architectural style:

the day roars black and empty
all dark. all light. all my
loves' deaths.
        to have been there, where
they talked tenderness. to have
seen it pass.[35]

The lightness created by whole blocks razed for new skyscrapers is also the "all dark" of loves' death. The poet has seen enormous transformation of the built environment, and it has changed relationality and ultimately shaped cultures. As he puts it in "The End of Man Is His Beauty," the next poem in the volume, "Your world shakes / cities die / beneath your shape."[36]

Who is this "you"? In this set of poems, Baraka clearly characterizes the force that is shaking the world and killing the city: something abstract, unstoppable, ubiquitous, and in service of a vision of the United States that privileged white people at the detriment of people of color. In her writing about the literature of urban renewal, Myka Tucker-Abramson helpfully connects this moment in New York City to what Jodi Melamed usefully terms "racial liberalism." Both urban renewal and racial liberalism describe "the twenty-year period of racial reforms that sought to counteract widespread international criticism of US racism by creating an image of America as harmonious and inclusive, and thus formally enacting an alignment between decolonization, self-determination, and capitalist democracy."[37] For Baraka, returning from a trip to Cuba to an increasingly corporate, homogenous, and racially violent Manhattan, the harmonious façade is very thin. "A Long Poem for Myself" stages this conversation of urban renewal and loss and attempts to figure where art fits into the predicament. The poem ends:

      Thank each
      the other
that we are alive, "Thank you, Señor Jones
you make me weep with your music." Let us
look out from the terrace, at the city
let us wish
we were everyone

> and could suffer or taste
> each man's limited flesh.
>      Let us stare out
> at the city. It is ours
> finally, the white spokes
> of its will. Its sun/
> and sea too pulling
> at the moon.
>     "Look down
> from such a height, the eye
> has its own
> static. To look down
> so,
>   and still see
> each
> his own face.
>
>    How lovely"[38]

The speaker is conversing with a theory of art—here represented by a Spanish-speaking musician—that holds it to be collectivizing. The Spanish speaker argues that art and music provide a vantage point from which to see community and retain individuality ("to look down / so, and still see / each / his own face"). The speaker had previously been using the city itself as a way to feel connected and to understand movement (he had heard his friend Jimmy talking to himself as "singing"). Yet when he encounters the Spanish speaker, he owns the "white spokes" of the city's will, a complex metaphor for what Samuel Zipp calls "the metropolis's mythic postwar image of itself" that was built at this time.[39] From this vantage of connection and relation as a result of communal art, the speaker can see the true gravity of the city: the white spokes of proto-neoliberalism churning just beneath the façade of connective Cold War democracy.

## FRANK O'HARA REBUILDS THE SEAGRAM BUILDING

In Frank O'Hara's 1964 poem "Walking," the poet gets "a cinder" caught in his eye. New York City's fresh air and sunlight "pushes it aside," clearing his vision. Then he drops his "hot dog / into one of the Seagram Building's / fountains" before deciding "the country is no good for us." Assuming that the "cinder" is city filth or cigarette ash, the poem is participating in an urban-planning debate about sidewalk-level space, air quality, and light, a debate in which the Seagram Building was a major interlocutor. The phallic public health hazard of the hot dog is styled as charmingly American and healthy, preferable to the denser parts of the city with cinders and less light and also preferable to the open country. The speaker prefers the Seagram Plaza because in "the country":

> there's nothing
> > to bump into
> > > or fall apart glassily
>
> there's not enough
> > poured concrete
> > > and brassy
>
> reflections[40]

As the poem pushes out the cinders of dense city streets, and modernist buildings "move over" and "stamp" the previously built environment, a clear picture of urban renewal comes into view. Blocks had been razed and people displaced while New York City claimed a nationalist cosmopolitan supremacy of corporate style and poured concrete. By the time O'Hara wrote this poem, urban renewal had drastically changed the landscape of Manhattan. As the speaker of "Walking" praises the tall buildings of Park Avenue, he also defiles them by littering and complains of the pain and discomfort caused by so much pavement and wind. The poem ends with an exalting tone, "and I see it rising there / New York / greater than the Rocky Mountains." As O'Hara pays tongue-in-cheek homage to this history, "Walking" also points out the specific role that the Seagram Building has in the story. The Seagram Building shaped nationalist and corporate private interests by creating a "public space" that was in fact exclusionary, branded nationalist and elite.

The history of the Seagram Building—and its interconnection with O'Hara's poetry—begins in the 1950s, when Mies van der Rohe collaborated with Philip Johnson under the direction of Seagram's whisky heir, Phyllis Lambert, to create what would become a modernist architectural landmark. The Seagram Building was completed in 1958, while O'Hara was writing *Lunch Poems*. It is this section's contention that O'Hara's poetry engages specific architecture and urban-planning examples—in this case, the Seagram Building and debates about preservation and obsolescence—to intensify fraught political spaces and probe the role of poetry in public. O'Hara's poems about architecture are both political and participatory. I argue that O'Hara's Seagram Building—steeped in modernist ideologies and corporate interests—works to open the possibility for an ethics of queer encounter within midtown Manhattan as it displays the pitfalls of the major theories of urban planning in Manhattan in the 1950s and 1960s.

Deriving a connection between O'Hara's "I do this I do that" poems and the politics of architectural space shows the need for O'Hara's poems, and New York School poems, to be resituated. They are not only poems that chronicle the city, critique participation in commodity culture and white-collar capitalism, or recapitulate various notions of action or gesture.[41] These important frames can be utilized best if the poems are read more broadly, as akin to contemporaneous event scores and happenings. Like Fluxus works, this poetry problematizes the difference between interpretation and enactment while it works as poetry in general. In other words, O'Hara's poems use urban referents to "do" things in and beyond urban planning and architecture, outside the realm of representation to instead explore poetic language as dynamic, not stable. This poetry does not mirror the quotidian or use pieces of the city to make something else; through participation, it instead makes the structures of corporate midtown, as Gilles Deleuze remarks about the making of a minor literature, "vibrate with a new intensity."[42] This vibration comes from tactics of building and rebuilding dynamically, changing real spaces as the poems "do this and do that," spinning Cold War urban history into active participatory critique.

---

The Seagram Building, with its plaza, is the model for what has come to be known as privately owned public spaces (POPS). Seagram was a pioneer of "incentive zoning," when many midcentury architects used a 1916 zoning law to corporate design advantage.[43] The zoning law mandated a certain amount of public space per square foot of vertical private space, thus protecting light and air quality for pedestrians, discouraging overcrowded conditions, and providing minimum public access. The Seagram's architect, Mies van der Rohe, made an opportune move: he could build taller if he included some light, airy square footage of the building at street level. The innovation of the Seagram Plaza allowed for corporate density that was technically legal but previously unseen in 1958. This trick was later codified in the 1961 zoning resolution, which awarded up to 20 percent of bonus space through a floor-area-ratio system to private buildings that provided public plazas as part of their design. This zoning density bonus would become a given for major development projects; in the years between 1961 and 1973, New York City constructed over one million square feet of plaza space (more than the total of all other U.S. cities combined), a benefit that resulted in increasing the buildings' value exponentially because of their rentable space.[44]

Although plaza spaces are technically permeable to anyone, their boundaries are maintained by private interests, sometimes through direct exercises of power like security and closures, as well as the soft power of cultural norms and corporate schedules.[45] Sociologist William H. Whyte was the first to study the way these plazas were used, and he concluded as much. Although Whyte praised the Seagram Plaza for its dynamism in 1970, his research demonstrated more largely that bonus spaces were not truly welcoming to the public.[46] His work catalyzed a series of amendments that pushed for more accessible spaces in New York City through the enforcement of regulated seating, trees, and signage. The decades following brought changes to the zoning laws, and private rules for specific POPS. For example, following the Occupy Wall Street movement in 2011, many POPS posted signs banning sleeping and items related to sleeping. POPS are "public" in a highly contradictory way, and they continue to be an illuminating space for cultural understandings of access.

The Seagram Plaza of the late 1950s and early 1960s is a cypher for Cold War politics of nationalism and a signal of policies to come. This is because the Seagram Building had an early stake in neoliberal rationality as it corporatized democratic spaces. O'Hara's poetry of this moment presses on these contradictions of the Seagram space in particular and public-private spaces more generally. When the poet of "Walking" throws his hot dog into the fountain, he is using the space as intended, at least to a certain degree. The Plaza, located just around the corner from MoMA, was a place for O'Hara to have lunch on break from the museum when he worked there as an assistant curator in the international program, just the sort of white-collar worker welcomed there. Yet the line breaks of "Walking" show the dynamism of the space, recalling its permeability, and the poem queers the plaza by creating visible phallic waste in its "watery" periphery.

"Personal Poem," written in 1959 and published in *Lunch Poems*, covers this set of issues clearly, depicting the Seagram Building as a dynamic space while lampooning nationalism. The second stanza begins:

> I walk through the luminous humidity
> passing the House of Seagram with its wet
> and its loungers and the construction to
> the left that closed the sidewalk if
> I ever get to be a construction worker
> I'd like to have a silver hat please[47]

The city animates desires in this rapid passage. The possessive "its" in the third line shows that people belong to the building and even the seeming arbitrary weather ("luminous humidity" and "wet") are governed by the built environment. The "wet" here plays on Seagram's whisky as a "wet" product but also the visual pun of the building itself, which was likened to a highball because of its bronze caramel-colored exterior and shape.[48] The pervasiveness of the building is a nod to the dominant and prevailing nature of skyscrapers on city infrastructure at this time, and Seagram specifically. Likewise, the silver hats of the workers seem truly extravagant. Instead of fetishizing or objectifying labor and laborers, as this line is often read, I suggest that O'Hara is garnering a sensibility about Seagram specifically as a luxurious and perhaps frivolous site.

If a construction worker were to wear a silver hat anywhere, it would be at the House of Seagram. When the Seagram Building went up, it embodied luxury in its use of materials, its detailing, its extraordinary artistic acquisitions for its interior, and the spectacle of its opening. Seagram's interior support beams are visible on the exterior, yet they are sheathed in costly, customized bronze. The curtain wall, which begins above the lower stories, is composed of decorative pink-amber-gray glass; the plaza is made with pink granite; and the whole thing was lit with "spectacularly orchestrated" perimeter night-lighting.[49] This contradiction of functionalist modernist style and extravagance was an apparent and highly politicized critique of the International Style. Newspapers listed facts and figures of Seagram's expense, its need for custom technology, and the technical feats the building would accomplish.[50] The Seagram Building brought wealth into a functionalist modernist discourse, and it also combined cultural prowess with nationalism and capital-driven technology: it introduced the first automatic bill changer, and it was the first corporate business to fly an American flag.[51] For the dedication of the Seagram Building in 1959, a symposium on the new values in the nuclear age was held at the building. Speakers included an odd mix of cultural and scientific luminaries: Robert Frost, Bertrand Russell, Milton S. Eisenhower, and a heterogeneous handful of banking executives and anthropologists.[52] In 1962, the spectacle of the marriage of geopolitics, wealth, and high art culture reached new heights when a full-scale model of a Polaris missile was shown in the lobby, presumably for patrons of the stylish Four Seasons Restaurant located there. In the Seagram Building, corporate America easily slides into "culture," with the vehicle of a wealthy version of the International Style vying for Cold War primacy. As Benjamin Flowers writes, the Seagram Building was "engaged in the construction of both a business entity and a particular way of life."[53] This way of life was defined by material power, newness, and cleanliness that the building embodied. Flowers writes, "In the face of the threat of nuclear war, the Seagram Building was welcome evidence of the powers and ingenuity of American engineering and design. The wealth, imagination, and advanced technology necessary to construct it were cast as the very forces that would serve the United States on the geopolitical stage and preserve the vitality of American business, culture, and society."[54]

This potent mixture was present in the Seagram Building's construction. In other words, the building of the House of Seagram was a major capitalist and nationalist spectacle. During construction, the company generated interest by hiring "sidewalk superintendents," or people who peeped in on the construction through Plexiglas holes at various heights and intervals in the fences around the site. To encourage more peeping, the company broadcast information about the construction in multiple languages and displayed a model of the completed building near the site.

The construction advertised the rich, modern, and clean spectacle of corporate America at every stage. For these reasons, architectural historian and theorist Felicity Scott reads the building as a "sort of switching point, a symptom of modernism's ever-more complete integration within the globalizing and spectacular forces driving . . . postmodernization, forces at once social, economic, technological, aesthetic, informatic, and geopolitical."[55]

Whether the construction work that "closed the sidewalk" in "Personal Poem" alludes to the initial raising of the building or to a moment of repair, the spectacle of abundance is made clear through the aestheticized construction workers in rich materials. Yet without criticizing or undercutting the image of wealth and power, the poem inflects it with a queer reference: the silver hat as object of desire. Later in the poem, after discussing their literary tastes, the poets in the poem discuss aspiration and reputation: "we don't want to be in the poets' walk in / San Francisco even we just want to be rich /and walk on girders in our silver hats." Rejecting prestige in favor of spectacle, the poets want to be watched from below ("on girders"), not commemorated abstractly—they want their poems to be like the Seagram with its Plexiglas peepers in style but somehow not part of corporate culture or national recognition. As Michael Davison argues, O'Hara's "insouciant, queer, celebratory" register provides an important antidote to contemporary nationalism, even, in this case, as Terrance Diggory has suggested, upstaging a corporate spectacle that was nationalism's backbone.[56]

In other poems, the critique of corporate nationalist culture, as symbolized by modernist architecture, is blatant. "Nocturne" dated 1955, is a melancholy poem about obsolescence and clearance that seems to accept modernism as it laments it.

> There's nothing worse
> than feeling bad and not
> being able to tell you.
> Not because you'd kill me
> or it would kill you, or
> we don't love each other.
> It's space. The sky is grey
> and clear, with pink and

blue shadows under each cloud.
A tiny airliner drops its
specks over the U N Building.
My eyes, like millions of
glassy squares, merely reflect.
Everything sees through me,
in the daytime I'm too hot
and at night I freeze; I'm
built the wrong way for the
river and a mild gale would
break every fiber in me.
Why don't I go east and west
instead of north and south?
It's the architect's fault.
And in a few years I'll be
useless, not even an office
building. Because you have
no telephone, and live so
far away; the Pepsi-Cola sign,
the seagulls and noise.[57]

The poem, itself shaped like a skyscraper, laments the ineffectual glass curtain walls of buildings like Seagram's. Mirroring common complaints as the International Style office building became widely copied, the windows are weak, impractical, and consumptive. A melancholy lover, missing his beloved, is irrelevant and becoming obsolete, like a modernist building in a changing era. The speaker is "built the wrong way" for his environment and "it's the architect's fault." In other words, "Nocturne" interrogates the ideology of increasingly common modernist architecture in Manhattan. New York may be rising, greater than the Rocky Mountains, but once it is up, it has a melancholy tone. In the poem, this tone is not the result of relations between lovers but rather the space between them. Unlike the previous density of the city, this architecture allows the sky to be visible.

The speaker-building improbably seems to be facing the UN building, the first International Style skyscraper built in Manhattan. Designed by Le Corbusier and Oscar Niemeyer in what was considered a cutting edge but immutable modernist style and built in 1950, it sits overlooking the East River in the Turtle Bay neighborhood of New York City. Samuel Zipp studies the UN building as paradigmatic of the beginning of urban renewal, meant to serve as evidence of New York as a "cultural capital of the world."[58] The mixed-use area that was cleared to create the space for the building was publicly depicted as violent, abject, and mostly made up of slaughterhouses, allowing the UN site to represent the highest fulfillment of the logic of replacement and progress behind slum clearance. Although it represented the possibility and promise of the city-rebuilding ethic for Manhattan, in reality, 179 families and several meatpacking plants needed to be relocated as the renewal projects attempted plazas with tree-lined paths.[59] The space created here, the poem illustrates, is melancholy and bare.

Looking out over the vastness of Cold War American "progress," the speaker sees "a tiny airliner drop its "specks over the U N Building." Whether propaganda is being dropped from a real airliner or the war image is a metaphor for a bird defecating, these lines actively undermine notions that the UN is impenetrable to foreign attack. The lines "And in a few years I'll be / useless, not even an office / building" seem to speak directly to Le Corbusier's ideals of modernist architecture's potential for ultimate endurance, or its ability "to pass the crisis."[60] If the obsolescence of the previous neighborhood in Turtle Bay represented the superiority of capitalism, the modernist buildings built in its place were meant to endure. Yet the poem points out a fact that was becoming increasingly true in the 1950s, the fact of what Daniel Abramson calls "the promise of obsolescence" which, he argues, infused much architectural thought during this period.[61] By the mid-1960s, architects, from avant-garde practitioners to mainstream builders, were beginning to embrace obsolescence as part of capitalist optimism. But in 1955, the obsolescence—especially of modernist buildings—was unnerving, a threat. In the poem, relation and connection between lovers is foreclosed by corporate style, and emotional durability is rendered precarious by architectural obsolescence. However, unlike the argument of Jane Jacobs's *The Death and Life of Great American Cities*, which along with other texts in the early 1960s, inspired a preservationist trend to protect quality of life for pedestrians, the poem accepts the premise of modernism in the built environment. The poem and the speaker are both skyscrapers, after all.

O'Hara's "The Lay of the Romance of the Associations," written three years later, in 1958, illustrates not only the melancholy of urban renewal and obsolescence but also the pitfalls of preservation in New York City at this time. As Daniel Abramson explains, "Preservationism and obsolescence were in fact two sides of the same modernizing coin. Both rationalized change in elite interests."[62] The poem satirizes the elite notion of purity and tradition that kept the East Side of midtown Manhattan from demolition and development in the 1950s. While residents were not being displaced there at the same levels as they were in other parts of the city, this area resisted public use and commerce that would benefit large numbers. In the poem, urban planning is both the stuff of a love relationship and resistance to its consummation. The poem begins:

> *High above Manhattan's towers*
> *gilded like Camelot in every weather*
> *I heard the cries of the Park Avenue and the Fifth Avenue Associations*
> *trying to get together.*
>
> If only, if only, cried the Fifth Avenue Association
> bring the less elite of the two, and therefore
> the first to come on, I weren't so rushed all the time!
> I have so much to say to you but we are far apart.
>
> I hear you, yodeled the Park Avenue Association
> in Westchester accents cracked with emotion,
> and I too am harried even in my very center and a strange
> throb of emotion fills the towering Seagram Building
> with a painful foretaste of love for you. But alas,
> that bourgeois Madison Avenue continues to obstruct
> our free intercourse with each other.[63]

The Fifth Avenue Association, though perhaps "less elite" than the Park Avenue Association, is a long-standing group of New York merchants, property owners, and investors with a penchant for preservation. From its inception in 1907, the association was dedicated primarily to reinforcing the image of Fifth Avenue between Thirty-second and Fifty-ninth streets as a high-class shopping district. The group advocated against noise, factories, traffic, and tall buildings, often campaigning for or against laws and ordinances according to this mission.[64] As a self-published history from 1957 puts it, the Fifth Avenue Association formed to rescue the avenue from "gaudy signs . . . loiterers, beggars, and peddlers [who] hung around in doorways . . . desultory and untidy garbage removal . . . and heavy trucking."[65] Through the years, the association achieved its aims: it banned and removed unhoused, poor, Black, and foreign-born people and their potential for livelihood, and they halted many projects and transportation that disrupted expensive private property and notions of comfort for a small few. Or, as the association puts it, "the cheap, the tawdry, the raucous, the ephemeral, have been spotted quickly by the Association, which has been helped to buttress the dignity to which the thoroughfare has laid claim for a century and a half."[66]

The Park Avenue Association, although founded a little later, in 1922, had a similar mission, which included publishing a social review and "keeping the avenue free of commercialism and unwanted motor traffic."[67] Both associations had enough sway to change the type of development that happened on their streets—the Fifth Avenue Association was partially responsible for halting the development of several skyscrapers in the area—as well as imposing policies such as banning motorbus traffic and taxi whistles on the avenues.[68] The poem plays on these class and race signifiers as the associations seem kept in place by the geography of the avenues, and the avenues bear metonymic relation to their inhabitants. The "lay," a short lyric poem intended to be sung, has a long history in medieval French romance poetry of the courts, the highest of the feudal classes. The title, punning on "lay" as a sexual act as well as aristocratic practice, keeps the associations apart from each other through courtship. Like the space in the poem that obstructs their "free intercourse with each other" through a gratuitous double set of articles, the two streets and associations are not able to touch.

The poem continues:

> Intercourse!
> cried Fifth Avenue, all I want to do is kiss you, kiss
> your silver grey temples and your charming St. Bartholomew's
> ears. What would Sak's think, and De Pinna, much less Tishman
> if such things were to go on in the middle of Manhattan?

You must not be untrue to your upbringing, even if
your suit is torn and your tailor hasn't delivered the new one.

Suit-shmuit, said Park Avenue, our joining will fecundate
this otherwise arid and sterile-towered metropolis!
the alliance of aristocrat with parvenue has always been
the hope of democracy, not to mention bureaucracy. You
don't think I need you, my plants are green. But look!
I don't have many plants. And you, even in the depths of
winter, are covered with lights under which like basking collies
grow your tender evergreens of love and commerce. Come!

I can't, for stern Madison Avenue has me in thrall
and won't divorce me even though I've offered "no settlement."
Why don't we rendezvous in Central Park behind a clump of
   cutthroats
near the reservoir and there we'll kiss and hold each other
sweatily as in a five o'clock on a mid-August Friday in the dusk
and after, languorously bathe, to sweeten city water for all time.[69]

When, in the poem, Fifth wants to kiss the ears of St. Bartholomew's, a church built in 1830, the philosophy of "protecting isolated urban treasures" is likened to a personal sexual fetish.[70] Yet policies to honor old buildings were widely adopted soon after the poem was written, in particular in this area. As preservationism was becoming a more popular urban-planning tactic, in 1965 the Fifth Avenue New York City Landmarks Preservation Commission formed to protect Fifth Avenue's limestone buildings, largely built in the early 1900s. Fifth Avenue's depiction of Park as haggard although well bred ("You must not be untrue to your upbringing, even if / your suit is torn"), illustrates why "the towering Seagram Building" is the phallus in the poem, complete with "a painful foretaste of love." Though the Park Avenue Association was committed to elitist tactics of capturing public space in private interests, the Seagram Building stands for Park's dirty modernization that compromised preservationist ideals. However, Park knows that the Seagram Building—with its bronze trappings and modernist status—only helped maintain its elitism and it wants Fifth, a newcomer to preservationist wealth (a "parvenue"), to join the preservationist impulse, which would secure the "hope of democracy."

The end of the poem, proposing a half-dangerous sexual encounter in Central Park, queers this romance between the associations and aims to undercut the ideology of both renewal and preservation. This is a scene of "criminal intimacy," in Michael Warner's sense that "the discourse contexts that narrate true personhood have been segregated from those that represent citizens, workers or professionals."[71] The love relationship is set apart from the grid of Manhattan streets; it takes place at the end of the workday and near potential violence (a "clump of cutthroats"). The poem suggests that the dominant ordered culture, once it breaks, or loosens its hold on the physical structures of both real space and normative consumer spatial practices, allows an activation of a separate futurity ("for all time"). After the streets break out of their grid, they wish to "sweeten city water" through the reservoir water supply. This infectious but improbable image of the sweat of sexually fulfilled collective-singular avenues—their associations and inhabitants represented—entering drinking water rings of Cold War containment paranoia. Deborah Nelson writes about the dominant understandings of private and public spheres in this era: "The potency of American democracy in Cold War rhetoric was, therefore, not its cultivation of a vibrant and free public discourse but its vigilant protection of private autonomy. Furthermore, the stakes of this conviction were typically apocalyptic: either we preserved the integrity of private spaces and thus the free world, or we tolerated their penetration and took the first step toward totalitarian oppression."[72]

Despite the apocalyptic penetration imagery, the poem flips the usual narrative about containment because the farce around nationalist rhetoric of containment—in this case, containing the sanctity of elite neighborhoods—comes from the Seagram Building made queer. The depiction of the penetration (and possibly ejaculation) from the otherwise moral, clean, and very American Seagram Building into the entire city points out that the war cannot be with either new architecture or with the preservation of precious old buildings. By making both modernism and preservation the contaminating agents for the city, the poem undermines various notions of purity associated with both. Instead, the poem claims that the culture of privileging certain forms of life over others in a spatialized sense ("the tender evergreens of love and commerce") criminalizes bodies for the sake of capitalist enterprise. As Myka Tucker-Abramson argues, while some dominant scholarship still maintains that the Cold War ideology of this time was focused on "containment," that might not be the best term to describe policies at home or abroad. She writes about "containment":

> From its construction of the Bretton Woods agreement that laid the basis for the global financial order of the present day, to its import of scientists and engineers into the Third World to create and develop market-based economies, to its use of CIA operatives to manipulate the affairs of foreign countries up to and including coups and assassinations, to its overdevelopment of white suburban areas and underdevelopment of urban space, and also its use of programs like COINTELPRO [counterintelligence program] to destroy Black, queer, feminist, and class-based liberation movements—of this suggests that "intervention," "invasion," "expansion," "penetration," "displacement," or "dispossession" might be more accurate terms around which to base a study.[73]

Indeed, the "sweetened waters" of the city are brewed uptown in the Park, and "the hope of democracy" comes from an unlikely union of interests. Yet both interests seek to destroy the populations made vulnerable by Cold War policies. This uneven sense of democracy can be traced through *Poetry in General*—readers can think back to my discussion of Yoko Ono's instructions and scientific management (chapter 1) or George Brecht's interest in suburbanization and commodification (chapter 2)—but is perhaps most easily surfaced here. Poetry in the current chapter embodies these very sites of dispossession.

These "real" spaces surrounding MoMA become capable of being manipulated within this New York School style. The poems accomplish an act that spatial practice cannot: built environments are shaped, clarifying how privatization forces operate in ways that are often purposefully silenced in the privatizing impulse itself. The poems of human-skyscraper lovers and groups of buildings in queer sexual relationships use the rhetoric of privatization to generate new possibilities. With elite consumer associations comes intercourse that subverts Cold War ideology, with the spectacle of national wealth and cleanliness comes queer desire, with architectural critique comes the possibility of a valuable love relationship. Each poem asks us to participate in an event in the places that we know in order to transform these very places. My reading of O'Hara's work and the Seagram Building points out the resonance between a public poetic tradition and "I do this I do that." This genre of "I do this I do that" was created within the pages of *Locus Solus* through national imaginaries, and it manipulates cities through action, calling into question the ideologies of urban landscapes. These lists of actions, like Fluxus events, show us the possibilities just outside the everyday. They act as scores to illustrate how to activate our environment, taking the expansion of poetry as their subject.

# 4

## FEMINIST PROCEDURE AND DURATIONAL CONSTRAINT

Reproduction, Welfare, and "Losing Myself"

In 1971 and 1972, three women in different but overlapping artistic milieus experimented with hunger over the duration of one month. One documented a moderate diet, one studied theories of presence through fasting, and one wrote about food as a state of mind. These works have been written about separately in relation to feminist body art, photography, and poetry. Bringing them together as poetry in general, this chapter suggests that these artworks interrogate the government regulation of women's bodies through welfare, health care, and work.

In their experimentation with diet, these procedures register the literal imprint and impossibility that 1970s political economic conditions make on bodies. By centering cisgendered women's bodies in procedural practice, these experiments illustrate how they are constructed through various government regulatory schemes—welfare and antiabortion laws in particular—to facilitate capitalism. Uniting these works by their use of food as a procedural device illustrates their political stakes within a dominant trend of constraint-based art and poetry that began in the 1960s and lasts through today. Although these works obviously speak to each other, reorienting our gaze to see them as part of the same genre is only possible through an exploration of two critical conversations: one about procedural writing and the other about feminist body art, conversations that have previously been mired in ideas about apolitical experimentalism and biological essentialism, respectively. The introduction to this chapter will briefly sketch some socioeconomic conditions at play for these artists in the early 1970s and then turn to the troubling categories of analysis in which their work is usually placed. After laying the groundwork for an expanded field for procedural artwork, I will then analyze the poetry, photographs, and performances together. Examining body art alongside poetic constraint illustrates that the femme bodies on display in performance are just as constructed as poems. Furthermore, these experiments direct constraint to expose the strategic construction of realities otherwise normalized by the state. As I put the works in conversation, I conjecture about what drew these artists to food as a procedure in 1971 and 1972. As a mechanism for thinking about social limitations, food will move from the actual effects of eating or fasting to a figure of sustenance provided by welfare and reproductive rights.

By the early 1970s in the United States, various strains of the women's liberation movement—from local welfare rights organizations to popular literature—were questioning a previously naturalized condition of women as unwaged laborers in the home.[1] The feminine gender, tied to constructions of race and class as well as capitalism, was revealing itself to be a personality shaped by the labor market, and designed to remain unwaged or low waged. In other words, the purpose of reproducing workers through cooking, cleaning, childbearing, and rearing was not culturally valued as productive; this fact was only becoming more obvious with the decline of the family wage and reorganization of the workforce. Increasing numbers of women entered the workforce, and it responded with wage stagnation, shrinking social welfare, and devaluation of domestic labor.[2] Women, incentivized into the workplace, were also punished there.[3] As the Endnotes Collective puts it clearly, women are cheaper short-term labor due to the potential of leaving the sphere of waged labor (whether they intend to have children or not).[4] At the same time, neither abortion nor contraceptive pills were legal or safely available, putting many people in an impossible bind.[5] Welfare and food assistance were increasingly stigmatized at this moment, and this process of stigmatization dovetailed with debates about population growth and workforce cultivation (sometimes in other terms, about abortion and birth control) to reinforce normative structures of existing wage systems.[6]

These large and abstract battles were mapped most concretely onto the site of cis-normative, feminine gendered bodies. Silvia Federici theorizes that "women's bodies have been the main targets, the privileged sites, for the deployment of power-techniques and power relations." She continues, "Many of the feminist studies which have been produced since the early 1970s on the policing of women's reproductive function, the effects on women of rape, battering, and the imposition upon them of beauty as a condition for social acceptability, are a monumental contribution to the discourse on the body in our times."[7] One place this discourse shows itself most clearly is in the use of constraint and procedure in women's art of the era. When critics discuss procedure and constraint, they are generally referring to poetry. However, by studying feminist body art that uses procedural techniques alongside poetry, an important story about this type of work emerges. Unlike procedural poetry, which is thought to be apolitical, the 1970s includes a wave of body art that speaks directly to labor deregulation, privatized public services, and welfare cuts in the United States.[8] Amelia Jones defines body art as work that "exacerbates, performs, and/or negotiates the dislocating effects of social and private experience in the late capitalist, postcolonial Western world," and it is worth pointing out that it often uses constraints on the body to do so.[9]

In the decades following, 1970s women's art that centered the cis-normative, feminine gendered body—or most especially, the emancipation of this particular body—has been criticized for reifying a second-wave essentialism, especially as feminists of the 1980s and beyond eschewed notions of sexual liberation in favor of seemingly more structural modes of analysis.[10] In other words, these works have been critiqued for equating the notion of "women" with a specific biological body, which although the race may have been unmarked, was often white. As Helen Anne Molesworth argues, a false critical distinction was drawn between "emblematic 70s art," which featured biologically based femininity, and artwork of the 1980s that focused on the category of women as constructed through various cultural and economic categories. Molesworth shows that this spurious distinction has obscured the focus on political economy in 1970s feminist art across the spectrum. She argues that works by Mary Kelly, Mierle Laderman Ukeles, and Judy Chicago that center care work, maintenance, and the domestic sphere deconstruct the categories of public and private through interrogating women's labor as much as they are "about" women's biological bodies.[11]

Molesworth's reorientation informs my contention that aligning political economy–focused body art with linguistic practices in what is usually considered the field of poetry and poetics undoes essentialist readings without disallowing a focus on the body. Examining body art alongside poetic constraints reveals that, across an expanded field of durational works, artists were exploring how cis-normative women's bodies are in fact shaped by questions of political economy. For example, performance artists like Ukeles created constraint-based artworks that focused directly on stagnating wages and the location and devaluation of women's labor or, as she puts it in her 1969 manifesto, "The culture confers lousy status on maintenance = minimum wages, housewives = no pay."[12] In her "I Make Maintenance Art One Hour Every Day" (1976), her unit of procedure was temporal; the hour as the unit of the waged work pointedly becomes the artist's generative rule. Other artists used the everyday constraints of women's beauty practices as their procedures. Examples include "Leah's Room" at *Womanhouse* (1972), where a performer worked to apply, remove, and then reapply makeup constantly in a nightmarish cyclical routine meant to recall the absurdity of the traditional feminine toilet.[13] Where a procedural method like N + 7 robotically works to replace noun after noun, in this room, makeup becomes an arbitrary and unrelenting "generative process." Similarly, works by Shigeko Kubota, Hannah Wilke, and later Lorraine O'Grady and Cindy Sherman show the constructed nature of the feminine face and pose by use of excessive constraints, overposing, or overfalsifying the appearance. Mary Kelly's *Post-Partum Document* has likewise been written about as a central site for the connection between performance, conceptual art, and theories of reproductive labor because it catalogs the work of childbearing and child-rearing.

Within literary studies, constrained poetry is often viewed in purely formal terms, without consideration for the accepted political gestures of constraint. Perhaps this elision stems from the fact that all writing is constrained, and poetry, of course, even more so.[14] Yet when we discuss "constraint," "procedure," or "generative device" (and for my purposes here, these are synonyms), we are not usually talking about the rules that govern certain forms or genres of poetry like sonnets, ballads, or even sestinas. Although the rules that govern these forms might be likened to bondage, they do not center a procedure created by the artist to help generate them and then accepted as artifice throughout the work. For Joseph Conte, procedural form is "a generative structure that constrains the poet to encounter and examine that which he or she does not immediately fathom."[15] Likewise, in his book about Oulipo writing, which is often considered the primary example of constrained writing, Daniel Levin Becker quotes Gilbert Sorrentino's syllabus: "'Generative Devices' are consciously selected, preconceived structures, forms, limitations, constraints, developed by the writer before the act of writing. The writing is then made according to the 'laws' set in place by the chosen constraint. Paradoxically, these constraints permit the writer a remarkable freedom. They also serve to destroy the much-cherished myth of 'inspiration,' and its idiot brother, 'writer's block.'"[16] If some generative devices eschew bourgeois notions of genius in favor of "freedom" made possible by more rules, other types of constraint might impose rules to expose and reject existing social constraints. One can hear the Oulipian philosophy of *potential* ringing through these definitions in a way that differs from the engagement of known generic forms.[17] In other words, with procedural form, the rules of creation are set before the result is fathomed, and they are set in part to make it less likely that anyone can fathom the end-result. As Conte explains, these forms are "primary to the creative process."[18]

For most of the scholarship on procedural poetry since Conte's book, the use of constraint or procedure is tied to "postmodern forms."[19] Poetics scholarship about procedure and constraint often ends with an identification of the generative device used in a particular example, an exclamation that the work is oriented toward process rather than product, and sometimes even a suggestion that constraint-generated work is most useful as a writer's exercise.[20] The poststructuralist insistence that a readerly output matches a writerly output is often the endgame of this style of criticism, and it rarely includes either materialist analysis or close reading of the text itself. Yet if authorial potentiality is leaned on too heavily in poetry criticism, it is undertheorized in literature on body art. As art historians like Molesworth and Jones have made clear, essentialist and reductionist interpretations arise when body art is considered without questions of potential or structure at play.

These symptomatic methods of interpretation—methods that elide material considerations of the works themselves—expose that previous definitions of the aesthetic practice of constraint are too narrow. Simply put, this means that scholars have been looking for constraint only in writing, and when similar rules apply to bodies and spaces, we call it something else and interpret it very differently. Yet if we link aesthetic constraint to social systems of constraint, then we can see beyond metaphors of creation to a larger interpretive horizon for individual texts, and we unearth an expanded field of procedural texts. By widening durational constraint practices to include texts beyond what we usually think of as poems, I start this process of forging a larger category, one that is linked to social forms of constraint, a category that can help us fathom what material and social possibilities aesthetic constraints might generate.

My interest in putting these works together is inspired by Juliana Spahr and Stephanie Young's charge to create what they call "foulipo," a new group formation that engages the "relation between formalism and body art and sees both as part of a tradition that was complicated and interconnected."[21] At a 2005 conference otherwise about experimental writing, Spahr and Young brought attention to body art that emerged around the same time as Oulipian constraint; as they explained, they brought in body art as an antidote to what they saw as an inauthentic engagement with politics in procedural literature. They write about the feminist politics of Eleanor Antin, Mierle Laderman Ukeles, and Valie Export and then "slenderize" their own writing, an Oulipian technique of removing one letter from the entire text (in this case, the letter "r"). As their essay was recited at the conference, actors took off their clothes and put them back on again in a cycle that Bruna Mori suggests was meant to show the "disrobing of language."[22]

Part of their point in asking for this new type of art called "foulipo" is to show that it is very difficult to discuss formal procedure, politics, and the body together; their literal undressing and abstract redressing of the field of procedure illustrates this fact. I agree with Spahr and Young and here hope to recover the way that procedural body art and procedural writing are ultimately connected. Despite the scholarship on formal constraint as existing mostly in apolitical literary fields, ritualized constraint and procedure was a central aspect of the explosion of 1970s political body art.

To use Spahr and Young's terms, a "foulipo" has been right in front of us the whole time. This chapter considers these practices together within a category of constraint, an element of poetry in general. This tactic brings a political lens to the field of constraint-based practices as a whole. I will argue that body art and procedural poetry together are uniquely well positioned to expose and critique how the state's facilitation of capitalism had a clear stake in sex and gender at a moment parallel to the women's liberation movement. Constraints with food in particular expose and critique the state rationality of welfare and pregnancy beyond what then burgeoning feminist theory allowed.

This chapter will closely analyze Eleanor Antin's photography, *Carving: A Traditional Sculpture*; Adrian Piper's loft performance, *Food for the Spirit*; and Bernadette Mayer's book of prose poetry, *Studying Hunger*. In 1972, Antin photographed her body over the period of thirty-eight days through the loss of ten pounds; Piper fasted in isolation while doing yoga and studying Immanuel Kant's *Critique of Pure Reason* over the summer of 1971, stopping only to record her image in a mirror and her voice on a recorder; and Mayer attempted to document what she called her "states of consciousness" over the course of one month, April 1972. Mayer's work is usually considered poetry, Antin's as photography, and Piper's as performance art. Each of these artists at one point or another were classified as conceptual artists and feminist artists, though Piper's work is understood to most explicitly critique racism and gender stereotypes through the 1980s and 1990s.[23] Mayer and Antin are white and from working-class New York backgrounds: Mayer was an orphan raised by nuns in Brooklyn. Antin was the daughter of newly immigrated Polish Jews in the Bronx (she moved to San Diego, California, three years prior to creating *Carving*). Piper is a light-skinned Black woman from an upper-middle-class Black family.[24] In the midst of the New York City art world fascinated with women's liberation theory, they each employ the durational constraint of hunger to make art.

Each artist set a procedural rule that was meant to facilitate the artwork in question: either fasting or eating for a month. The monthlong formal constraint is crucial to the social forms these artists explore. Each work attempts the duration of roughly a menstrual cycle while *Roe v. Wade* was debated on the national stage and abortion rights were further restricted in backlash. The month in question is also the duration of a food-stamp allotment when work incentives and home surveillance were first introduced to welfare services. By interrogating the rules of welfare and health care, these works show how the labor force and the bodies within it symbiotically sustain each other. By manipulating hunger, the ultimate rule of sustenance and reproduction, these artists eschewed the constraints imposed by the state welfare system and the ideas of normative gender embodiment it produced. I interpret these works to suggest that support for people who can get pregnant must include reproductive health care. In this way, *Carving*, *Food for the Spirit*, and *Studying Hunger* interrogate how bodies are constructed not only by biology but also by the state.

## AESTHETIC CONSTRAINT: GENDER, WORK, AND THE DOCUMENTATION OF DIET

### ELEANOR ANTIN'S DIET

Eleanor Antin's *Carving: A Traditional Sculpture* (1972), the rigorous documentation of a diet that the artist underwent to lose ten pounds, shows a particular corollary to constraint-based processes from literature (figure 4.1). One hundred forty-eight clinical photos of nude Antin from the front, back, and sides (four per day) depict a white door and wall around her body getting larger as her body gets smaller. The photos are arranged in deadpan documentary style, and Antin herself dons a blank expression and vaguely scientific posture with her legs and arms set slightly apart. Because the photographs are hung horizontally according to time and vertically according to pose, they can be read like a film strip, and they recall Eadweard Muybridge multiples that illustrate movement. Unlike Muybridge studies, however, in which figures move forward between photos, Antin's body recedes, and the white space opens as she loses weight. Unlike a filmstrip, which might depict a few seconds of footage, Antin's experiment lasted thirty-eight days.

In part, *Carving* is a joke about medium—Antin was asked to submit a sculpture to the Whitney Annual Exhibition of American Sculpture,

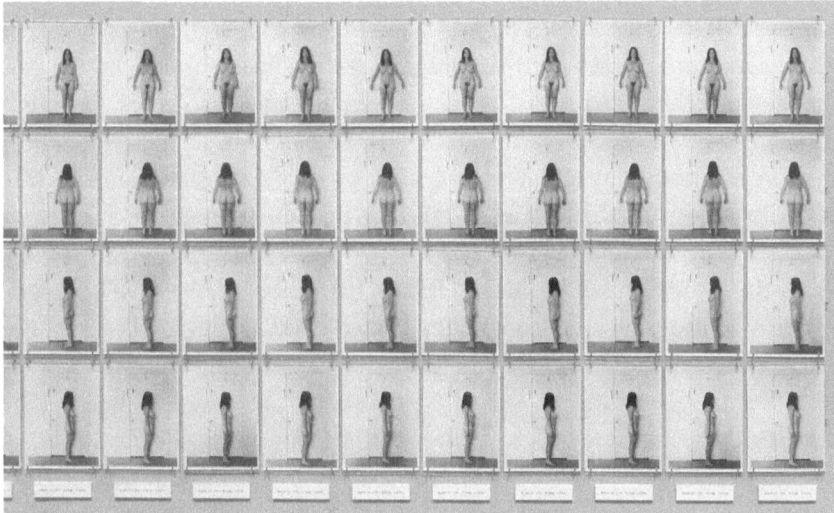

FIGURE 4.1 Eleanor Antin, *Carving: A Traditional Sculpture*, July 15 to August 21, 1972. 148 gelatin silver prints, 31¼″ × 204″ (each 7″ × 5″). Art Institute of Chicago. Copyright Eleanor Antin. Image of detailed section used with permission.

and this was her contribution. In a draft of a letter to the Whitney, Antin wrote:

> There is one work especially I thought you might be interested in for the Whitney Annual. It's a large sculpture I call CARVING. It consists of photographic documentation . . . of my unclothed body in the process of "carving" down during a strict regimen of dieting and exercise. . . . The piece is actually carried out technically in the manner of archaic and classical Greek sculpture which proceeded to peel small layers off an overall body image until the image was gradually refined to the point of aesthetic satisfaction. While I may have a different aesthetic for the female body than Greek sculpture exhibited for the Korai I think the work articulates the aesthetics of carving as a sculptural mode.[25]

It was rejected from the Whitney because it was not a sculpture, but the message is clear: Antin wanted viewers to know that she is both the artist and the artwork.[26] Like the technique of chiseling bits of stone away to create a form, she is "carving" her body through constraining the amount and type of food she eats. The art object is personal and it is procedural. As Helen Anne Molesworth writes about the advent of conceptual art, in *Carving* "the managerial impulse to document and survey is shown to permeate women's lives differently, bound as it is to the production of women's bodies as a consumable commodity."[27] Antin's diet rule was set with a consumable result in mind: a particular image of beauty or "aesthetic satisfaction."

Antin exposes the political efficacy of constraint-generated work to critique not only notions of constructed gender but also the way the art world was organized. Just as dieting was part of the beauty ideal that thinkers like Shulamith Firestone, writing two years earlier, called "a cultural tool to enforce sex class," here it is apparent that this constraint is a symptom of patriarchy "borrowed" for the purpose of Antin's experiment.[28] At this time, the Wages Against Housework campaign urged women to recognize the fact that women must worry about their looks on the job—whether that job is waged or unwaged—and that it needs to be "considered a condition of the work."[29] With *Carving*, Antin documents conditions of work on the body, linking those conditions to artwork and illustrating that marketization of gender is central not only to the boundaries of medium enforced by art institutions at this time but also to the material constraints of women's livelihood.

When the work was exhibited, it was shown with a wall text that explains the procedure in detail and that ends with a reference to the sculptor Michelangelo: "It should be kept in mind that two considerations determine the conclusion of a work: (1) the ideal image toward which the artist aspires, and (2) the limitations of the material. As our great predecessor once said: 'non ho l'ottima artista alcun concetto che el marmo solo non in se sircoscrive' or to paraphrase in English: 'not even the greatest sculptor can make anything that isn't already inside the marble.'"[30] There is plenty of irony to the piece as Antin addresses the notion that, no matter how hard she worked during the process, she could not archive an ideal image because her body ("the material") was inferior to begin with (has "limitations"). Even if conjured cheekily to tease the art world, the tradition of Ancient Greek and Renaissance art is attached to notions of ethnic whiteness. Lisa Bloom and Cherise Smith have pointed out that Antin's Jewishness is at stake, or that it is in fact Antin's Jewish body that is ironically suggested should be critiqued or remade.³¹ There is some truth to this, as Antin measured herself against a fabricated ideal body type. However, although it does point out limitations and suggest failure, the choice of Michelangelo Buonarroti's Sonnet XV complicates any idea that the medium is insufficient. The speaker in the sonnet cannot win his beloved's favor, and the sonnet likens his inability to make her love him—or to draw love from her—to a sculptor failing to make a sculpture beautiful, even though it contains beauty within the material. The poem ends: "Since in thy heart thou carriest death and grace / Enclosed together, and my worthless brain / Can draw forth only death to feed on me."³² In the poem, failure is not the fault of the material but the fault of the artist or of the lover's "worthless brain." In *Carving*, the lover and sculptor, artist and artwork are one and so the final image of "feeding" death further indicates that an external regime is shaping the body. Although she may aspire toward an ideal image or even indicate a desired result at the beginning, she also knows that the true result of imposing hunger is only death. She is slenderizing, even disappearing, her body to illustrate impossible external constraints.

*Carving* was created while abortion restrictions were deliberated throughout the United States. As Emily Liebert observes, "Against this political backdrop, [*Carving*'s] depiction of a subject literally diminished by regulating regimes reads as a protest against state control of women's bodies."³³ In fact, Antin had personal experience with not only subtle means of control of women through the labor market but also the way that lack of access to abortion disciplined women's lives and bodies. In her mock-memoir, she writes that at sixteen years old, God answered her prayers to terminate an unwanted pregnancy.³⁴ The fear of another unwanted pregnancy in the 1960s made her move in with David Antin, her later husband and longtime partner. As she explains in an oral history interview, "I thought I was pregnant and I didn't know who the father was. No, I thought I knew but he was such an asshole I didn't even want to tell him. So I figured, uh, oh, I need an abortion. But I didn't know how to get one. It was illegal then."³⁵ After she entirely changes her life course, she later finds out that she "was not pregnant, fortunately."³⁶ For Antin, the documentation of the body serves as a way to explore the possibility of transformation under debilitating constraints. In an essay criticizing conceptual artists for spuriously assuming that documentation is a "neutral list of facts," Antin explains that her "interests in transformation were inextricably bound up with the nature of the documentation process itself."[37] In *Carving*, diet serves as an agent to both protest and display the making of bodies. The photographs that Antin creates are not just documentation of hunger but the utopian horizon of transformation or genuine bodily autonomy. The concept of slenderizing or disappearing is underscored by the fact that the diet that Antin used for *Carving* consisted of cutting out certain foods rather than introducing a weight loss regime such as the then popular grapefruit diet or the Weight Watchers program.[38] In other words, this is a diet of restriction, a constraint of taking out.

Antin's *Eight Temptations*, made the same year, is an attempt to depict the constraint itself. A companion artwork to *Carving*, *Eight Temptations* consists of color photographs of Antin heroically denying herself food that is not allowed in the diet she performed for *Carving*. The project calls our attention to the myriad areas of everyday sexist constraints (her yogurt, banana, and peanuts are "temptations"). The comically overposed nature of Antin's face and gestures in this series contrasts with the serious tone of *Carving*, perhaps a comment on the heroism of formal constraints themselves. If Oulipians felt themselves to be the *opérateur* of a constraint until the work is completed, Antin's work illustrates that the artist is a product of the constraint. Constraint is the political agency behind the artwork, which exposes and critiques the unlivable aspects of social life. The tone of *Eight Temptations* demonstrates that separating the procedure from the events and spaces of everyday life is a little silly. Throughout her career, Antin would continue to expose the constructed nature of categories like gender, even developing personas or whole identities in her artwork, which included archetypes or characters like the King, the Ballerina, and the Nurse. She writes, "Gratuitous or random choices, as well as quick violent forays to the edge, are equally limitations on my understanding. I wanted to work with nuclear images, magnetic gravitational fields—geocenters of the soul."[39] Just as Oulipians belittle chance-based writing, Antin is discouraged by "random choices." In *Carving*, the constraint itself is the archetype of the restrictive, feminized diet that her rules expose and transform. Antin's work suggests that gender is performative and linked to artistic practice, but also that the body, and all the ways it is shaped publicly and privately, is part of the production.

## ADRIAN PIPER'S FAST

In July 1971, Adrian Piper became so immersed in her study that, as she put it, "I thought I was losing my mind, in fact losing my sense of self completely."[40] She explains the project as a "private loft performance continuing through summer, while reading and writing a paper on Kant's *Critique of Pure Reason*, fasting, doing yoga, and isolating myself socially."[41] This combination of study, fast, isolation, and yoga was so immersive that she frequently had to "make sure [she] was still there."[42] She elaborates on the performance: "To anchor myself in the physical world, I ritualized my frequent contacts with the physical appearance of myself in the mirror.... I rigged up a camera and tape recorder next to the mirror so that every time the fear of losing myself overtook me and drove me to the 'reality check' of the mirror, I was able to both record my physical appearance objectively and also to record myself on tape repeating the passage in the *Critique* that was currently driving me to self-transcendence."[43] *Food for the Spirit* consists of this "private loft performance," the record of which is a spiral bound notebook of pages torn from Kant's *Critique of Pure Reason* (translated to English by Norman Kemp Smith) alternating with fourteen photos of her body in various states of underexposure.[44] The photos were taken with a Brownie camera, and they appear small, gray, and grainy yet exude enormous presence. In each one, Piper's body recedes into darkness and shadow, and her face is obscured. In her notebook, the sequential arrangement of the photos from lighter to darker suggests the gradual disappearance of her body throughout the course of the fast.[45] A note in the front of the notebook explains that, while she was at the mirror, Piper would "repeat aloud the passage in the *Critique* (underlined on the following pages) that was shaking the foundations of my self-identity until it was just (psychologically manageable) words."[46] The note also explains that the recordings have since been destroyed, but the pages of Kant's *Critique* included in the notebook are underlined and annotated by Piper (figure 4.2). In 1997, after careful consideration of intentions and effects of the originals, the small photos of the notebook were blown up to a larger size using Piper's negatives.[47] Since then, the full set has been exhibited many times without the notebook or passages from Kant's text and, in some cases, a few photos are shown without the accompaniment of the full set (figures 4.3 and 4.4).[48]

80  KANT'S CRITIQUE OF PURE REASON

B 55 and that too by those who have nothing very convincing to say against the doctrine of the ideality of space, is this. They have no expectation of being able to prove apodeictically the absolute reality of space; for they are confronted by idealism, which teaches that the reality of outer objects does not allow of strict proof. On the other hand, the reality of the object of our inner sense (the reality of myself and my state) is, [they argue,] immediately evident through consciousness. The former may be merely an illusion; the latter is, on their view, undeniably something real. What they have failed, however, to recognise is that both are in the same position; in neither case can their reality as representations be questioned, and in both cases they belong only to appearance, which always has two sides, the one by which the object is viewed in and by itself (without regard to the mode of intuiting it—its nature therefore remaining always problematic), the other by which the form of the intuition of this object is taken into account. This form is not to be looked for in the object in itself, but in the subject to which the object appears; nevertheless, it belongs really and necessarily to the appearance of this object.

Time and space are, therefore, two sources of knowledge, from which bodies of *a priori* synthetic knowledge can be

A 39 derived. (Pure mathematics is a brilliant example of such knowledge, especially as regards space and its relations.)

B 56 Time and space, taken together, are the pure forms of all sensible intuition, and so are what make *a priori* synthetic propositions possible. But these *a priori* sources of knowledge, being merely conditions of our sensibility, just by this very fact determine their own limits, namely, that they apply to objects only in so far as objects are viewed as appearances, and do not present things as they are in themselves. This is the sole field of their validity; should we pass beyond it, no objective use can be made of them. This ideality[1] of space and time leaves, however, the certainty of empirical knowledge unaffected, for we are equally sure of it, whether these forms necessarily inhere in things in themselves or only in our intuition of them. Those, on the other hand, who maintain the absolute reality of space and time, whether as

[1] [Reading, with Laas, Adickes, and Vaihinger, *Idealität* for *Realität*.]

FIGURE 4.2 Adrian Piper, *Food for the Spirit* (1971). Portfolio edition of fourteen silver gelatin prints (photographic reprints 1997) and forty-four annotated book pages torn from a paperback edition of Immanuel Kant's *Critique of Pure Reason*, 15″ × 14.5″ (38.1 cm × 36.8 cm). Detail: page 3. Collection Thomas Erben © Adrian Piper Research Archive Foundation.

FIGURE 4.3 Adrian Piper, *Food for the Spirit* (1971). Fourteen silver gelatin prints (photographic reprints 1997), 14.95″ × 14.56″ (37.7 cm × 37 cm). Detail: photograph one of fourteen. Collection of the Museum of Modern Art, New York © Adrian Piper Research Archive Foundation.

FIGURE 4.4 Adrian Piper, *Food for the Spirit* (1971). Fourteen silver gelatin prints (photographic reprints 1997), 14.95″ × 14.56″ (37.7 cm × 37 cm). Detail: photograph fourteen of fourteen. Collection of the Museum of Modern Art, New York © Adrian Piper Research Archive Foundation.

For a project that seeks to "record physical presence objectively," these photos are remarkably opaque.[49] As Laura Larson puts it, "*Food for the Spirit* performs a 'reality check' on the medium's claims to objective representation. What's lost in an underexposed film photograph is detail in the shadow and Piper's photographs are all shadow."[50] Like Antin's body in *Carving*, Piper recedes in these pictures, but unlike *Carving*, *Food for the Spirit* is playing against, not with, rubrics of objectivity. The shots are ritual not clinical; although all the photos are taken in the same place with the same camera angle, sometimes Piper wears underwear, sometimes nothing at all. The wall shadows create a decorative frill, the presence of which sometimes changes the punctum of the image.

Piper, who later earned an MA and PhD in philosophy and became a philosophy professor, summed up the first part of Kant's *Critique of Pure Reason* as "a discussion about how space and time are in fact forms of perception" and noted that, before encountering Kant that summer, she had similar intuitions through LSD, yoga, and meditation.[51] Critics have read *Food for the Spirit* as a meditation of a racialized and gendered body's attempt to "pass" for Kant's universalized subject, on which the perception of space and time depends.[52] Piper herself has said that she appreciates Kant's universalist assumptions and that she believes that racist and imperialist theories that rely on his work misinterpret him.[53] She has also said that she made this work at a time that she began "thinking about her position as an artist, a woman, and a black."[54] As her image disappears in these photos, I also recall what she would later describe as a "triple negation of colored women artists," which functioned not only to exclude Black women artists from the canon but to obscure or misread their works.[55] The effect of the essay that describes this phenomenon (entitled "The Triple Negation of Colored Women Artists") is to further obfuscate her own image, perhaps referencing these negations that she herself performed. At this point in her career, Piper had already become part of a conceptual art and writing scene with works appearing in *0 to 9*, a magazine edited by Vito Acconci and Bernadette Mayer. In the spring of 1970, she had also recently undergone what she called a political awakening, which changed her art and sense of herself immeasurably.[56] The issues that she cites as having "changed everything" are "The Women's Movement" along with the invasion of Cambodia; the Kent State and Jackson State shootings; and student rebellions, including at City College of New York, where she was studying.⁵⁷ In 1971, Piper created *Food for the Spirit* and later that year was in a consciousness-raising group with Rosemary Mayer (Bernadette's sister and feminist artist) and others, immersed in women's liberation theory.⁵⁸ I imagine that to insert a Black woman's body into these worlds meant a process of both revealing and obscuring—starving into nonexistence and also "proving" existence. It was not long after *Food for the Spirit* that, due in part to the hostile racism and sexism of the art world—or, as she put it, getting "kicked out of the art world" when people found out she was a woman and Black—Piper would decide to continue her philosophy studies in graduate school.⁵⁹

*Food for the Spirit* literalizes the way that Piper is being killed or her body is being disappeared by various (and sometimes subtle) social constraints. Underscoring the importance of loss, or "losing myself," as Piper put it, the title of the artwork includes the word "food" while Piper herself was fasting.⁶⁰ This is one indication that she was attempting to find the boundaries of bodily demands that Kant describes as necessary for self-knowledge through the apprehension of an object outside oneself. Piper's work relocates sensuous experience to the "spirit" because, as she puts it, she was on the "verge of abdicating my individual self on every level" and afraid to enter a state of "transcendent reality of disembodied self-consciousness."⁶¹

Turning these themes of disappearing and revealing outward, Piper's *Catalysis* series from the same period was intended in part to see how people reacted to her body's disruptive presence.⁶² Her *Catalysis* works required her to perform antisocially in public: wearing a stinky mix of cod liver oil, vinegar, and rotten milk and eggs on the subway; rubbing wet paint or rubber cement onto store displays; putting towels in her cheeks; and attaching balloons to different parts of her body.⁶³ Although her *Catalysis* series does not include written instructions, carrying out these actions resonates with Fluxus scores discussed in my first chapter. Similar examples, which fit squarely with constraint-based literature, procedural writing, and the work of the other artists I analyze here, are Antin's *4 Transactions* (1972) and *Domestic Peace* (1971–1972), which revolved around a set of written instructions. Less explosive than Piper's *Catalysis*, for *4 Transactions*, Antin made written and notarized plans to perform certain uncharacteristic actions with her women's encounter group. These actions included wearing a dress and only addressing people from the rear with the goal of seeing how it transformed the group's dynamics. *Domestic Peace* consists of instructions for how to get along with her mother on a seventeen-day visit with "a daily set of conversational openers consisting of carefully chosen stories" and maps that tracked the success of the tactics.[64]

Both Antin's and Piper's works are usually paired with feminist body art that centers identity. When Lucy Lippard asked Piper what the *Catalysis* series had to do with being a woman or being Black, Piper replied that the work was "a product" of her as an individual and "the fact that I am a woman surely has a lot to do with it. You know, here I am, or was, 'violating my body'; I was making it public. I was turning myself into an object."[65] This comment mirrors another that she would make in 1974 about deciding, because of current events, "to become an art object."[66] When in alignment with the social world, the artist must be seen as an object in objective light. From Piper's position as "a woman and a black," one could understand the body as constantly violated, always precarious, on the edge of nonexistence.[67] While Antin's instruction-based action work from this period took place in more intimate settings (with her mother, with her consciousness-raising group), Piper's relies in part on being anonymous; erasing; or, as she wrote about *Food for the Spirit*, "losing" herself.[68]

John Bowles argues that *Food for the Spirit* illustrates something that photography fails to capture, that is, "the artist watching herself being watched," and that Piper purposefully creates a failure of empiricism.[69] I agree, and I will add that the failure also seems to be that of the fast. Piper cannot defeat the conditions that are producing her body, even while controlling and limiting some of them. Bowles explores this Foucauldian paradigm as an experience of "being watched," but it is also the experience of being produced. Any control the artist puts on her diet—any hunger she enacts, which results in a metaphorical illustration of real gender and racial confines—cannot defy this shadowy production. In the mid-1980s, after Piper further developed her philosophies of race, presence, and the role of the body in perception, she would abstain from meat, sex, and alcohol permanently.[70] This time, she was trying to defy the "drag of the body," by which I believe that she meant pleasure, desire, but also socially produced constraints.[71] The front note in the *Food for the Spirit* notebook reads, "I recorded these attempts to anchor myself . . . these attempts did not succeed, so I eventually abandoned them."[72] Later she became increasingly reclusive about her personal life, and then in 2012, she "retired from being black."[73] *Food for the Spirit* did not provide the sustenance required then or later. Her experiment "to anchor" herself by rules of the fast "did not succeed," or, I argue, it only made her lose herself differently.[74]

## BERNADETTE MAYER'S HUNGER

Unlike Antin's neatly "scientific" study of diet, gender, and sculpture or Piper's bounded inquiry into the relation between self and sustenance, Bernadette Mayer's project, *Studying Hunger*, is sprawling and somewhat unfocused. The piece begins:

> Listen
> I began all this in April, 1972. I wanted to try to record, like a diary, in writing, states of consciousness, my states of consciousness, as fully as I could every day, for one month. A month always seems like a likely timespan, if there is one, for an experiment. A month gives you enough time to feel free to skip a day, but not so much time that you wind up fucking off completely.
>
> I had an idea before this that if a human, a writer, could come up with a workable code, or shorthand, for the transcription of every event, every motion, every transition of his or her own mind, & could perform this process of translation on himself, using the code, for a 24-hour period, he or we or someone could come up with a great piece of language/information.
>
> Anyway
> When I began to attempt the month-long experiment with states of consciousness, I wrote down a list of intentions. It went like this: First, to record special states of consciousness. Special: change, sudden change, high, low, food, levels of attention
> And, how intentions change[75]

Mayer was no stranger to procedural works, the autobiographical recording of consciousness, or even art governed by the duration of one month. In July 1971, she had completed *Memory*, a work of photography and text documenting her life. In her poems in *o to 9*, the experimental magazine she edited with Vito Acconci, she cycled through various poetic constraints, and her book *Story* (1968) was governed by a single procedure.[76] Here, however, her emphasis on "code" and information is remarkable. Mayer continues to explain that, unlike her other projects, *Studying Hunger* would not be a "pose." Its intention was in fact the opposite of "accumulate data" (a reference to the introduction to *Memory*, which describes that project's purpose), and it was not for the purpose of telling oneself to "keep going" (a reference to "The Way to Keep Going in Antarctica," a poem that would be published in her collection *Poetry* in 1976).[77] Mayer claims that the hunger referenced in the title is partly related to "regular hunger, which I felt in the extreme because my parents had died young (there was nobody to feed me)," from a synesthesia concept of eating words and colors, and from a condition she was experiencing as she started the project: "I couldn't swallow, perhaps as in 'I couldn't swallow it.'"[78] As with the hunger, the swallowing condition is both real and metaphorical as she tries baby food to soothe a presumably inflamed esophagus and also discusses everything that she cannot accept—or, idiomatically, "swallow"—about her life.

Despite its promise as a procedural piece, on April 2, 1972, Mayer writes that the "experiment went badly, real bad," by April 13, she "can't focus," and by April 20, Mayer writes that she "gave up the project." As she explains in the 2011 version of the journal, what ends up being published in 1975 as the collection called *Studying Hunger* are selected portions of her journal to her psychoanalyst, which she worked on from this moment in 1972 through 1974.[79]

In other words, Mayer's *Studying Hunger* is a piece of procedural writing that went terribly wrong, a failure. Instead of studying hunger for a month, as the constraint suggests, Mayer's project spans years and ends as a study of eating. In fact, the book culminates in a cemetery where the speaker seduces and cannibalizes David, a character that presumably refers to David Rubinfine, Mayer's psychoanalyst. The speaker pretends to be drunkenly seducing him and then drives a thorn from a rose bush into the pineal gland of his brain. The book ends: "I take out my other instruments & proceed to do what I have already related; I do not ignore the genitals, as some would ignore females. As the dawn comes I take all evidence of my crime & drive away in David's Mercedes Benz. I bring some of the flesh with me to survive on, exclusively, until I am arrested."[80] It all certainly seems out of the opérateur's control. At points in the text, the speaker laments that, beginning in July 1972, she became "a prisoner of this work," which is described as a "notebook of my crime."[81] She later describes the project as a journal *for* the analyst that she was seeing, the same person whose flesh she survives on exclusively at the end of the text.

It is worth noting that Mayer does do some of the things she set out to at the beginning of the experiment. She does record states of consciousness, with a special emphasis on a "workable code" suggested in the beginning. Except for the category of "change," which she admits at the end of the 2011 version that she "forgets to speak of," she seemingly sticks to her definition of "special," which includes the noun "food." Food is talked about throughout. Food is sex, incest, a measure of emotional well-being, and seemingly relates to babies and baby food as Mayer tries to eat normally but is unable to do so. In *Studying Hunger*, there are hints at not being able to eat, at being a baby incapable of eating solid food, dreams and dialogue about pregnancy and abortions, and questions about the inability to distinguish and sustain the self. In the more complete *Studying Hunger Journals*, Mayer's pregnancy and failed attempt to obtain an abortion are narrated in a matter-of-fact time line; in that text, Mother's Day is a "time to hide the bad feelings."[82] In both books, food becomes the creative process of the text itself: "By this time & it was a long time, I knew a couple of things. I figured that what I was doing created a funny need for repeating, but I was used to repeating since I had been a poet. What was even stranger was the need to review, re-read, re-use, recycle what had already been written. My own work was never finished & it was always leading back to itself & to older work. Not a system of feedback but a system of feeding."[83] Like Antin's photos, *Studying Hunger* is not the experiment itself but a journal about the experiment, and in fact just a portion of the journal of the experiment.[84] Instead of existing in the clinical world of documentation, *Studying Hunger* becomes a being in need of food. As Antin's diet is not her art, but the photographic evidence is, Mayer creates "a system of feeding" that must cannibalize itself.

Mayer is living on a government subsidy as she is writing *Studying Hunger*, and she is anxiously thinking about who is funding the project: "I am a ragamuffin, I depend on the U.S. govt. that murders Allende, it's council on the arts supports me, I cant remember, 30 bucks a week, from the copper mines of Chile, I dont know. I am trying to change the world. I'll take anything I can get for food, if I can eat it."[85] Food is what sustains the art, which is designed to change the world, and yet Mayer is clear-eyed both about her complicity with violent U.S. foreign policy ("from the copper mines of Chile") and about the efficacy of the art itself to change the world. A little later, on the same page, she writes:

> & we are not in power
> we just paint slogans on the wall
> & we are not in power
> we just try to change the fucking language
> & we are not in power
> but we take money for food if we can eat it: whose mother you are
> cause then you feed it too
> & then only then
> you can eat
> horseshit[86]

Mayer tries to change the world but the text returns to its core hunger, its need for food and constant feeding, a reflection on destabilized conditions of bodily cultivation.

---

Two years after Mayer finished *Studying Hunger*, she performed another monthlong project, this time collaborating with Lewis Warsh, with whom she was living and raising a child in Lenox Massachusetts. The project is called *Piece of Cake*, and the constraint was that Mayer and Warsh take turns each day writing one chapter of this book for the entire month of August 1976. When they begin, their baby, Marie Warsh, is eight months old and their days are split between caretaking and writing (Mayer does all the food preparation and cleanup for the household). Lewis's parents come to visit, and friends come to visit, which are the only deviations from their schedule. Where *Studying Hunger* is abstract, *Piece of Cake* is straightforward. It chronicles the couple's lives as parents and writers, and it works as easily as its name implies. Unlike *Studying*

*Hunger*, Mayer differentiates dream from reality from fantasy, and the sections written by her shed light on many of the abstractions in *Studying Hunger*. For example, here she chronicles and explains her love for her psychoanalyst, David Rubinfine, and also tells the full stories of her unwanted pregnancies, which include a childbirth experience in the 1960s and several abortions after that. It is also here that we get a more complete picture of how Mayer's finances govern the day-to-day.

Warsh and Mayer are on welfare, specifically food assistance, as they write *Piece of Cake*, the fact of which looms over both their writing. Echoing Mayer's abstract calculations in *Studying Hunger*, Warsh muses early in *Piece of Cake* that "food stamps, $130 worth a month, give us the freedom (we only pay $71) not to think about how much we buy so we tend to buy what we want, though the novelty of spending sixty dollars at one time wore off after a while."[87] Yet toward the end of the month they run low on cash and then run out about a week before the end of the month, which spurs a long discussion about how to ration their food and money better in September.[88] At different points in the book, Warsh and Mayer conjure memories from earlier parts of their lives. About ten years prior, Warsh had worked for the Department of Welfare. He describes going into the Bushwick and Ridgewood neighborhoods of New York City (incidentally where Mayer was born, which he points out) to check on women with multiple children and seemingly no help with caretaking or providing.[89] He wouldn't ask the invasive questions that his boss told him to, instead trying to get his clients the most amount of money that he could, which he said "was hardly enough to live on."[90] He would stretch funds for his clients, sometimes applying to the Department of Welfare for emergency funds for necessities for his clients that they could actually use for entertainment, which he explains is an important part of life. Warsh muses that he felt close to his clients and left the job after eight months because of the draconian rules of the welfare system.[91]

While Warsh was discovering the inhuman rationale of welfare, about ten years prior to *Piece of Cake*, Mayer was accidentally pregnant. She was unable to obtain an illegal abortion, and she was therefore saving for medical bills to give birth to a baby. She names the baby Bernadette and gives her up for adoption because she is "broke" at the time and "all [Mayer] wanted to do was write."[92] She had gotten pregnant with her boyfriend,

Ed Bowes, who had just flunked out of school and moved home with his parents. She writes:

> Neither of us really wanted a baby but, while the thought truly terrified Ed, to me it seemed just confusing. Ed kept saying he'd be back to Syracuse and I kept our apartment there till late in February when I gave up on him and finding an abortion. My sister and I had even gone to Puerto Rico, not really knowing what we were doing, but the scene there was a little too horrifying, cab drivers handing us cards that said "Dentista" and one low stone building, painted yellow, where they said, "Yes but your father must sign for you."[93]

For a month before the baby was born, she was too angry to see Bowes, but she ultimately forgives him and they reunite, even getting pregnant again together, but this time obtaining a legal abortion.[94] While Warsh chronicles his disillusionment in the welfare system and ultimately extracts himself from it, Mayer illustrates how her life is tied to these systems, whether she works in them or actively tries to avoid them. She ends up losing about a year of writing and work as well as some savings to her 1966 pregnancy, and it shapes the way she experiences much of the rest of her life.

*Studying Hunger*, or the obsessive constraint of food, is a way to bring these issues of welfare and health care together, not with different speakers, chapters, or memories but through the experiment itself. Mayer studies food as a constraint imposed by receiving welfare benefits that both limit her intake and tie her to forms of government that she finds unconscionable. The hunger experienced is a metaphor for reproductive needs that are unmet or unfed, and they mirror her experience of real food scarcity and neediness as a child. The larger assertion is that women's lives and bodies are in crisis. Several times in *Studying Hunger*, Mayer describes giving birth to herself in dream sequences. With the full picture of her 1966 baby, Bernadette, these stories have a particular traumatic resonance. As Mayer puts it, she is without the ability to "swallow" it all; it is unreasonable when one cannot be a writer and, at the same time, a person who can get pregnant. The world of *Studying Hunger* makes Mayer into a murderer when she kills her analyst at the end; the larger claim is that all women are criminals under the rationality that separates livelihood from bodily autonomy from work.

## STATE CONSTRAINT: HEALTH CARE, WELFARE, AND THE WORK OF GENDER

While Antin, Piper, and Mayer were studying hunger, debates about women's bodily autonomy dominated American discourse. *Roe v. Wade* reached the Supreme Court in 1970 after it was first argued in a northern Texas District Court. In the Supreme Court, it went through two rounds of arguments before the 1973 decision. As the Court deliberated, many states increased antiabortion restrictions and further criminalized abortion in local enforcement.[95] However, New York passed a law in 1970 that made abortion legal up to twenty-four weeks of gestation, which meant that people of means who wished to terminate a pregnancy could travel from other states to New York for the procedure. That obtaining a safe abortion could be possible was a watershed moment in women's health, both for the country and for New York. Previously, in 1965, abortion was so unsafe that 17 percent of all deaths due to pregnancy and childbirth were the result of illegal abortion. Other statistics draw that figure higher: "In New York City, in the early 1960s, one in four childbirth-related deaths among white women was due to abortion . . . [and] abortion accounted for one in two childbirth-related deaths among nonwhite and Puerto Rican women."[96]

My chapter has situated this art within a history of reproductive rights (alongside labor and welfare rights) in part because Eleanor Antin, Adrian Piper, and Bernadette Mayer have each referenced their experience with abortion access, pregnancy, or childbirth in New York in the late 1960s and early 1970s.[97] As Mayer narrates directly in *Piece of Cake*, intimates in *Studying Hunger*, and chronicles in *Studying Hunger Journals*, she had at least two unwanted pregnancies in this period. In an interview, she describes "taking a year off" to carry an unwanted pregnancy to term.[98] In *Piece of Cake*, Mayer tells the story fully: she had traveled to look for an abortion but could not find a way to have a safe procedure, so she covered the hospital bills herself, gave birth, named the baby Bernadette, and put her up for adoption immediately.[99] For her second unwanted pregnancy, which occurred during the period that she wrote *Studying Hunger*, she obtained a legal abortion.[100] Eleanor Antin had a child in 1967, but it was the fear of an unwanted pregnancy in 1960 that entirely changes her life.[101]

While Antin and Mayer have publicly written about the way that constraints on reproductive health shaped the material conditions of their life and work, as far as I know, there is only one small clue that abortion rights were on Adrian Piper's mind during this era. A piece written in 1972 points out a "coincidence": "the building where I went last month for my abortion USED TO BE the hotel in which the discotheque where I worked was located."[102] Framing her abortion this way normalizes the choice to terminate her pregnancy, but it may also suggest that there is something seedy about it—that it is in some ways similar to when Piper was paid to dance in a glass cage—because of its shadowy legality before *Roe v. Wade*.[103] Piper does not discuss her abortion in her autobiography or other art that I know of; Piper has remarked that, before 1972, she avoided any overt references to race or gender in her work, which she has called an unconscious attempt to avoid becoming a target of racism.[104]

To return to the discussion that began this chapter, another active conversation at this moment was about a different type of state control of bodies: what was termed a "welfare crisis" in popular media.[105] The number of never married, divorced, and single women receiving welfare (like Mayer) alarmed commentators through the 1950s and 1960s. Stoking the fire of public concern, several studies that aimed to connect poverty to moral traits ended up targeting "broken families" as part of the problem of both hunger and criminality.[106] Congress responded by passing the 1967 Social Security Act, which established mandatory maternal work requirements through the Work Incentive program (WIN) and provisions to curb out-of-wedlock births, creating "both a carrot and a stick to encourage AFDC [Aid to Families with Dependent Children] mothers to perform wage labor."[107] Although WIN did not succeed in moving recipients into the wage market, this amendment introduced new elements of moral surveillance and also put a freeze on federal AFDC funds to states for children of unwed mothers.[108] As Jennifer Mittelstadt sums it up, "Drawing on the precedent of rehabilitation, welfare law after the 1960s increasingly focused on forcing poor 'dysfunctional' women out of 'welfare dependency' and into mandatory 'self-support.' 'Rehabilitation' evolved into 'responsibility' and welfare became workfare."[109] Warsh's comments about the inhumanity of the welfare office he worked for in the 1960s clearly reflect this history.

The public rationale that welfare needed to be more actively policed flared in the early 1970s and coincided with a recession, oil crisis, and massive unemployment for all, making low-income women and people of color even more vulnerable to poverty.[110] As Melinda Cooper illustrates, when Nixon's 1970 family assistance plan—which, by extending welfare to men, was supposed to secure the family wage and repair the supposedly harmful effects of earlier policy on families—was defeated, it signaled a new era.[111] This moment marks the end of expansionist politics on both sides of the aisle. Both welfare and counterculture came to be seen as harmful to normative family structures (or "family values," as it came to be called around this time), but instead of remedying these influences with renewal of the family wage, the public conversation shifted to an attack on welfare recipients.[112] Racist stereotypes about welfare were created in this era, with notions that support had to be earned through work and that it should be given only to the "deserving" and the "appropriate."

Historians have painstakingly illustrated the ways in which welfare in the United States has always been a tool for controlling otherwise marginalized populations. Because wage and benefits are tied to employment, and employment favors able-bodied white men, support for those outside these categories is often shaped by surveillance and disciplinary power surrounding race, gender, and ability. Premilla Nadasen, Jennifer Mittelstadt, and Marisa Chappell observe that, throughout the history of the welfare state and AFDC, two "critical features of US aid to the poor have remained consistent. First, welfare broadly defined has always been shaped by distinctions between the 'worthy' and 'unworthy' poor. . . . Second, because of deep suspicion about the worthiness of impoverished Americans, AFDC also has been used to shape and even control their behavior."[113] But, this particular set of restrictions of the 1960 and 1970s, which targeted people of color, women, and counterculture together, brought a welfare rights movement with it. In the mid-1960s the National Welfare Rights Organization (NWRO) was established primarily by African American women; functionally part of the civil rights movement, NWRO began organizing to defend welfare recipients' rights.[114] Building from this momentum, the women's liberation movement tied together a constellation of issues including political, economic, and bodily autonomy. Reciprocally, the movement further empowered activism targeting welfare, health care, and public housing policies.[115] The radical Wages Against Housework movement along with best-selling forms of feminism were built from tying together these otherwise separate spheres.

It is clear how the interests of capitalism dovetail in repressing abortion and criminalizing welfare support.[116] Scholars have shown how abortion and birth control debates are always tied to issues of population growth and the future desired workforce, and similarly the carrot-and-stick welfare discrimination grapples with normative structures of existing wage systems.[117] However, despite the explosion of women's liberation theory in the 1970s, abortion and welfare are rarely part of the same conversation. Antin, Piper, and Mayer experimented with hunger, desire, work, and where food might come from—Antin and Mayer in the wake of their criminalized pregnancies and stigmatized welfare experiences—during this moment of awareness around government cultivation of bodies and behavior. By choosing the durational period of one month and each failing their constrained experiments uniquely, these artworks nod to how the state cultivates bodies and behaviors. These artists study the ways in which their bodies are specifically linked to not only social practices embedded in wage labor structures (like diets) but also the various forms of labor to which they might be indentured, like childbearing and rearing. Mayer's interest in the "information" of objective "states of consciousness," Piper's aims to "record [her] physical appearance objectively" during a period of intense study during which she otherwise feared that she would "lose herself," and Antin's attempt to make herself a classical sculpture use procedure as feminist practice.[118] The objective, informational, or documentarian impulses of the state are tempered by rules created by artists specifically to ensure that the authors and bodies in question had no sense of what might be fathomed for the artwork beyond the rules. Their hope instead was a transformation beyond the art and the self.

The failed nature of this hope is crucial to the projects. Mathematically inclined readers may have noticed that Eleanor Antin's diet lasted thirty-eight days and with four photographs each day, the project should have included 152 photos. However, Antin skipped one day of photos when she was traveling, giving the piece thirty-seven rows.[119] This was not a mistake but rather another life constraint. Antin wrote a letter to Henrietta Ehrsam in July 1972 (before she had finished creating *Carving*) to see if Ehrsam would be interested in showing it at the Henri Gallery. Antin described the piece this way: "It consists of photographic documentation (120 photographs in all) of my unclothed body in the process of 'carving' down during 30 days of a strict regimen of dieting and exercise.

4 photographs were taken of me each day, front and back view, right and left profile, which graphically detail the loss of 15 pounds of the 30 day period."[120] Despite writing about the piece in the past tense, Antin had not finished creating it. All other official descriptions of *Carving* define the goal as losing ten, not fifteen, pounds and include the longer time period.[121] In other words, the archive reveals that *Carving*'s procedure, or generative device, was to document a one-month diet with a set goal of a fifteen-pound weight loss, but it lasted longer and did not achieve the original intention. Antin gave up the diet before losing fifteen pounds, likely because the experiment was dragging on much longer than she originally intended. Similar to Mayer's monthlong project spanning years and Piper's "abandonment" of *Food for the Spirit*, an aspect of failure was part of the project.[122]

The place of failure has been continuously theorized in relation to procedural poetry; the Oulipian term for this sort of failure is the "clinamen." The notion comes from Lucretius's Latin for the Greek klesis, meaning "a bending" or "swerve." For Lucretius, the clinamen was a bending of falling atoms that allowed for free choice. For the Oulipians, it is the idea that every rule must be broken somewhere in a perfect procedural work.[123] Scholars and poets have noted that this swerve away from the rule is often what allows the reader to detect the true symmetry of the rule, that a purposeful mistake highlights the rigidity and the constructed aspects of the rule.[124] In the case of these three procedural pieces, failure signals the way that this moment brought impossible constraints and that people's lives depended on improvisation—around types of reproductive labor—despite layers of artificial constructions. It is notable that two of the three artists returned to these pieces to try again later in life: Antin reperformed *Carving* with different intentions in 2017, after David Antin died. As she puts it, "Perhaps as a desire to escape myself, to lose myself even, so I could create the new self I now needed to be, or perhaps even something of a punishment for remaining behind when my lover and closest friend had already left."[125] Mayer published the entire hunger notebook (*Studying Hunger Journals*) rather than just the selected parts in 2011. In her introduction to it, she explains that it may seem odd that she published *Memory* and *Studying Hunger* in such short succession but that she was "in a great hurry." She continues, "I figured I'd die like my father did, at age 49. I did have a cerebral hemorrhage at that age just like him but I didn't die. I had brain surgery and lived to eat more oysters."[126] Both women indicate that there was something unfinished about their earlier projects, and both expose themselves to self-definition once again later in life.

As far as I know, Adrian Piper has not returned to *Food for the Spirit*. However, in her 2018 memoir, in part about the abuse and harassment she experienced at Wellesley College in her career as an academic philosopher, she writes, "No matter how often I return to inspect pictures of myself, I never seem to be able to establish a connection between what I am seeing and the person I experience myself to be. I have this problem when looking in the mirror, too."[127] Because Piper states her intention for *Food for the Spirit* as anchoring herself in actualized self-image, even her memoir could be seen as another attempt. She writes: "Transferring those images [of pain] from my mind to the page in front of me. That is the purpose of this memoir. It has nothing to do with you."[128] I interpret this passage as a reminder to the reader that Piper continues to exist despite visual obscurity, fasting, and transference.

Mayer ends the *Studying Hunger Journals* with what could be both a rationale and a definition for feminist procedural or constrained artwork in an expanded field. When she admits at the end of the 2011 text that she neglected to cover "change" as a special state of consciousness, she writes: "I have not changed. I have no private property. Nor are these journals a diary of change. They are a simple recommendation to be driven to the present with the chances that may allow to change not one's self but the world. We cannot begin to know science and poetry until we understand the people and the machines with which they work, the eyes, a glance, the hands."[129] Mayer suggests that studying the technologies that generate poetry or examining the people who construct experiments exposes subtle details about the workings of larger systems that make and unmake us. I hope this chapter has shown that constraints may be both embodied and linguistic, but if we are attentive, the procedures that govern them show us how "to be driven to the present with the chances that may allow to change not one's self but the world."[130] I echo Antin's purpose in *Carving* to say that poetry in general transforms not merely documents, and I repeat Piper's stated intention for her artwork to make manifest: "to anchor."[131] The poetry in general of this chapter has engaged literal, material bodies; it has detailed how artistic constraints, even as reflections of social constraints, are trumped by the reality of public forms. The failure of each experiment shows that public form is its fodder rather than an abstract idea. In this way, poetry in general paradoxically stands as opposite of what Jane Blocker refers to as "the body in general," the pure idea of a body—a body that precedes any signification and also sets the terms of signification of the body . . . the "hoped for," "always sought and imported from outside"—that is often discussed in 1970s performance art.[132] The bodies implicated by the poetry in general of this chapter are a social and public form.

# 5

## DOCUMENTAL POETRY AND THE PRIVATIZATION OF INTERPRETATION

In the 2000s and 2010s, experimental literature circles were preoccupied with poetry that reframed and interpreted public and semipublic materials. These type of projects were seemingly everywhere at once: a book of verbatim testimony from coal miners interspliced with newspaper accounts of mining disasters and coal-sponsored curricula; a collection of captions from the United States Holocaust Memorial Museum curated without images or explanation; a meticulous transcription of state-captured final words of people about to experience capital punishment in Texas; a poem exploring documented reasons and solutions for unexplained crying at office jobs; a book that reproduces the author's email; a book that captures the gaze of public statues carrying weapons alongside drone transcripts; poems that use as word banks the Department of Defense Dictionary, archives from prisons and asylums, text of congressional statements, transcripts of legal decisions, and full newspapers.[1] As I suggested in the introduction to *Poetry in General*, writing like this relies on methods of accumulation, absorption, and combinatory processes to sift through forms that are provocatively public, such as internet searches, surveillance data, court transcripts, email, manuals, and dictionaries. These works instigated conversations about plagiarism and expression that crested and mostly fizzled around 2012 (my coda will briefly take these conversations up). But the techniques of repurposing public material—techniques that were not new, just very exciting at this moment—only became more ubiquitous after. Poetry that manipulates and assembles public and semipublic material wagers that it can inform our present not by recuperating this material but by interpreting, animating, and processing it.

This chapter argues that the explosion of this poetic form in the beginning of the twenty-first century helpfully refracts and estranges the material conditions of interpretation, most especially in the post-2008 recession era. By "material conditions of interpretation," I mean both the process by which poets employ poetry variously as a tool to interpret the documents and effects of policy and also the shape and contours of the communities that do interpretive work. I adopt Michael Leong's term "documental poetry" for poems that share a formal process of archival work with a preoccupation of what makes the public.[2] In his book *Contested Records*, which examines how poems like these engage with a current crisis of cultural memory, Leong writes, "Documental poets cite mostly publicly available texts in order to return them, rhetorically transformed, to the public sphere."[3] I appreciate the coinage of "documental" (it is a portmanteau of "conceptual" and "documentary") because the term includes conceptual poetry, conceptual writing, and "uncreative writing," but it also includes poetry that is referred to variously as documentary, investigative, and socially engaged.[4] This taxonomy skirts the spurious notion that conceptual poetry—by figureheads including Vanessa Place, Robert Fitterman, Kenneth Goldsmith—is inherently conservative, whereas forms of documentary poetry—understood as Mark Nowak and Jena Osman from the legacy of Works Progress Administration (WPA) era works by Muriel Rukeyser and Langston Hughes—are inherently leftist or enable a Marxist political approach.[5] Yet pointing out that politically diverse poetry shares a formal process does not mean ignoring its political differences. Rather, the term "documental poetry" highlights an archive that diversely engages public texts to index how neoliberal policy and its reflection in institutions is in conversation with the production and interpretation of poetry. In other words, many of these projects point out that, although texts are "public," people do not have access to them or the tools to interpret or shape them. The category of the public—and how it manifests through public documents—is an arena that moves with neoliberalism, and examining why and how formal procedures that engage documents became central to poetry in the twenty-first century, and indeed shifted and solidified after 2008, have much to tell us about both the definition of the public and the definition of poetry.

In every chapter, *Poetry in General* has considered the rematerialization of public forms into poetry or poetry's capture of state and bureaucratic policy. This context puts twenty-first-century documental poetry into a constellation of other postmedium, interdisciplinary works, beginning in the 1960s. My argument is that the category of poetry has been contending with forms of privatization by becoming more "public" since a moment broadly known as "art in general" or intermedia expression. Earlier chapters argued that poetry is a helpful place to examine government policies about the facilitation of capitalism because its category is sutured to the public and to institutions in ways that reflect logics of livelihood. Thinking with Leong's contention that documental poetry is uniquely positioned to directly address a nexus of issues related to the public at large, this chapter offers a close look at several works that perform a post-2008 recession-era grappling with the privatization of poetry itself. I suggest that documental poetry affords an opportunity to explicitly consider academia as part of the category of poetry. In the post-2008 moment, attention was brought to what counts as "public" through thinking about academia as part of a larger system of government redistribution of risk to individuals and away from institutions.[6] Although this process began in the 1960s, the regime change was later illuminated by student debt and winnowing government support for education in general and for the arts and humanities in particular, all of which have a profound effect on practices of interpretation and on practices of poetry. These issues surrounding education policy and where poetry is studied or employed make and unmake poetry communities themselves. In the most material sense, this process is borne out within the poetry world through the rise of debt-accruing MFA programs that rarely lead to employment and through the increasing unavailability of outside grant support.[7]

Within this precarious environment, poetry in general, as the documental poetry that I discuss here, considers the privatization of its own production and interpretation. It asks how its privatization—reflected in curtailed arts and education funding, for example—interacts with the smooth workings of state and corporate public forms. This chapter will discuss M. NourbeSe Philip's *Zong!* (2008), a rewriting of the 1783 English legal case involving the murder of 150 enslaved people onboard the *Zong* ship; Mathew Timmons's *CREDIT*, which documents credit offers from the 2007 economic bubble and rejections after the 2008 crash (2009); and Counterpath's *Let Her Speak: Transcript of Texas State Senator Wendy Davis's June 25, 2013, Filibuster of the Texas State Senate*, a rewriting of the dialogue of an eleven-hour filibuster to thwart antichoice legislation (2013). These texts ask questions about the afterlives of slavery, the contemporary problem of debt, and the need for abortion access as a form of health care through a consideration of the role of poetry in the public sphere. How can poetry disrupt the opacity of public language that makes state power function cleanly? *CREDIT* reframes the work of the debt-saddled poet both in and outside the institutions where poetry is written and interpreted; *Let Her Speak* works to undo notions of biological essentialism that have previously been tied to discussions of abortion rights; *Zong!* offers a portrait of the unrepresentable violence at the center of racial capitalism.

These disparate examples take up legal documents (an eighteenth-century legal case, a twenty-first-century state senate hearing) and personal financial documents (correspondence from credit card companies) that are available to the public but are not usually accessible to most people. State and financial documents are the bedrock of neoliberal and racial capital power, but they are often hidden, fragmented, and partial; furthermore, when they are available, legal and financial documents are often only within the interpretive purview of trained specialists. Timmons, Counterpath, and Philip each offer a decontextualizing process and a series of interpretive supports by way of poetic production. Like other documental works, a reliance on digital, data-driven, and informational glut frames these works; it is clear that technological "speed up," or the role that digital information plays in creative and critical production, is a central concern.[8] Timmons uses optical character recognition (OCR) technology to create his work, Counterpath employs Amazon's online task firm Mechanical Turk, and Philip discusses how her complicated relationship with digitally available information spurred the project of *Zong!*. In each case, the poems probe the role of digital technology and how it implicates labor in and outside the university. Taken together, these three texts suggest that the material reality of poetry communities are built on and through contending with privatization and the government support of capitalism. When seen as part of "documental poetry" and poetry in general more widely, these texts suggest that poetry's future has a stake in interpreting neoliberal language—often through digital, bureaucratic, and administrative technologies to automate certain aspects of a reading process—and also thinking beyond that very language to create new poetic alphabets.

## INTERPRETING EDUCATION ECONOMIES

Mathew Timmons's *CREDIT* (2009) is an example of documental poetry's everyday confrontation with the brutality of bureaucratic documents. In particular, *CREDIT* probes the paradox of both the personal and impersonal nature of bearing witness to the rise of debt that elicited both the financial boom of the early 2000s and subsequent crisis after 2008. It contends with how to interpret a moment in political economic history—the 2007 bubble and 2008 crash—by curating its documents. As Michael Leong and Moberley Luger have claimed about conceptual writing of this period, *CREDIT* provides a way to witness painful traces of public record.[9] Here, I suggest that *CREDIT* uses an interdisciplinary poetics in order to resituate the role of both the poet and the critic. Using double-entry bookkeeping as medium, *CREDIT* stages a critique of the growing business of poetry MFA programs and the poetry economy these programs produce. Ultimately, *CREDIT* reframes the work of the indebted poet both in and outside the institutions where poetry is written and interpreted.

Timmons's *CREDIT* is an eight-hundred-page, hardback, coffee-table-style book that costs $199 for material purchase or $299 for download from Insert Press. The tome is divided into two parts: "Credit" and "Debit." In "Credit," the twenty-six letters of the alphabet reproduce different offers for credit lines and cards, all of which Timmons seems to be preapproved or "prescreened" to obtain, and all of which he received during a three-week period in 2007. In this section, all proper names and numbers, except for the names of the companies, are redacted. The second section of the book, "Debit," is organized by numbers 1 to 10 (rather than lettered like the first section), and it consists of overdue payment notices that Timmons received over a two-week period in 2009. In this section, the author's name and address are visible, as are the statement numbers,

DOCUMENTAL POETRY AND THE PRIVATIZATION OF INTERPRETATION 131

amounts, phone numbers, and addresses of the companies; contrary to "Credit," the information redacted in this section appears to be only the terms and conditions of the overdue payments (see figures 5.1 and 5.2). The book ends with two appendixes (A and B) that appear to include everything that was redacted from each section. The "joke" of the book is summed up on the website blurb as "offer turned to obligation"; in 2007, Timmons was flush with credit, but two years later, after the financial crisis, he has only debit.

Timmons situates his work in a lyric tradition as well as outside it, and *CREDIT* is playful about what might categorize personal and public subjecthood. If at first it seems like Timmons's account information is redacted to save him from identity theft, then it is put back in later for epic effect in the appendixes. Spoofing what might be a more sincere poetics of witness or confession, the book is described on the press's website as a "highly revealing and emotional work chronicling a personal tale of credit."[10] Jokes aside, although there is not a word of "original" writing authored by Timmons in *CREDIT*, we do glimpse an image of a poetic subject's desires and the contours of his life by the offers he receives. An offer

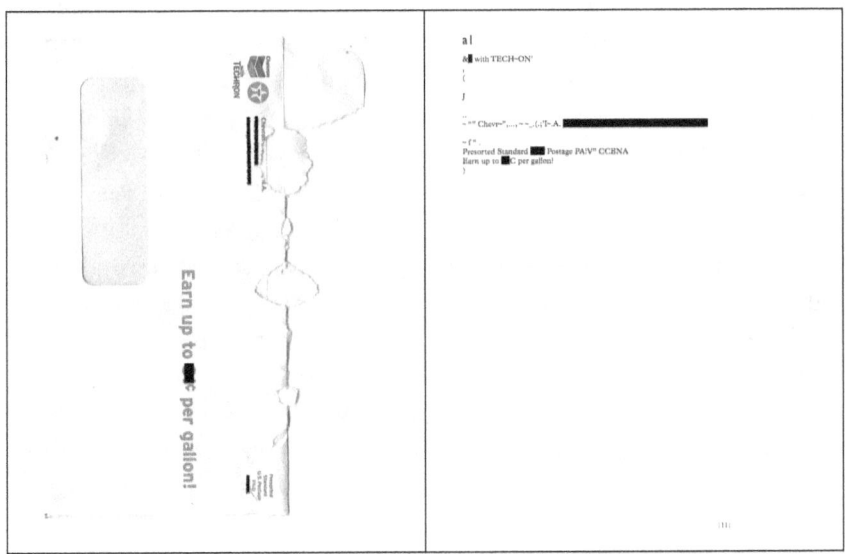

FIGURE 5.1 Mathew Timmons, from *CREDIT*, "Credit," pages 10–11. Used with permission.

132  DOCUMENTAL POETRY AND THE PRIVATIZATION OF INTERPRETATION

FIGURE 5.2  Mathew Timmons, from *CREDIT*, "Debit," pages 750–51. Used with permission.

for a credit card that earns baseball tickets and one that earns points toward pet food, for example, tell us something of the profile of Timmons that financial institutions might keep. Furthermore, Timmons's overdue bills for utilities and specific loan amounts give us a sense of his daily life (some are for hundreds of dollars, others are for thousands). Commenting on this concealing and revealing of expressivity, Annie McClanahan argues that "*CREDIT* plays out the oscillation between the personality of credit's ideology and the impersonality of its actual material functioning."[11] In other words, even though credit itself is staked on notions of individualized, personal, moral fitness (think here of the exuberance of "preapproval!"), the way it affects us all is a matter of the collective, especially as the 2008 recession showed. Timmons's book certainly reveals this paradox. But *CREDIT* also takes up the form of documental poetics in its most abstract and excessive form—forms increasingly inherent to the category of poetry—to attempt to interpret this moment through curation and reproduction.

The length and cost of the book are clear suggestions toward the discourse of interdisciplinary media. The Insert Press website boasts that

*CREDIT* is the longest, most expensive book publishable through the digital print-on-demand service Lulu.com. Then follows an origin story: "In late spring 2007 as an irrational exuberance and promise of financial fortune hung in the air, mailboxes were filled with generous and gracefully worded offers of credit. Just over two years later, in midsummer 2009, the shape of the financial environment changed radically and mailboxes still filled up with statements of credit. Something had to change, offer turned to obligation. Retailing for $199.99, *CREDIT* is a book the author himself lacks the cash or credit to buy."[12] With this sound-bite explanation of the book, Timmons portrays the poet as both suffering from the crisis of capitalism during the crash of 2008 and as a capitalist exploiter himself. The project trades in a sort of serious irony—on the one hand, from the rhetoric of the origin story we understand that capitalism, in an unexplained way, is bad for all of us. On the other hand, the author's vampiric answer to the recession is to create products from its detritus to sell at an unreasonably expensive price.

This sort of trick of the financially unstable artist-turned-capitalist is reflected in other documental poetry of this period. For example, both Dana Teen Lomax and Brian Kim Stefans reproduce the author's personal financial records as poetry at roughly the same moment.[13] In 2013, Vanessa Place launched vanessaplace.biz, with its proud tagline "poetry is a kind of money."[14] Operating as an art installation, the website sold products such as "Poetry Pays," an art object in the *l'art pour l'art* tradition, and a book project called *$20*, which consists of twenty single dollar bills sold for $50.00. Place spoofs the notion of poets "selling out," even as the debt that many poets take on is staggering. The subtext for these works is the combination of government disinvestment and the growing business of MFA programs—the only credential for poets—in the 1990s and early 2000s at such a rate as to recharacterize what Mark McGurl called "the program era" to "the debt era."[15] To be a poet is to be in debt. If an indebted poet is successful by finding a job in academia, that poet will be later tethered to an education system that generates debt for others.[16] Both Timmons's and Place's work arrived when the language of debt came into view more broadly because of the 2008 crisis and when art critiquing the art world had begun to feel out of touch. Coming at the same problem as Timmons but from a different vantage, Place's "biz" critiques poetry as commodity in a world where the poet is desperate for livelihood.[17]

Whereas Place's project targeted the poetry economy, Timmons's attempt to sell his credit and his debit orients his work to interpret the debt crisis as itself a crisis of interpretation. Probing the role of digital archives, Timmons used OCR technology to scan and replicate his offers and bills, often leaving mistakes in the text. These mistakes seem a testament to the unreadability of credit offers and financial statements. He also performs a critique of techno-determinism in his pricing structure. Although both book prices—digital and print—are unreasonably expensive, it is significant that the version for download costs more than the print copy, an act of transmediation cutting against technoeconomic structures.[18] Whereas the economic dimension of remediation is to repurpose older material and thus change it, Timmons's project throws a wrench in our understanding of media "reform." Instead of going from expensive print book to cheaper eBook—indeed, on Troll Thread, another conduit of conceptual poetry, the downloads are free—*CREDIT*, does the opposite. These tricks seem to interpret facts about the increasingly digitized poetry economy itself by pointing back to the formal techniques in the poetry, and its interpretation.

Further monetizing abstraction, *CREDIT* traffics in cultural capital as well as finance capital. For the book promotion, Timmons collected thirty blurbs from established poets whose names are listed under "Praise for *CREDIT*" on the Insert Press website. Some blurbs are cheeky, like Harold Abramowitz's musing that "credit is not cheap" and Sawako Nakayasu's offer that she "will send a very special, one-of-a-kind, only-available-via-purchase-and-full-completion and proof-of-reading-of-this-book, to all who purchase and read this book. Offer not valid in Kentucky." Others try to present the stakes of the book sincerely, like Holly Myers who writes about "consumer capitalism's fine-print underbelly" on display in the text. Timmons graduated from the CalArts MFA program at the School for Critical Studies, and the other poets on his list mostly have both MFAs and current academic credentials. Like the uneven circular logic of Timmons's creditors, and like the poetry MFA programs meant to eventually "pay" through jobs in academia that have become scarce and adjunctified, *CREDIT* is a closed system. It seals itself off from public interpretations while also suggesting that it requires them.

*CREDIT* contends with the material left by the financial crisis while eliding the crisis itself. In other words, the book displays the abstract excess of the 2007 bubble, then eclipses the 2008 crash entirely, memorializing instead its paper trail in 2009. Finding the crisis unrepresentable directly, Timmons creates a new language, a new medium, an alphabet of abstraction that mirrors the abstraction of the financial crisis itself. The offers for credit that make up "Credit" from *a* to *z* seem to exist, frozen for claim by Timmons, but in fact are a mirage containing only toxicity, as we see two years later in "Debit" 1 to 10. The choice of the word "debit"—as opposed to the more common "debt"—emphasizes Timmons's dialectical critique. "Credit" and "debit" represent a double-entry bookkeeping system, where "debit" covers the side of the account on which debts are entered.[19] The poetry of CREDIT is the bookkeeping, not the settling or even the representation of a system of prestige and debt that doubly obscures the work of poetry and its interpretation.

## INTERPRETING REPRESENTATION

Documental poetry projects often probe the relationship of the practice of poetry and poetics to government support, connecting weakening arts funding to other policies and privatization regimes. Where CREDIT grapples with education policy and debt, Counterpath's *Let Her Speak* performs this work in regard to health-care and abortion access. Rendered as a poem, the transcript of a filibuster directly contends with feminism that foregrounds white experience and with notions of biological essentialism that have previously been tied to abortion rights discourse. These issues become clear in *Let Her Speak* due to its writing practices and production—crowdsourced transcription—and because it deconstructs metonymy and apostrophe, figures that are hallmarks of poetic form.

The book is a print version of Davis's eleven-hour filibuster to block Senate Bill 5 (SB5), a Texas bill that would close most women's health clinics in the state due to new regulations, ban abortions taking place after twenty weeks, and force restrictive oversight on doctors. The Texas State Senate had called a special session to pass the bill, and Davis planned to stall the vote for thirteen hours until midnight, when the special session would end, with the aim of thwarting the bill entirely. The Texas State Senate requires filibustering senators to stand while speaking, abstain from food or water, and keep their speech relevant to the issue at hand. To perform the filibuster, Davis had a catheter inserted by a physician the morning of the session and she wore pink running shoes, presumably shoes suited to standing for long periods of time. News coverage in advance and during the filibuster mentioned that she was a runner, an athlete accustomed to uncomfortable feats of endurance. She read prepared testimony on the subject of women's health, and when that testimony ran out, she read abortion stories that were sent in ad hoc to her office. She would not concede the floor when repeatedly asked to do so. Senate Republicans had secretly come up with a system of taking turns to catch her in a decorum mistake, so the filibuster was particularly harrowing.[20]

Davis did not achieve the goal of talking until midnight because Senate Republicans ended it after eleven hours, on a "three strikes and you're out" rule, claiming that she had violated regulations twice by straying off topic and once by allowing a colleague to help her with a back brace. A long deliberation ensued before the vote to end the filibuster, and Texas Senate Democrats did their best to slow the process, filling more time. By this time, the news coverage was extensive, and Democratic senators were taking suggestions about how to stall from social media.[21] The filibuster ultimately prevailed as a community effort, making it to thirteen hours with the help of disruption from a local crowd at the chamber, which chanted, "Let her speak," until the clock ran out.

Although this episode ignited energetic activism in Texas, the bill was signed into law less than a month later.[22] SB5 gained a majority vote in the second special session held by then governor of Texas Rick Perry in light of what he called a "breakdown of decorum" in the first. In 2016, the Supreme Court would throw out the restrictions of the bill, ruling that the restrictions put an undue burden on what was then a constitutional right to an abortion. Then, in 2022, the Supreme Court reversed federal protection of abortion, allowing bills similar to SB5.

Counterpath Press, a small press known for publishing documental poetics, released *Let Her Speak: Transcript of the Texas State Senator Wendy Davis's June 25, 2013, Filibuster of the Texas State Senate*, in September 2013. The text consists of the unaltered chamber proceedings. It was transcribed from the video of the filibuster on the Texas State Senate website through the use of an anonymous crowdsourcing employment platform. Tim Roberts, Counterpath's director, explained that, after the

DOCUMENTAL POETRY AND THE PRIVATIZATION OF INTERPRETATION 137

Texas State Senate claimed that no official copy of the transcript existed, the editors turned to crowdsourcing.[23] Counterpath was able to make a full transcript by posting the video in ten-minute clips and paying $5.00 per clip to anonymous transcribers and later double-checking the transcript for errors.[24] Shortly after publication, Counterpath held a public marathon reading at its venue in Denver, Colorado, with parallel readings at Innisfree Books in Boulder, Colorado; the Spider House Café in Austin, Texas; and Bluestockings Bookstore in New York City. Readings were open to the public, and each reader was given about six pages of the transcript to read. The Counterpath website explains that these events were meant to "celebrate and extend Davis's act of protest."[25] Not only did Counterpath perform an interpretive and archival service otherwise absent from the public sphere—the record of the transcript—their events repeated previous engagement and protest at a time when abortion rights activism was otherwise losing steam.

The project *Let Her Speak*—its production, celebration, and textual artifact—meditates on the importance of telling abortion stories and how they are told. The filibuster itself was created from a simple impulse to speak. Davis had planned to use her time on the floor reading testimony from people who were unable to testify in advance of the special session about the bill. There was a long list of written stories because, after waiting up to ten hours to speak about their experiences with abortion, many were sent home because Texas State House committee chair Byron Cook said that the testimony "had become repetitive."[26] Cook implied that the stories were so similar that they did not warrant attention. Davis's assertion that these stories needed to be told contains a political message about respecting the experiences of those who needed abortion care. After this moment, and in the years leading up to the *Dobbs* decision in 2022, talking about abortions in public places became more and more common as abortion rights were under national and local siege. The simple statement of people's stories of pregnancy and pregnancy termination seemingly became the central conduit of public activism. In 2015, the social media campaign #ShoutYourAbortion would encourage people to share their abortion stories over social media in order to destigmatize and normalize them. Culling stories from this project, the book *Shout Your Abortion* was published by PM Press in 2018. Although it bears some relation to *Let Her Speak*—both books are crowdsourced abortion stories—the modes in each are different. In *Let Her Speak*, there is already a layer of mediation as each story is retold, first by Davis during the filibuster, then by the transcriber processing the story, and then often by a reader at a public performance.

A form of synecdoche happens within Davis's performance, which commentators at the time—reporters and others who had seen the spectacle but had not read the text—noted. The spectacle of Davis's discomfort on the senate floor recalls and sometimes mirrors the stories she reads aloud. Whereas commentators of the video event used Davis's body in particular to perform synecdoche—a white, cisgendered body, blonde and trimmed with much-remarked-upon pink—the text *Let Her Speak* implicates other types of bodies as well, suggesting that other bodies can represent the issue and cause of abortion access.

The project refracts the white, heteronormative representative politics on display and calls for more nuanced and communal understanding of the issues of bodily autonomy at stake. In other words, *Let Her Speak*, as a text, creates rhetorical tropes where there were fallacies of equivalents before. This synecdoche of the live event and the recording is fraught: Davis had been reading other people's stories, and yet is standing up—standing in—for them. *Let Her Speak* asks questions about the politics of representation (how is it helpful for one to recite the story of many?), and even animation. The text begins, "Yes, Mr. President. I intend to speak for an extended period of time on the bill. Thank you very much."[27] The vocative follows the decorum of the Texas State Senate, but in the context of the synecdoche otherwise performed—that this is a poem with multiple mediations of voice—the vocative serves as apostrophe. In 1986, Barbara Johnson carefully parsed the relationship of this particular rhetorical figure to the political issue of fetal personhood. She writes, "Can the very essence of a political issue—an issue like, say, abortion—hinge on the structure of a figure? Is there any inherent connection between figurative language and questions of life and death, of who will wield and who will receive violence in a given human society?"[28] Her answer ultimately is yes. Johnson defines apostrophe as "a form of ventriloquism through which the speaker throws voice, life, and human form into the addressee, turning its silence into mute responsiveness."[29] In other words, even though Davis speaks, "Yes, Mr. President," she is not really addressing the Texas State Lieutenant Governor and Senate President David

Dewhurst, and she does not concede the floor. She addresses him to make him responsive to a specific rhetorical situation that she engineered. As Johnson explains, with apostrophe, the speaker always controls the discursive situation in the poem. For this reason, apostrophe is an inherently political tool—who can inhabit which discursive position (that of the mother, the child, the dead child in Johnson's examples)—becomes the lynchpin of the argument Johnson subsequently develops. Johnson ultimately argues that there is something different in how poems by men and poems by women imagine the relationship of the speaker to the text. She suggests that because everyone has been a child and thus can project a child's voice or speak to a child and that the other discursive positions are difficult for some, this means that male writing is procreative and female writing is infanticidal. Johnson's equation of gender to childbearing possibilities performs a cis-normative biological essentialism (much in the same way that, during her filibuster, Davis suggests that she is able to talk on this matter of abortion because she has got "the equipment").[30] Through the interpretive function of the text, however, *Let Her Speak* keeps the animating politics of the rhetorical figure and rejects essentialist gender-based claims.

It is the fact that Davis is speaking to the president of the special session that makes it possible for her to tell other people's stories. The speaker ("Davis" but also the transcribers and the readers) do not express shame or inhibitions telling these stories. Apostrophe is one of the "strange temporalities of projection into an enabling object that is also disabling," that Lauren Berlant takes up in *Cruel Optimism*.[31] Berlant makes much of the idea that the speaker is the agent in this particular rhetorical figure: apostrophe is "a turning back, an animating of a receiver on behalf of the desire to make something happen *now* that realizes something in the speaker, makes the speaker more or differently possible, because she has admitted, in a sense, the importance of speaking for, as, and to, two—but only under the condition that the two are really (in) one."[32] Berlant writes that "a lyrical address to the dead—apostrophe—works best when they are absent and you are affectively and mentally in sovereign control over the ways in which they are 'in' you."[33] The absence of the senate president, created by multiple mediated layers, enables both frankness and emotional attachment to the stories, which would not otherwise be possible, in the transcript and its readings.

Through these devices, Davis's body becomes one of many and her struggles a little less sex- and gender-specific. Toward the end of the text—after Davis has gone without food or water for over ten hours, when she has not sat down or even "leaned on the desk," which she knows would disqualify her despite her back pain—there is a very long debate about whether a senator helping Davis with a back brace breaks the rules.[34] The word "respect" is repeated in regard to Davis's body, and she is "respectfully commended" by Senator John Whitmire for being "very statesman-like, doing something that I know most of us couldn't do."[35] Whitmire is referring to the extraordinary physical feat Davis has been performing, and we can also read this line as calling attention to the physical feats of both pregnancy and abortion. In this section of the transcript, Whitmire is suggesting that senators respect decorum but not become unkind, he argues that the "greater good" will be achieved if they do not disqualify Davis from accepting friendly assistance. He asks, "Isn't there a greater good of respecting a woman?," seemingly reminding the room that this is a bill about respecting bodies of constituents.[36]

Yet the courtroom shows an interest in the spectacle when Senator Eddie Lucio concedes that "Senator Davis does have the right to oppose this bill until she drops."[37] As the room debates whether to disqualify Davis, she begins to read a study related to the so-called fetal pain part of the bill, which bans abortions before twenty weeks. Davis reads a portion of the bill: "'The findings indicate that the State has a compelling state-interest in protecting the lives of unborn children from the stage at which substantial medical evidence indicates that these children are capable of feeling pain.' And what I have here, members, is a study specific to that particular issue."[38] As she goes on to read the study and to explore the bill further, the irony builds. Davis is experiencing pain as she discusses people needing abortions experiencing pain, and yet the pain of a fictional or absent fetus—scientific evidence aside for whether the existence of this notion is warranted—is the primary concern. By speaking to members of the Texas State Senate in the apostrophe above, Davis is throwing her voice, ventriloquizing a senate that might be interested in the science of a particular study. She maintains the bodily autonomy to feel pain, indeed perhaps to "drop," and also garners worlds beyond that specificity.

In addition to the citational apostrophic technology of ethical imagination in the text, the very production process of the book—crowdsourcing—brings in another layer of mediation along with important questions about community, globalization, and representation. The Amazon service Mechanical Turk, which was utilized by Counterpath, offers a crowdsourced way for people to perform small tasks for money. On it, employers, or "requestors," set up small jobs, or "human intelligence tasks" (HITs), for contract-style employees (Turkers) to perform. Jeff Bezos began Amazon Mechanical Turk in 2005 to exploit the fact that humans can sometimes easily perform certain tasks that are difficult for computers to do. The name comes from an eighteenth-century chess-playing device—"the Turk"—that opponents believed was a machine but in fact was a human in disguise. Bezos has called Mechanical Turk "artificial artificial intelligence" to indicate that the tasks come from the computer and go to humans.[39] In truth, the requestors are a mostly anonymous mixture of academic, business, and nonprofit entities using the unregulated platform to their advantage, and the workers are mostly younger, college-educated people—underemployed poetry MFAs among them—looking to supplement their incomes.[40]

Multiple studies and reports have shown that requestors often renege on agreements, perform wage theft, and that Turkers, on average, make less $5.00 per hour and receive no other benefits, security, or compensation. These factors, along with a slew of protests in 2014 that were meant to bring attention to Turkers' plight, made Mechanical Turk a symbol of the worst of the unregulated gig economy. The anonymity supported by the digital platform seems to allow, or even promote, predatory and exploitative labor practices.[41]

The pay structure that Counterpath set for their HIT, $5.00 per ten-minute clip, although nowhere close to minimum wage, is not as exploitative to Turkers as most of the work on the site. It treats these workers much like the readers performing six-page sections of the text at bookstore and book-center celebrations, as participants in activism and interpretation. Both the readers at bookstores and the Turkers transcribing the stories seem to have a stake in them. After publishing *Let Her Speak*, Counterpath continued to use Mechanical Turk for their *Reading @realDonaldTrump* series. The project published a series of seven volumes during his presidency (between November 2016 and November 2018), each consisting of Turkers' interpretations of Trump's tweets. The Counterpath website explains, "Tweets are posted to Amazon Turk as 'human intelligence tasks' (HITs) with the prompt to write at least 100 words describing the surface meaning and subtext. These readings are then collected in a short book devoted to a given @realDonaldTrump tweet. Proceeds from sales of titles in the series are donated to nonprofit causes."[42] The promotional material notes that worker identification numbers are included with each reading, and the page at the print-on-demand service Lulu.com further explains that workers were paid $1.00 for their one-hundred-word descriptions.[43] Paying workers through the Mechanical Turk service for the work of interpretation, rather than rote tasks, is a break from the way the service is conceptualized and often used. The modest but not exploitative wage structure ($1.00 for one hundred words), is also significant because the service is famous for legally skirting the Fair Labor Standards Act to ask workers to perform long tasks for meagre compensation.

The anonymity of the service here was not in this case used to exploit, but rather as part of a literary tactic. This technique is similar to Counterpath's restaging of the transcript with readings around the country with members of the public—multiple genders and bodies with and without childbearing possibilities—standing in for Davis, standing in for each person's testimony. Together, and along with the formal apostrophe of the text, *Let Her Speak* performs something of Jacques Derrida and Gayatri Spivak's notion of teleiopoesis. Spivak describes the Derridean term as "imagining yourself, really letting yourself be imagined (experience that impossibility) without guarantees, by and in another culture, perhaps."[44] This is an act of being made by reading rather than making when engaging with the other worlds of a text. For Derrida, the vocative case and citations—especially multiple citation—allows this practice. Teleiopoesis is most clear in sentences that turn back on themselves through the apostrophe; his *Politiques de l'amité* is a meditation on Aristotle's "o philoi, oudeis philos," or "O my friends, there is no friend." Derrida and Spivak's interest in teleiopoiesis is, in part, a call to attend to mediation.[45] For Spivak in particular, it contains the key to remaking the discipline of comparative literature to be more radically open, singular, and ethical, which she sees as an antidote to globalization. In this case, the terms of the abortion debate are not ceded to antiabortionism or to essentialism (as both Barbara Johnson and Wendy Davis unwittingly do in their discussions). Rather, as Margaret Ronda writes about abortion as a poetic figure: "Abortion, in its very presence, serves as deconstructive figure for the normative politics and meanings of family as property relation and

DOCUMENTAL POETRY AND THE PRIVATIZATION OF INTERPRETATION   143

social form."⁴⁶ These performances not only suggest deconstruction of the often white cis-feminist trope but also what might lie beyond race, capitalism, and patriarchal notions of autonomy and care.

*Let Her Speak* begs Spivak's question: How are we made within the eyes of the other?⁴⁷ In this project, we are all people who can get pregnant, people who have experienced birth and miscarriage, people who want to carry pregnancies to full term or do not, people who have made decisions about their bodies. The figures of apostrophe and citational vocatives create this teleiopoetic possibility. *Let Her Speak* is a poem about how abortion is a labor issue, a global issue, and a technology to be wielded.

And yet there is a troubling incoherence at the heart of this seemingly complete project. The video on the Texas State Senate website does not end the same way that Counterpath's *Let Her Speak* does. The final page of *Let Her Speak* reads:

> Dewhurst: Thank you, Senator Davis. [*Extended pause*]
> Dewhurst: Members, after consultation with the Parliamentarian and after going over what, what people heard as far as discussion, Senator Campbell your point of order is well taken and is sustained.
> Gallery: [*Extended yelling, shouting.*] Bullshit! [*Increased yelling, shouting.*] [*Various attempts to speak by members.*]
> Dewhurst: Can you hear me? Senator Watson, can you hear me?
> Gallery [*chanting*]: Let her speak! Let her speak! Let her speak! . . .
>
> [*End filibuster.*]⁴⁸

Although Davis does not speak again, the video recorded by the Texas State Senate, and arguably the filibuster itself, goes on for more than five hours after this moment. Perhaps more pressingly, there is five hours of the Texas State Senate video left when "the point of order is well taken and is sustained" (the point of order to end the filibuster due to the three strikes rule), followed by just a few minutes of chanting, "Let her speak."⁴⁹ Part of the five hours may be represented by the ellipses above because there is certainly chanting of "Let her speak" later in the video as well. What we don't see represented in *Let Her Speak* is that several Democratic senators quibble about the rules and in fact appeal the ruling of the chair, opening a debate about the motion. Incredible collective politicking ensues. Dewhurst steps down and puts Senator Robert Duncan in the chair's position. Duncan, as the new chair, requests that the protestors are cleared from the gallery—he is ignored by security or law enforcement—and then Democratic Senator Leticia Van de Putte requests to be filled in on what she missed while she was attending her father's funeral. There is a discussion about why certain members have been recognized and others have not, and there are more appeals against the initial point of order. Senator Van de Putte is interrupted and told that she is not "in order" by Duncan in a few tense moments. What is perhaps summarized above as "various attempts to speak by members" is in fact lengthy and complicated.[50]

This is important because, in other many accounts of the day, Senator Van de Putte's question to Dewhurst (this entire part is elided in the Counterpath text), "At what point must a female senator raise her hand or her voice to be recognized over the male colleagues in the room?," is what started the sustained chanting of "Let her speak!" by the crowd. In fact, many consider this utterance by Van de Putte, a Latinx female senator from San Antonio, Texas, the catalyst for the failed vote. In the video created by the Texas State Senate, the room certainly does get wilder after Van de Putte's question.[51] This moment of drama occurs about two hours after *Let Her Speak* ends. Directly after Van de Putte's question, Duncan yells, "If we cannot get order in the chamber, we will suspend the roll call vote!"[52] This is what seemingly happens, and the last two to three hours of the senate video displays senators milling around the floor while people scream and chant off-screen. Many sources would later call this filibuster the "people's filibuster" for this reason: Van de Putte's question galvanized the people to run out the clock, disallowing the order to vote. Finally, Dewhurst returns to the podium to say that the session has expired so the vote cannot take place, and to add somewhat menacingly, "It's been fun, but we will see you soon."

It is not clear whose choice it was to elide the last few hours of the debate and Van de Putte's key contribution from the Counterpath poem. Did Counterpath get a shoddy or even racist Turker who ignored key moments in the video, erasing this crucial contribution from a woman of color?[53] It seems more likely that Counterpath did not post the last five hours to Mechanical Turk to be transcribed, deciding to end the poem with the end of Davis's voice.

Imbricated in the transforming power of documental poetics, *Let Her Speak* mirrors the logics of white supremacy. Indeed, this aspect of the book reflects the logic of public language of finance and the state, allowing some voices and stories and not others. Assuming that the transcript provided was the video itself, and not even the complete video, the documents of the documental poetry here were entirely bureaucratic, ensconced in administrative aesthetic and therefore contained the brutality of the state even as the poetry might ellipse it. This brutality continues to function even if, or maybe especially because, these documents exist within the privatized world of poetry. To confront the noise of these logics, poets have attempted to reinterpret, reproduce, and reframe the language of the state (here, represented through ellipses, reading performances, and even Turkers). But as poets summon and expose the global technologies of documents, transforming them into imaginative devices, might they also strive to, as M. NourbeSe Philip puts it, "*Break the words open . . . explode the words to see what other words they may contain*," resurfacing drowned voices and even animating voices that were previously frozen by neglect?[54]

## LIMITS OF DOCUMENTS AND THE DREAMS OF BUREAUCRACY

By documenting, exploring, and performing Wendy Davis's transcript in ways that nuance and reorient the multipart struggle for bodily autonomy, *Let Her Speak* performs a crucial public function otherwise missing from the public sphere. Where other accounts of Davis's filibuster make evident that her advocacy for bodily autonomy insists on her body as part of the work of the state, even as methods of describing state power try to obscure it, *Let Her Speak* repositions the body as a collective figure, a figure that deconstructs harmful racist and essentialist logics. In doing this work, the transcript, as poetry, contains elisions, absences, and holes. Grappling directly with how the logics of white supremacy are imbricated in the logics of bureaucracy, many post-2008 texts turn to collective authorship as they work out philosophies of listening, hearing, speaking, telling, and untelling.

In the coda, I will discuss a suite of texts from this era that ask questions about interpretation through employing and probing the silenced voices and gaps in bureaucratic state documents. First, to conclude this chapter, I will briefly examine *Zong!*, which M. NourbeSe Philip coauthored with ancestral voice Setaey Adamu Boateng, to consider how documental techniques specifically fathom the unrepresentable and the unreachable. Unlike the other texts discussed, *Zong!* thoroughly illustrates what needs to be rendered invisible to make racial capitalism operate seamlessly. It asks directly how to engage documents of history that elide the very atrocities that they historicize. Published in 2008, *Zong!* opened the doors to a popular mode of documental poetry that pursues absented voices, and the book quickly became the center of conversations about the future of poetry, affect, and appropriative practices. Philip is a Canadian writer from Tobago. Although she calls these two places home, she explains that she is "indigenous to the world" but remains "exiled, possibly permanently."[55] In addition to writing poetry, she writes young adult fiction and nonfiction and practices law. She has garnered international acclaim and has written extensively on race and racism in Canadian cultures and institutions.

Although it might seem counterinitiative to the argument of this chapter to conclude with a writer set apart from the United States and a text that was published on the precipice of the financial crisis rather than when it was more largely felt, both *Zong!* itself and its institutional reception shed light on the place and role of ideology critique during the neoliberalization of higher education. *Zong!* was published simultaneously by Mercury Press, a Canadian publishing company, and Wesleyan University Press, a U.S. academic publisher. Its U.S. reception was phenomenal; it was discussed widely in U.S. poetry and experimental writing circles and then became a syllabus favorite for all kinds of university classes and even by professors who did not usually teach poetry. Philip herself has located the United States and the U.S. political context as a crucial home for her work and that it makes it possible for her, living in Canada, to write at all.[56] Canada, she argues, seemed without a tradition of Black writing, and if she were in the United States and also writing about the United States, she would have to perform an engagement with "the long history of writing by African Americans, beginning with the enslaved poet Phillis Wheatley."[57] Unlike her other works, *Zong!* was coauthored (or "as told to the author") with Setaey Adamu Boateng, an ancestor. The ancestral voices involved in the production of the work and the unreproducible textual format of the poems are crucial to the project.[58] I hope to show how Philip's vantage point and these factors of textual production make *Zong!* a helpful cypher for other documental poetry, including documental poetry more clearly seated in the United States.

Although much has been written on silences and gaps within Philip's *Zong!* as a philosophy of history, far less discussed is how her use of an administrative aesthetic directly interprets the globalization and financialization of the twenty-first century.[59] Contemporary political economy and inequity were on Philip's mind as she wrote *Zong!*. In a 2007 interview, she explains:

> One of the things I've found as I've worked on this project is that this is very old and yet very, very present with us. How do we make sense of living in a world where 1 percent of the people living in the United States, for instance, make as much as 90 percent of the rest of the population [combined].... And so much of what we're living with today is linked to that first experience in globalization where the currency of globalization was the black body. Black bodies could be taken anywhere in the world, at any point in time, sans passport, sans visa. That was the currency of globalization then and I don't think we have had a reckoning on that yet, and this is why we keep recycling and returning to these moments, to which we will continue to return until (if ever) and unless we come to some kind of reckoning.[60]

Like Counterpath and Timmons's projects, this reckoning takes the form of rewriting the language of the state. The poems of *Zong!* look like poetry created within the Language tradition—they are difficult, include language play, dominate the page in fantastical patterns—but, as Philip explains in the book's "Notanda," although the poems here "employ similar strategies to reveal the hidden agendas of language" to Language poetry, in Philip's work, "the strategies signpost a multifaceted critique of the European project."[61] *Zong!* is written from a source text, which the book also reproduces in full at the end.

The source text is a report of the decision of an English legal case of 1783, *Gregson v. Gilbert*, in which Luke Collingwood, the captain of the slave ship *Zong*, ordered 150 enslaved Africans to be drowned in the ocean for the purpose of collecting insurance money after their deaths.[62] The voyage was taking longer than expected, and many enslaved people had died through illness and lack of sufficient water. Captain Collingwood assumed that, because his "cargo" was insured, if the Africans were thrown off the boat, he would be able to collect money, whereas if they died of natural causes, restitution was not guaranteed. After the insurers refused to pay, a jury found them liable for compensating the ship's owners for the "lost cargo." The insurers then appealed the decision, after which three justices decided that a new trial should be held to determine the ultimate fault. The court document that states the judge's decision—absolute payment of costs—is referred to as *Gregson v. Gilbert* and it provides the language that Philip uses for the poems. Historians of transatlantic slavery know this horrific case as an important step on the way to abolition.[63] The logic of high finance enshrouded in the language of bureaucracy made the slave trade possible—as Ian Baucom writes, it is because of this "modern system of finance capital capable of converting anything it touches into a monetary equivalent" that slavery can exist to begin with—but this particular episode, as a limit case for these logics, helped transform the system.[64]

Constrained by this short bureaucratic court document, Philip's collection consists of reiterations, imaginings, and meditations about what cannot be known about the historical event that took place on the *Zong* ship. The "Notanda," Philip's essay that ends the book, contains additional historical background, culled from several other sources, as well as a philosophy of history. Although very different from the conundrum of Timmons's *CREDIT*, when faced with the unrepresentable, Philip, like Timmons, creates a new language, a distinct alphabet with twenty-six characters. The "Notanda" explains that Philip is haunted by the story of *Zong*—she reads, rereads, and researches the case and its evidence—which forces her to enter a "different land, a land of language," and also an understanding of silence.[65] Faced with the fact that she must tell the story of *Zong* but also cannot imagine it told, she employs only the words that were used in the courtroom decision to create the poems "Zong! #1–26," which make up "Os," the first section of the text. Then Philip writes translations of these highly compacted first poems to make up the subsequent sections of the book.[66] The *Zong* case is a "story that cannot be told, yet must be told"; as Philip explains "we want the bones."[67] The poetry book begins with "Os," the Latin word for bones, and also a lament, sob, and address.

The poems of *Zong!* #1–26 each have a different lineation and a different logic. By isolating phrases or grammatical elements of sentences, a new way of telling appears: the gaps and holes that language usually further obscures become illuminated as absence. For example, *Zong!* #26 probes at the obliqueness of what "was." Containing no grammatical subject, it begins "was the cause was the remedy was the record was the argument / was the delay was the evidence was the overboard was the not was the."[68]

Limited not by the words within the case but rather by their letters, the other sections of the book include words in Arabic, Dutch, Fon, French, Greek, Hebrew, Italian, Latin, Portuguese, Spanish, Sonha Twi, West African patois, and Yoruba. They are broken across the page, and in some sections type oversets type and also creates undulating patterns.[69] The names of the murdered people do not appear in any of the historical documents, and to repair this omission, Philip breaks the textual constraint that otherwise governs *Zong!* by creating possible names and lists them, submerged below the poems on each page of the book.

The section entitled "Manifest" presumably lists the ship's cargo. As the constraint tells us, however, the "manifest" is only a list of the words that Philip could create from the extant text. This document then works as an origin for the other poems because it illuminates what could be told and what could not. The list is divided into "African Groups & Languages," "Animals," "Body Parts," "Crew," "Food & Drink," "Nature," and "Women Who Wait." These categories provide guidance to the backstories that Philip creates in the text. For example, under "Women Who Wait," Ruth and Claire are listed. In the poems, these two women appear repeatedly in correspondence from a white crew member. This "manifest," or the invoice detailing the contents of the ship, is the medium that creates the alphabet of *Zong*. The manifest, like the double-entry bookkeeping system, is part of what Baucom considers the central logic of empire and, when employed, creates a "monetarizing anatomization of the body."[70] Like Philip, Baucom argues that the financialized case of *Zong* illuminates present systems. He writes, "Our present moment is, thus, more than structurally like the antecedent high finance moments who value forms and capital logics it recuperates. It is a moment which does not merely resemble that equally financialized moment in which the *Zong* sailed. Our time, I want instead to suggest, is a present time which, in a fully Benjaminian sense, inherits its nonimmediate past by intensifying it, by 'perfecting' its capital protocols, 'practicalizing' its epistemology, realizing its phenomenology as the cultural logic 'of the entire social-material world.'"[71]

The question of *Zong!* is how to interpret atrocity, an atrocity of financialization and globalization that, as Philip suggests, is "very old and yet very, very present with us."[72] Her book also asks, How do we engage with documents of history that elide the very atrocity that they historicize? Philip's documental poetics suggests a postmedium language—created by the manifest—that also reaches beyond the bureaucratic administrative aesthetic of its creation. Suggesting that how this incident in 1781 is interpreted has much to tell us about our own moment, Philip manipulates the epistemologies of bookkeeping but does not refuse them.

If Philip's *Zong!* employs the financialized logics of empire to create something else (an alphabet that spins a language of holes), Timmons's *CREDIT* perhaps displays an intensification and simple practicality of that logic through an alphabet less aesthetically wrought. Timmons's poetry of bureaucracy elides a subject, allowing only the specter of a pet owner with potential travel vouchers and a catchy sales voice on a website to suggest a philosophy of history. Counterpath's *Let Her Speak*, in aiming to create a state bureaucratic document in order to activate state protest, also replicates the philosophies of white supremacy, unfortunately glorifying a false subject, the heroine figure of Wendy Davis. Philip, sharing authorship and preserving manifest, maintains a strategy of interpretation, exploration, and nuance in *Zong!* Philip's technique makes space for future documental poetics and the continued relevance of poetry in general.

# CODA

The poetry that I have discussed within these pages works between disciplines and through media to refract and critique U.S. public forms. To make the argument that this robust category of "poetry in general" provides a helpful path for scholars of literature and across the humanities alike, I have traced poetic entanglement with institutions and government apparatuses. For some readers, my focus on more experimental texts may have come as a surprise, given what is sometimes seen as an anti-institutional or extra-institutional location of this type of poetry. Nevertheless, the poetry examined here is variously bound to state facilitation of capitalism, policy, and rationality, sometimes even taking institutional language as its subject and its fodder. I have not been discussing poetry that is addressed to a—or "the"—public per se; rather, I have been interested in poetry that is preoccupied with public forms.

My tactic, a focus on interdisciplinary poetic techniques that engage public forms, diverges from recent trends in poetry studies, where there has been much thought given to how poets engage a public audience and how contemporary deviations in engagement might differ from definitions of poetry that depend on privacy or solitude.[1] This interest has resulted in much scholarship on the institution of the lyric, the rise of lyric theory, and studies of its embeddedness in institutions. The last ten years especially have brought scholarship that connects lyric structures to whiteness and to state power; this connection is shot through the "new lyric studies" and also its trenchant critiques.[2] Likewise, many critics have argued that the most salient poetry of the last sixty years disrupts lyric forms and notions of solitary personhood in part by trafficking in versions of these very forms.[3]

The archive engaged in this book's pages—variously from Fluxus to documental poetry—offers one suggestion toward a separate trajectory of the category of poetry that also implicates architectures of race and state power. This trajectory may even share some of the same poets with lyric studies, but it is my hope that seeing them within the frame of poetry in general offers a fresh look at how they engage social questions of work, power, and relation to the state.[4] I hope this offering will attend to what I see as a lack of attention to experimental interdisciplinary practices like constraint, collage, and multimedia poems amid this surge of criticism about institutions.[5] Coming from the other side, scholarship on experimental poetry has largely passed over its institutional nature in favor of arguments that either equate experimentalism with revolutionary actions or place it outside institutions.[6] As I hope *Poetry in General* has shown, poetry of both experimental and lyric traditions participates in various institutions to comment on and shape public forms. Recall the avant-gardism of Yoko Ono's "Blood Piece" next to Frank O'Hara's love poem "Nocturne," for example.

This coda will suggest how we might bridge institutional studies that often center the lyric to scholarship on experimental poetry in order to build a more nuanced conception of the relationship between poetry and politics. As both lyric and experimental poems may be imbricated in public forms, to clearly gauge the process of interdisciplinarity at play in either type of poem—or poems that can be categorized as both lyric and general—we must be attentive to multiple lineages, practices, and categories. We must, for example, acknowledge lyric patterns of engagement as well as interdisciplinary techniques of experimentalism—like instructions, constraint, cut-ups, rewritings—to see the full range of poetry in general.

In regard to "documental" poetry in particular, the absence of this bridge is especially apparent from both sides.[7] Recent books about how poetry has worked with and against the prestige and safety of academia do not discuss documental poetry, despite its entanglement in English and creative writing departments and its categorization as the experimental writing of the early 2000s.⁸ Even Kimberly Andrews, whose incisive book focuses on avant-garde poetry, ultimately concludes that the academic avant-garde has created "a form of lyricized critical thinking" but that conceptual writing does not belong in that story because it "does not show up as a traceable form of *interaction* with those intellectual structures" in academia.⁹ The archive and the framework that I have delineated in this book shows that institutional study of conceptual and documentary writing—both best seen as part of documental poetry—illuminates the workings of this interdisciplinary poetry clearly and sheds light on the structures that produce it. With this framework in place, in this coda, I hope to briefly illustrate the traceable interaction between this poetry and contemporary academia. *Poetry in General* has covered government and private-sector institutions of immigration (chapter 1), office work and various types of suburban and urban development (chapters 2 and 3), health care and welfare (chapter 4), and financialization and debt economies (chapter 5). Within these foci has lurked the university, an interlocking site, along with the state and capital, to produce the forms of imperialism, patriarchy, and extractive ideology studied here.¹⁰

The connection between the university, the state, and capital is never clearer than when I discuss documental writing, much of which is produced directly under the contemporary conditions and intellectual structures of academia. The collections that I will discuss in this coda thematically link issues of higher education and its methods to imperialism, settler colonialism, and structural inequities. In fact, Andrews's helpful conclusions about how poetry has created certain forms of criticism and interpretation can be mobilized to illustrate that the ongoing world of documental poetics is one place where institutional questions are foregrounded and particular types of institutional expression emerge. Andrews's focus is on how crucial (and inefficient, or perhaps even anticapitalist) knowledge work is informed by an interdependence between poetic production and critical methodologies. Indeed, contemporary documental projects connect academia to the public in ways that look like public criticism, for example, critiquing the insular rise of debt-accumulating MFA programs, to bring poetry more broadly into the intellectual, social, and material life of the university and beyond. It may be that documental poetry projects are clearer about their commitment to critique as a method (more about documental poetry and a crisis in higher education in a moment), but these projects certainly respond to intellectual trends in academia and the conditions of classrooms and research.

In chapter 5, I argued that poetry in general, in the form of documental poetry, engages and critiques the neoliberalization of higher education. One way to see documental poetry's work of engagement with latent forms of ideology in public life, even more specifically, with forms of neoliberal ideology and language produced at the hinge between the state and the financial sector, is by looking at the particulars of its material conditions of production and circulation. The sustaining home for these conditions is academia; it is one space where (often precarious) livelihood can be found in poetic experimentation. Here I will note that during my research at the Gilbert and Lila Silverman Fluxus Collection Archives in the Museum of Modern Art, I sifted through pamphlets, letters, curricula, and reports from 1968 and 1969 when over forty Fluxus artists were brought to University of California, Santa Cruz on a Carnegie Fellowship to work, cocreate, and imagine higher education's futures with students and workers there. It is hard to imagine such a program now. The dearth of spaces for interpretation, experimentation, and critique has been driven by a diminishing support for art and poetry in many areas of the public. But it is nowhere clearer than in academia, where recent cuts, debasement of public standing, adjunctification, and a shrinking employment base has taken a toll.[11] After the 2008 crash, the poetry world was a facilitator of capitalism in interesting ways, and, as I hope chapter 5 has shown, examining poetry as an economy nestled within larger economies is a helpful response to queries about its autonomy and its relation to criticism. In other words, this dearth of supports within academia is reflected in documental poetry techniques and preoccupations because a central part of documental poetry—and the debates surrounding it—rests on the role of the poet in academia. The conversation about and study of documental poetry—infused through literature and creative writing programs alike—reflects and responds to devaluation, defunding, and privatization, especially as these trends are brought to an inflection point in the years following 2008.

As Leigh Claire La Berge argues, the expansion of MFA programs and decreased government funding for art practice—a process that exponentially increases student debt—are major factors in the general crisis. This is a multipart issue: the design of MFA programs is predicated on the notion of a future job in academia, but since the 1970s, universities curtailed tenure and long-term job security in favor of adjunct positions. At the same time, MFA programs expanded, and tuition increased (some calculations say 259 percent since 1971).[12] Although she does not discuss documental writing, La Berge provides a political economy of the studio MFA, simultaneously arguing that art has become more socially engaged as it thematizes its material structure. The MFA degree in creative writing, although central to the study and production of poetry, likewise does not function as a professional degree leading to a job "but rather as a costly extension of [students'] liberal education."[13] As Mark McGurl asserts in his 2009 landmark study, *The Program Era: Postwar Fiction and the Rise of Creative Writing*, about the impact of the creative writing degree on novels: "To contextualize a literary work in relation to [the campus or the classroom] can be as telling as connecting it to the global cultural flow."[14] At the end of *The Program Era*, McGurl suggests how teachers and practitioners of creative writing fit into the university (other than tuition revenue without expensive overhead costs):

> Inwardly, their jobs as teachers is to stand as inspiring exemplars of the unalienated laborer. In this sense, every artist on campus is half a performance artist: making his name, doing his job, owning the product of his labor of "self-expression," the artist or writer-in-residence is in a sense the purest version of the kind of worker, the white-collar professional, that so many college students are preparing to be. . . . Outwardly, the task of the academic creative writer is to produce, in her writings, unconscious allegories of institutional quality, aesthetically pure because luxuriously useless.[15]

Poetry in general, in its instantiation of documental poetry in particular, refuses this pattern of allegory, which might otherwise be recognized in lyric studies. For better or worse, documentary poetry is often produced within universities, and many of its projects engage the deteriorating conditions of higher education directly.

Given the deep thematic engagement of much documental poetry with its own social conditions, it is surprising that, just as studies of poetry and the academy have not included documental poetry, in studies of documental poetry, academic institutionalization has been an aporia.

For example, both Seth Perlow and Paul Stephens cover a clear trajectory of experimental writing as critique, knowledge work, and reflection of public structures, linking it directly to technology and flows of capitalism, but neither discuss the specific conditions of the academic poetry world or higher education.[16] Likewise, in Craig Dworkin's helpful essay about poetry's relationship to digital technology and the commercialization of affect, he examines poetry itself as outside institutional structures, even if it is often discussed within them.[17] Perhaps this aporia is because conceptual writing—a large part of documental poetry—has been mired in shallow explanations, sometimes from its own progenitors, that its central intervention has to do only with upending notions of original genius, lyric voice, or confession; indeed, some argued that it was purely "against expression."[18] With this initial packaging, discussions of appropriation burned hot in poetry debates and publications, but by the summer of 2012, conceptual poetry was declared dead in a number of academic and quasi-academic venues.[19] Its death—not too surprisingly, given its avant-garde status—coincided with its further institutionalization, at least for a moment; 2011 and 2012 brought two anthologies of conceptual writing, complete with manifestos and the look and feel of classroom textbooks.[20] In 2015, the widely decried racist poem "The Body of Michael Brown" by Kenneth Goldsmith, one of conceptual writing's most vocal proponents, made it so that few wanted the category on syllabi or publication titles.[21]

Before I turn to examples of documental poetry that illuminate the thorny tangle of issues in higher education, I now briefly examine the debate about conceptual poetry in academia. I would like to suggest that we see this debate itself as part of a traceable academic structure. Conceptual writing, even and maybe most especially the "brand-name" kind, in its faux-academic refusal of expression, will not abide by the aforementioned model that reinforces institutional quality or bolsters suggestions that unalienated labor can exist within the institution of academia.[22] The debates surrounding conceptual writing's demise expose a crisis of what counts as creative and critical labor, where it happens, and what it means to support it. The shift to a more socially engaged art that La Berge and Joshua Clover, in a different way in his critique of conceptual writing, evoke clearly takes place within the documental poetry canon as conceptual writing is pushed into a larger category.

This category of documental poetry uses all the techniques of the imperial economies that produce it.

The process of conceptual writing widening into documental poetry—alongside its wholesale academic rejection—sheds light on what has been called a crisis of methods within literary studies and the humanities.[23] Coming at these questions of social engagement and the material conditions of academia by studying its internal workings, Patricia Stuelke makes a persuasive argument linking the turn to affect in the humanities—including "descriptive" and "reparative" methods—to neoliberal racial capitalism and neocolonialist tendencies. She argues, "Response to US imperial formations—the casting of such formations as legible and evident, and the corresponding turn to feeling and care as ends in themselves and limit points of possible action—has a history, one that is inextricable from the cultural and social forms of US imperialism and anti-imperialism in the late twentieth century and the concomitant rise of neoliberal racial capitalism."[24] Stuelke puts practices like surface reading and debates about ethical reading practices into a broader hemispheric archive to argue that the valorization of reparative methods needs to be examined in relation to the "institutionalization of late twentieth-century US domestic and transnational social movements: their move into the academy, their shifting relationship with the state and the university."[25] During this moment, conceptual poetry was one of the only places in literary studies arguing "against expression," or claiming that there was a problem with "feeling and care as ends in themselves." In hindsight, it is shocking to see this critique emerge from creative writing and English departments during the complete saturation of the affective turn throughout the humanities at large.[26] Although the fact that conceptual poetry was "against expression" might not be the most interesting thing about it—indeed, might not even be correct—documental poetry as a whole staunchly positioned itself as performing ideology critique in a moment that otherwise eschewed it.

Seen in this light, many documental projects refuse the dominant neoliberal ideology of feeling as an end-goal as they draw attention to the economic crisis that feeds into these very methods. Of course, documental poetry's ideology critique is not always coherent and, in some cases, it is misguided and damaging (the aforementioned "The Body of Michael Brown," for example). As I hope my framing of documental poetics within poetry in general has shown, this category stems in part from other types of poetry with ambiguous entanglements in the institutions that help them produce poetry. For example, George Brecht and other New Jersey Fluxus members' research at the intersection of Johnson & Johnson, Bell Labs, Rutgers, and the avant-garde art scene produced some very cogent critiques about the borders between art and life as well as some that were less so, and they even suggested problematic appropriation (see my discussion of the role of "yams" in chapter 2).

At our moment, diminishing supports in higher education and the poetry MFA conundrum is only one example of what La Berge calls "decommodification" among many. And yet in the 2010s, it became an emblem of the problems of livelihood generally and of poetry communities specifically. As Stephanie Young writes about the Bay Area in 2011, "The mostly middle class poets I am and hang out with found one another in a moment where it felt important to insist again and again that nobody needs a degree to be a poet, most poets do not hold tenured teaching jobs, that the pipeline from degree to degree to publication to job was in fact broken, the boom only a blip in the long history of poets and poetry."[27] She goes on to explain that her role in the MFA pipeline as administrator for Mills College (since absorbed by Northeastern University) does not quiet her insistence that the MFA does not "work" and even that it *shouldn't* work, that the degree is predicated on a capitalist fiction rather than a truth about "the long history of poets and poetry." In the community itself, Young describes her status as someone who holds an MFA but not a PhD as "a weird mole." "I don't have the right degree," she continues, "[at an academic poetry conference] I'm inside, but not in the way others are. I feel outside, but I'm not. It would be easier to participate if I could project myself into the feeling of being one thing or another, one location or another, but I can't."[28] For Young, the MFA "seems largely reviled" across the board, a symbol of something that does not afford access but suggests it, that was designed with something other than poetry or community in mind. At the time that Young was writing, an explosion of poetry about its own publicness arose from inside and outside MFA programs across the United States. It was this moment of saturation that I began thinking about *Poetry in General*, and this type of poetry seems to have a robust future as well.

After highlighting the contributions of a few important but as yet unmentioned documental texts from the postrecession era that are preoccupied with the public, the remainder of this coda will briefly analyze the poetry of Lena Chen, Holly Melgard, and Vanessa Jiminez Gabb. The discussion of these three poets allows me to pinpoint how poetry in general participates in conversations about higher education and other perforated publics, illuminating how documental forms of knowledge making work within and outside academia.

Some crucial poetry collections of the last ten years that ask questions about interpretation through employing and probing the silenced voices and gaps in bureaucratic state documents include Claudia Rankine's *Citizen: An American Lyric* (2014) and *Just Us: An American Conversation* (2020), Kenji Liu's *Map of an Onion* (2016) and *Monsters I Have Been* (2019), Solmaz Sharif's *LOOK* (2016), Blunt Research Group's *The Work-Shy* (2016), Layli Long Soldier's *WHEREAS* (2017), Marwa Helal's *Invasive Species* (2019), Don Mee Choi's *DMZ Colony* (2020), Vanessa Jimenez Gabb's *Basic Needs* (2021), Holly Melgard's *Fetal Position* (2021), Tanya Lukin Linklater's *Slow Scrape* (2023), and Nicole Sealy's *The Ferguson Report: An Erasure* (2023). There are many more than the few I list here, and yet the list shows an incredible range of style. Of these works, Claudia Rankine's *Citizen* is a very popular example of poetry that is quintessentially interdisciplinary and focused on notions of the public.[29] Many of these works contain echoes of others I have discussed earlier in *Poetry in General*; several of them excavate North American histories and tie these histories to bureaucracy of public forms. Tanya Lukin Linklater is a Canadian Indigenous multidiscipline artist of Alutiiq descent whose book *Slow Scrape* includes event scores and documental poetry about experiences of Native Alaskan peoples. She weaves together found text about major devastations, her family memories, and instructions to "you" and to audiences to answer the question, "How do we traverse the slow scrape of time?"[30] The answer, she suggests, is through manipulating and holding "records," the work to "place one then another / until the gap is less."[31] The Blunt Research Collective's *The Work-Shy*, a collection composed from phrases drawn from the case files of inmates in the earliest youth prisons in California between 1910 and 1925, also speaks directly to readers of its project by questioning what it means to listen with and without permission. The collection uses the voices of inmates and their captors and also asks how any speaking can possibly be an ethical action in light of the eugenicist practices at these prisons. Long Soldier's *WHEREAS* meticulously rewrites a response to the congressional resolution of apology to Native Americans, which President Barack Obama signed in 2009, all the while interrogating what constitutes apology in the face of the genocide and dispossession performed on Indigenous communities. Sealey's *The Ferguson Report* doctors the Department of Justice's investigation of the Ferguson (Missouri) Police Department after the uprising of 2014 in the wake of the death of Michael Brown. Sealey, like Linklater, Blunt Research Collective, and Long Soldier, breaks open archives to form new U.S. public possibility. The way they chart this task challenges knowledge-making structures and archival methods in and outside academia.

Extending and clarifying the echoes of critiques of U.S. colonialism and philosophies of immigration that I wrote about in chapters 1 and 2, many of these collections excavate U.S. military expansion abroad and its rippling effects. Sharif's *LOOK* tells the story of U.S. intervention, specifically in relation to drone killing and surveillance, in the Middle East by using the terms of the U.S. Department of Defense Military Dictionary. Kenji Liu's "Deconstruction Papers" from *Map of an Onion* intervenes in official identity documents. It begins with "EXHIBIT A. / BIRTH CERTIFICATE WITH CHINESE INTERVENTION" where the punctuation on a line from a birth certificate is spelled out in English transliterated Chinese.[32] "EXHIBIT B. TAIWANESE PASSPORT WITH ENGLISH INTERVENION" begins "all caps Chinese consulate general end caps New York, N period Y period comma all caps," and continues with the English-language punctuation spelled out.[33] The last exhibit, "NATURALIZATION WITH LENAPE INTERVENTION" uses the Lenape words for pause, "kènu," seemingly for periods, and the Lenape word for stop, "alà," at the end of the certificate that otherwise seems to be quoted verbatim.[34] The Lenape's historical territory includes New York City as well as a large swath of New York State, New Jersey, Pennsylvania, and Delaware; their inclusion, like the inclusion of Taiwanese and Chinese for the other documents, maps identity into place. Liu, born in Japan of Chinese heritage, then became a settler on Lenape land when he became an American citizen. This poem exposes layers of identities into places that bureaucracy otherwise covers up. The method is "interventions," a technique gleaned from Theresa Hak Kyung Cha, which doctors the papers only so much as to estrange them further through the linguistic notation of punctuation, rooting documents in colonial histories separate from what might otherwise be available to view. As Liu's "Letter to Myself I" pleads partway through the collection, "Tell me how to say your name, because / documents won't protect us."[35]

Don Mee Choi's *DMZ Colony* uses journalism, interviews, memoir, government documents, imagined conversations, historical photos, and archives to interrogate Korean War history. Choi locates the project in U.S. academia at the beginning of the book; she was to give a poetry reading with an academic poet at an arts foundation in St Louis, Missouri, a location that happens to be parallel to the Korean demilitarized zone (DMZ), albeit on the other side of the world, when she heard migrating geese calling "return." These geese then told her, "SEE YOU AT THE DMZ."[36] She figures herself as a translator, her translations are only "mirror words," reentering Korea, the world of her youth. As a later poem explains, her translations, her mirror words, "are meant to compel disobedience, resistance . . . defy neocolonial borders, blockades."[37]

Choi's final poem of the collection, "(Neo) (=) (Angles)," rewrites captions of family and political photos, questioning what documentation means for those born during the Korean War. It ends with an echo of how the book began, "We are eternally motherless. We are your orphans. We are your angels. We are your mirror words. What's written on paper is obvious—See you at the DMZ!"[38] Unlike the other descriptors of the "we," the "mirror words" she names contain the hope of identity, selfhood, and resistance in an age wrought with what is supposedly "obvious" because it is "written on paper." As we know, paper records may purport to be transparent, but they also serve to obscure. The histories that Choi exposes are not recorded anywhere else; they illustrate the horrors of U.S. empire building more clearly than any singular bureaucratic account. The glib ending "See you at the DMZ!" punctuates this fact; it is only through a book of poetry that one may "return." Just as the book began, it is only through translating the voice of geese who appear in a moment fixed within the art and poetry economy—the Pulitzer Arts Foundation, the St. Louis Art Museum, an associate professor of poetry are all part of the first scene—that one can "see you" or truly see the DMZ.[39]

Chapter 4 covered several feminist performance poems produced on the precipice of *Roe v. Wade*, and now, two years after its repeal, there is an echo of poetry in general about abortion and health-care inequities. Lena Chen's *We Lived the Gaps Between Stories* is a ritual celebration of abortion providers, both the people who aid those seeking abortion and the abortifacients and emmenagogues that have served those who can get pregnant for centuries. The celebration is participatory and collaborative—it includes a wreath-making and thank-you note writing activity. Chen first created the work in 2021, has updated it several times since the *Dobbs* decision, and plans to repeat the project continually across the United States in the future.[40] The first iteration of *We Lived in the Gaps* took place in Cincinnati, Ohio, when Chen was the Vance Waddell Artist-in-Residence and as a response to Andrea Bowers's *Wall of Letters: Necessary Reminders from the Past for a Future of Choice*. In addition to an exhibition of thank-you letters to abortion workers and wreaths displayed in the Wave Pool Gallery, the piece included a celebratory march from the Wave Pool Gallery to Camp Washington Urban Farm (where the abortifacients and emmenagogues were grown) with the wreaths that the participants had made. A video on Chen's website shows this march with instrumental music and a poem read over the footage. The video ends with the participants in a circle, holding a giant wreath around one person, presumably an abortion worker, and bowing in thanks—"Thank you for giving us a shot at continuing our education, becoming financially stable, having a child under the conditions we wanted. . . . We honor your work," the voiceover says.[41] There is a solemnity and a beauty in the ritual; one of the participants is moved to tears, although it appears that no language is exchanged in real time.

The poem read over the video is in the second person and begins by describing "you," who grew up Catholic in a small town where most people were against abortions, including "you" who "wrote a high school paper against abortion and got an A on it."[42] "You" then supported a fourteen-year-old friend through an abortion and benefited from two safe abortions, one as a teenager, one as a married adult. After that, "you" becomes an abortion provider or abortion doula, and the poem is about "your" experiences in your work. The poem is in the past tense, but its second-person style is reminiscent of event scores. Like the Texas State Senate testimony discussed in chapter 5 and the interdisciplinary durational projects in chapter 4, the singular body becomes a communal body around the issue of abortion care. The poem is a documental work: Chen composed the poem using quotations drawn from interviews with abortion workers in Ohio and quotations drawn from letters thanking abortion workers.[43] Although the poem could be narrativized as describing one individual, Chen collaged the experiences of multiple abortion seekers together to make the first half, and the second half is drawn from interviews with a different set of people, abortion workers.[44] The two subject positions bleed into each other and don an instructional quality through the "you." The poem ends by blurring what is record, event, and future horizon: "Your love of humanity will continue to carry us forward. You are our past, present, and future."[45]

The subject matter of these works is the racist, sexist, and colonial violence that pervades the U.S. public sphere and also, we must read this poetry as embedded within higher education, itself a project of racist, sexist, and colonial violence. Many of the poets I have written about in this coda are employed in academia or in its fringes, and their work is a reminder about the ways that government support has dwindled and violence surges on within and outside the ivory towers. In other words, despite the fact that writers like Chen, Choi, and Sharif benefit from full-time or part-time work paid by creative writing programs, academic departments, and writer- or artist-in-residency positions, all of them refuse McGurl's suggestion of fifteen years ago that they inspire university students by modeling unalienated labor and producing luxuries. They write instead about the state of the U.S. university, and they chronicle how it participates in a larger series of failing publics. Their documental poetry and their positionality, what Stefano Harney and Fred Moten call "in but not of"—or Young's "inside, but . . . [feeling] outside"—the university creates the clearest possible portrait of contemporary intellectual structures in academia.[46]

Regardless of whether you have a PhD, an MFA, or both (Chen has an MFA and is earning a PhD, most of the other poets I have written about in the coda so far are MFAs), increasingly, the only possible relation for most in academia is antagonism, even as we cloak ourselves in institutional fodder. Of the group of books that I have mentioned here, *Basic Needs* by Vanessa Jimenez Gabb and *Fetal Position* by Holly Melgard most explicitly use documental techniques to think through questions of labor in higher education. Melgard's *Fetal Position* directly confronts contemporary dystopian work environments and the impossible, unmanageable, and uncomfortable feelings they induce. The sections "Reproductive Labor," "Divisions of Labor," "Child Labor," "Student Labor," "Lesser Person," and "Catcall" use a combination of found language from the internet, the street, and the office to explore what work means. Some of the sections explain their conceit, such as "Child Labor," which begins with an italicized passage that reads: "Pornographic descriptions of what it feels like to be inside of a woman cut up and re-ordered to form a composite narration of vaginal childbirth from the fetal point of view."[47] Other sections leave the reader guessing at how they are constructed, but they are all aimed at inducing discomfort with the patterns with which we usually think about labor.

"Student Labor" appears to be a conversation between a student worker and a professor, recorded only from the student side. In turns apologizing for not having finished something, letting on how much unrecognized labor they have already done, coaching the professor about how to do rote computer tasks, reassuring the professor about the professor's importance, and promising that they will perform more work later, the poem takes us through the horrors of doing "student labor." It illustrates the familiar truth that work done by students, graduate students especially, is variously considered professional development, mentorship, or even a gift to the student, despite its often grueling and exploitative demands. The poem follows a yes-no push-and-pull format to rhetorically illustrate this capitalist bind at the center of issues in higher education:

> Right, but well I mean if you really need this before your flight and it won't
> Uh huh. Yeah no, certainly not. I understand.
> No, exactly. No, yeah, no agreed. No. Understood. Yes.
> No, exactly
> No, you're right. They can't expect you to put together your own PowerPoint if they're also asking to throw you this reception. Yeah no, that makes total sense.
> Yeah, I can do that for you, but really though if you open it and just drag the mouse, I swear it will[48]

Glimpses of the professor's ineptitude and their unreasonable expectations are interspersed with assurances that the student will get the work done. The uneven bloat, which is a hallmark of contemporary academia—where some professors with tenure at rich institutions live luxurious lives while most in academia are just scraping by—is made apparent through the student's need to affirm the professor's choice to eschew the responsibility of a presentation because of a reception. There is an earlier section that promises more work, work that sounds like it should be done by the professor, not the student. But the student offers a chorus of thanks: "Seriously, if it weren't for you," and "I'm so thankful," along with the de facto "Thank you so much for the opportunity" that characterizes the conditions of student workers who are often not able to unionize with the spurious justification that their research or teaching positions are not work at all but opportunities.[49]

Like in Mathew Timmons's *CREDIT*, discussed in chapter 5, debt is pervasive in our era, and documental poetry gives us tools to examine it. These failures of contemporary higher education—exploitation and debt—are central to Melgard's collection, both thematically and stylistically. The section "Reproductive Labor," which is about whether the speaker wants to have children or not, laments that "I haven't managed to go to any dentist appointments in the last five years, how can I be trusted to follow through on vaccinations?" Only to, in the next stanza, come back with, "I guess it's not totally my fault that I haven't been to the dentist. My insurance only pays for one cavity a year, but I have at least 5 . . ."[50] Melgard's otherwise appreciative and more standard acknowledgments section at the end of the book includes: "Special *no thank you* to my student loan providers and other systemic facets that enable debt economies to thrive—They can go to hell."[51] Melgard, who earned a PhD in English at the State University of New York at Buffalo, lives in New York City, where she freelances and teaches writing classes at multiple universities. In *Fetal Position*, the precarity of humanities professors turned gig workers and the serious discontents of the workplace for today's students are visible in the work of creation, both in the making of poetry and in the varied work of birthing and raising children.

Very different in tone, if not theme, Vanessa Jiminez Gabb's *Basic Needs* is a book of poems that integrates text about the history of the labor movement in the United States along with theory about life under capitalism by Emma Goldman and Angela Davis. Between bursts of found writing, there is love poetry, lists, and scenes from the life of a worker (teacher, factory worker, parent, daughter). The poetry pulls at various threads of what we assume to be common sense about family and about making a living:

> I know my parents
> drove us west
> one summer these states
> I knew one was a teacher
> the other a professor
> that they were part of
> this system that there was
> this system because it was a word
> they used often
> and it meant something
> about who we'd become
> about the way they were
> allowed to love us
> and each other
> and keep getting paid
> every summer long[52]

Here the parents provide a map of the social forms and conditions of love—summer and family trips—through educating their children about the "system" of working for a wage in order to live, the system of contemporary capitalism. Their teaching jobs afford the luxuries of family and yet they manage to dispel the mystification of these luxuries to dispute the notion that it is acceptable to need to work in order to live and to love. In an interview, Gabb explains that she is a second-generation Marxist, a daughter of a professor and a teacher herself: "My writing comes out of this position, this academic class, then. It's at the heart of my poetic line. The tensions. The antagonisms. I love repetition as a device for this. We can't have excess without austerity on a systemic level. The poems are about similar contradictions on the personal level."[53] Many of these poems play out this idea of scarcity linked to abundance and experiences of consumerist alienation in academia:

> new products appear
> I've forgotten
> I bought them
> and worry
> about life and debt[54]

The familiar phrase "life and death" is distorted into what lurks behind the daily accrual of unneeded products, the constant experience of debt. Gabb's book charts socialist organizing and even worker revolution as something historical but also imminent and very possible. The poems take the forms of manufactured containers, epics, lists, dialogues, and love letters, enmeshing the documental, the everyday, and the lyric.

These projects are examples of documental poetries of antagonism that consider race, class, and gender inequities as central to matrices of power and capital accumulation. They employ the fodder of racial capitalism and everyday public life to engage U.S. public forms. I now return to Mark McGurl's summation that academic creative writers "inwardly stand as inspiring exemplars of the unalienated laborer . . . the purest version of the kind of worker, the white-collar professional, that so many college students are preparing to be" and outwardly produce "unconscious allegories of institutional quality, aesthetically pure because luxuriously useless" with a revision for documental poets in our moment.[55] Inwardly, those on the fringes of academia expose how all university labor is exploitation and extraction. This exposure is often unwelcome in literary studies especially, where many prefer the object of study to be free of the filth that otherwise coats the conditions for studying it. Outwardly, documental poets produce allegories of this exploitation that also contain an inherent contradiction: these poems are rich with research, history, information, data, and archival tools, but they are valueless to the disciplines that privilege those riches most of all.

In this way, these projects reject a line of thinking that some critics within literary studies have recently adopted: if interdisciplinarity has become a neoliberal tool of administrators, it must be resisted through clinging to its reverse, a rigorous disciplinarity. Instead, these collections suggest that critical interdisciplinarity can be an agent to disrupt dominant forms of institutionality.[56] They seem to build from Roderick Ferguson's conclusion to his study of the birth and development of the interdisciplines in academia. If academia is indeed part of the mechanisms of the state and of capital, and its very maneuvers have enforced a hegemonic affirmation, transforming minority difference into part of its smooth functioning, as Ferguson argues, we must "imagine critical forms of community, forms in which minoritized subjects become the agents, rather than the silent objects of knowledge formations and institutional practices."[57] By reorganizing and rewriting public forms through and with institutional tools of the university and the state, these poets employ an interdisciplinary interest not only in activating those forms but also in creating community around their activation.

This book has gathered works that grew out of a morass of documentation chronicling devastation, discrimination, and privatization of care, a morass that is sometimes called a history of U.S. postwar period. The archive represented here is constructed with poetry that lays record upon document, instruction upon list, rule upon constraint, sometimes igniting the possibility of communal public life. It is my hope that the light from it limns one way to proceed in poetry studies: by attending to interdisciplinary moments of culture and their poetic entanglements—contradictions and embodiments—with public forms.

# ACKNOWLEDGMENTS

In the years that I have lived with this book manuscript on my mind, at the tips of keyboard-clicking fingers, and in my mostly tender, always yearning heart, I have taught and learned with university students, mainly undergraduates at the University of California, Santa Cruz; Vanderbilt University; University of Southern Indiana; and the University of Maryland, Baltimore County. I am indebted to these various treasured classrooms in which we discovered or discussed some aspect of most everything of value that appears between the covers of this book.

When I finished my PhD in 2015, the profession for which I had trained was in such disarray that I did not think I would ever have the material support to write a scholarly book. However, after lecturing and adjuncting for several years—positions designed to exclude the material support for writing a book like this—I was extraordinarily lucky to land a job at the University of Maryland, Baltimore County (UMBC), which gave me ample time and resources for research. During this time at UMBC, I benefited from research time as part of my job, a start-up fund in the English Department, and multiple grants and fellowships: the Eminent Scholar Mentoring Program from the Office of the Provost; the Summer Research Faculty Fellowship from the Office of the Vice President for Research; the Humanities Residential Fellowship from the Dresher Center for the Humanities; and the College of Arts, Humanities, and Social Sciences Research Support during COVID-19.

The work that I have completed at UMBC built on some of the early research that was funded by summer fellowships from the Literature Department at the University of California, Santa Cruz (UCSC) and the Chancellor's Dissertation-Year Fellowship while I was a PhD student. A few UCSC faculty helped sow seeds of the ideas for this book. In particular, I am grateful to Angela Davis for her seminar "Critical Theory in the Marxist Tradition," which proved to be more formative than I even knew at the time; Christine Hong, whose thinking about my project truly helped it take the shape it has today; and Tyrus Miller, who found time to discuss weird poetry with me. Although I did not work on this book much at Vanderbilt, its little flame was protected and sustained there by friendships with Melanie Adley, Candice Amich, Pavneet Aulakh, Emily August, Elizabeth Barnett, Destiny Birdsong, Matthew Congdon, Lisa Dordal, Alex Dubilet, Jennifer Fay, Lisa Guenther, Jessie Hock, Scott Juengel, Sheba Karim, Michael Kreyling, Kenneth MacLeish, Karen Ng, Rachael Pomerantz, Freya Sachs, Mark Schoenfield, Anand Taneja, and Mark Wollaeger.

The material that I examined in archives is essential to this book, and I am indebted to librarians and staff at the following: Archives at the Art Institute of Chicago; Archives of American Art at the Smithsonian Institution; the Fales Library and Special Collections at New York University; Harvard Art Museum and Special Collections; the Museum of Modern Art Archives; the New York Public Library Archives; Special Collections at the Getty Research Institute; Special Collections at the University of California, Santa Cruz; Special Collections at the University of California, Berkeley; Special Collections at the University of Maryland, Baltimore County; Tate Britan Archive; and the Thomas Erben Gallery.

At UMBC, the mentorship of Jessica Berman, Lindsay DiCuirci, and Jennifer Maher helped me navigate academia. Among many other kindnesses, Jennifer patiently taught me the importance of a phone call, and Lindsay modeled how to do all of the things while also staying human. I am grateful for their friendship. Jessica often took me under her wing over the last six years, reading drafts, believing in me, and offering advice. She was the first to suggest that Columbia University Press might be a good publisher for this project, and for that I am immensely appreciative. I am also grateful to the following mentors who, during the process of working on this book, showed up for me in just the right way: Rebecca Adelman, Tamara Bhalla, Raphael Falco, Nicole King, Carole McCann,

Lucille McCarthy, Kathryn McKinley, Lia Purpura, Craig Saper, Marsha Scott, Sally Shivnan, and Mejdulene Shomali. Across the College of Arts, Humanities, and Social Sciences, Michael Casiano, Sarah Fouts, and Tania Lizarazo read and gave thoughtful feedback on parts of this work. They, along with the other members of our writing group—María Célleri, Courtney Hobson, J Inscoe, Charlotte Keniston, Thania Muñoz, and Yolanda Valencia—provided invaluable encouragement and important gossip on writing breaks. Within my department, I was fortunate to have a supportive cohort: Earl Brooks, Drew Holladay, Sharon Tran, and Emily Yoon. I am grateful to Evan Lincove and Grace Reeb for their work as research assistants.

I am indebted to Virginia Jackson for her mentorship and for organizing an enormously formative chapter workshop for me in 2021. Thank you to Candice Amich, Natalia Cecire, Craig Dworkin, Martin Harries, Christopher Nealon, Anthony Reed, Judith Rodenbeck, and Margaret Ronda, who participated in a generative Zoom discussion about an early version of chapter 2. I have called on Candice and Natalia for their feedback since then, and I am grateful for their generosity with their time and for their incisive comments.

Others who have read parts or versions of this work and provided crucial feedback include Karen Bassi; Kendra Dority; Sarah Dowling; Katherine Fusco; Jody Greene; Jo Giardini; Andy Hines; Davy Knittle; Madeline Lane-McKinley; Jane Malcolm; Joanna Meadvin; Heidi Morse; Yuki Obayashi; Stephen Pasqualina; Livia Woods; the Poetics|History|Theory lecture series at the University of California, Irvine; and the Poetry and Poetics Working Group at the University of Pennsylvania. Yuki's translation work and sharp analysis was crucial to chapter 1. I am grateful to the writers I discuss in these pages; every writer with whom I corresponded was magnanimous.

I would like to express gratitude to Columbia University Press for the smooth and rewarding publishing process. The Literature Now series editors, Rebecca Walkowitz, Matthew Hart, and David James, believed in the project, and Philip Leventhal truly ushered it into existence with his smart questions and care. I am appreciative of Emily Elizabeth Simon and to the Columbia production team who worked on the book. The two anonymous readers that Philip chose generously improved this manuscript from its earlier stage and also gave me confidence in its arguments.

As of late, I have found community in Baltimore that has sustained me: Luka Arsenjuk, Rebecca Armendariz, Samyra Cox, Brett Cox, Nicole Fabricant, Abigail Fendler, Jo Giardini, Beth Holladay, Drew Holladay, Ailish Hopper, Casey Lurtz, James Lynch, Lindsey Muniak, Madeline Rubenstein, Stuart Schrader, Christy Thornton, and Anneliese Van Arsdale.

To my family, both chosen and blood, my deepest love and gratitude. My whole life I have been held by my mother, Jeanne Finberg's loving care and inspired by her dedication to fight for what is right in the world. I am especially grateful for her fierce feminism, without which I would be nowhere. I am appreciative to her and my stepfather, Bob Stalker, for their incredible support and generosity as I have worked on this book. My father, Kem Holland Cook, passed away while I was editing the manuscript, but he would have been proud that I finished it. He was the first to model to me that intellectual pursuits may be frivolous, but they are also worthwhile. Kendra Dority has been my partner in imagining other worlds in life and literature—as Gayatri Spivak's mandate that we learned together: "imagining yourself, really letting yourself be imagined (experience that impossibility) without guarantees, by and in another culture"—for many years; she has become aunt to my children and an anchor for me. My beloved Sheba Karim and the Karim-Taneja family have cared for me during times of depletion, showing me joy, great warmth, and teaching me to chill. Andi and Colin Winnette periodically materialize to explain what we are all doing here on this planet: my deepest thanks to them for reminding me. I have been fortunate to marry into a wonderful family during the process of researching this book: Marcy and Jack Hines have been enormously caring and kind. All the Hines and Fenton love from both sides has kept us afloat, and Nancy Hines's interest in the manuscript has felt important to the process. Olive Dog Finberg-Hines came into my life as I was finishing my PhD, and she has taught me an enormous amount by taking me on walks every day and being a very good dog.

My children, Zev and Muriel, monkey and moon: thank you for showing me how everything is poetry, for giving me reason to write and also many good reasons in any particular moment not to spend my time writing. These gifts are my greatest joy.

Thank you to the people who took care of these treasures while Andy and I worked: Sally Becker, Ebony Brown, Ellie Hamilton, Amanda

Kaniowski, the staff of Bolton Hill Nursery, Downtown Baltimore Childcare Center, and the Calvert School.

I am lucky enough to have a few readers with whom I am in true collaboration, people who read multiple drafts and saw this writing at early, even embarrassing stages, people I think *with* and who have learned, read, and written along with me. Their sentences or phrases surely appear in the manuscript, and the best ideas here are likely born of their insightful feedback: Craig Dworkin, Davy Knittle, and Andy Hines. Craig has been a beacon of brilliance, joy, and kindness from afar—I do not think I would have finished graduate school, let alone a scholarly book, without him. Davy became my wing person just as I was starting to think of this project as a real book, and his friendship has advanced the flight in me.

And last, my first and best reader, my partner in life and intellect, Andy. I met you before this book was even a desire, and its various forms have grown along with our life together. Thank you for your genius and for inspiring me to think about the worlds contained here. Thank you for believing in me and this work even when I did not, for reading it over and over, and for nourishing me while I wrote. Thank you for caring for our children and our home while I revised and kvetched. Thank you for reminding me often to trust myself and for telling me that I do have something to say. This one is for you.

---

An earlier version of chapter 1 appeared in Keegan Cook Finberg, "Assimilating the Arts: On Poetry and Difference in Yoko Ono's Grapefruit," *Amodern* 11: *Body and/as Procedure* (October 2023), https://amodern.net/article/assimilating-the-arts/.

Earlier writing on the same O'Hara poems covered in chapter 3 appeared in Keegan Cook Finberg, "Frank O'Hara Rebuilds the Seagram Building: A Radical Poetry of Event," *Textual Practice* 30, no. 1 (February 2016): 113–42.

A different version of the argument about Counterpath's *Let Her Speak* that appears in chapter 5 was first published in "All the Women in the State of Texas" in "A Symposium on Repetition: A Discussion About (Usually) Books as They Relate to a Theme of Interest," *The Believer*, no. 115 (October/November 2017): 74–75.

The following textual permissions are gratefully acknowledged:

Excerpts from *Grapefruit*, by Yoko Ono, including "Blood Piece" and "Supply Goods Store Piece," © 1964 by Yoko Ono.

"Mandatory Happening," by Ken Friedman, © 1965, 2024 by Ken Friedman.

Excerpts from "Style" and "A Long Poem for Myself," by Amiri Baraka, first published in *Locus Solus III–IV*, 1962. Permission by Chris Calhoun Agency, © Estate of Amiri Baraka.

Excerpts from "Walking," "Nocturne," and "The Lay of the Romance of the Associations" from *The Collected Poems of Frank O'Hara*, by Frank O'Hara, © 1971 by Maureen Granville-Smith, administratrix of the Estate of Frank O'Hara, copyright renewed 1999 by Maureen O'Hara Granville-Smith and Donald Allen. Used by permission of Alfred A. Knopf, an imprint of the Knopf Doubleday Publishing Group, a division of Penguin Random House LLC. All rights reserved.

Excerpts from "Student Labor," and other quotations from *Fetal Position*, by Holly Melgard (Roof Books, 2021). © 2021 by Holly Melgard.

Excerpts from "You and me, forever," in *Basic Needs*, by Vanessa Jiminez Gabb (Rescue Press, 2021). © 2021 by Vanessa Jiminez Gabb.

# NOTES

## INTRODUCTION

1. In order, the books described are: Solmaz Sharif, *LOOK* (Graywolf, 2016); Craig Santos Perez, *From Unincorporated Territory [Åmot]* (Omnidawn, 2023); Don Mee Choi, *DMZ Colony* (Wave, 2020); and Layli Long Soldier, *WHEREAS: Poems* (Graywolf, 2017).
2. Jena Osman, *Public Figures* (Wesleyan University Press, 2012).
3. I borrow the term "documental," a portmanteau of "conceptual" and "documentary" poetry, from Michael Leong's scholarship. I fully define and discuss this type of post-recession poetry and how it engages the public in chapter 5. Michael Leong, *Contested Records: The Turn to Documents in Contemporary North American Poetry* (University of Iowa Press, 2020), 34.
4. Stephanie Young, *Ursula or University* (Krupskaya, 2013), 22.
5. I am thinking here, for example, about Kasey Silem Mohammed, who rearranges internet forums, Noah Eli Gordon's book that reproduces his e-mail, and Diana Hamilton's combining of public and private records. See also Jacob Edmond, "Copy Rights: Conceptual Writing, the Mongrel Coalition, and the Racial Politics of Digital Media," in *Make It the Same: Poetry in the Age of Global Media* (Columbia University Press, 2019), 151–93.
6. Andy Fitch, "An Interview with Craig Dworkin," *The Volta: Tremolo, Issue 4* (blog), accessed April 3, 2015, http://www.thevolta.org/tremolo-issue4-cdworkin.html.
7. "Capacious, Adj.," in *OED Online* (Oxford University Press), accessed June 22, 2023, https://www.oed.com/view/Entry/27360.
8. Nancy Fraser, "Rethinking the Public Sphere: A Contribution to the Critique of Actually Existing Democracy," *Social Text*, no. 25/26 (1990): 57.
9. Kathi Weeks, *The Problem with Work: Feminism, Marxism, Antiwork Politics, and Postwork Imaginaries* (Duke University Press, 2011), 4.

10. Despite the productive scholarly discourse about "form" as ontologically distinct or as the organizational principal for political life, here I mean to use the term specifically to help answer how the process of poetry became more interdisciplinary as it became preoccupied with the public. In this sense, I agree with Jonathan Kramnick and Anahid Nersessian in their review of some of this very scholarship: "Explanations are bound to questions, questions are bound to disciplines, and disciplines are bound to the rules they make for themselves—nothing more." Jonathan Kramnick and Anahid Nersessian, "Form and Explanation," *Critical Inquiry* 43, no. 3 (March 2017): 669.

11. Friedman had discovered Something Else Press while working on his radio show at Shimer, which began an interest in Fluxus and in events as art form. Estera Milman, ed., "Ken Friedman: Art[Net]Worker Extra-Ordinaire," in *Alternative Traditions in the Contemporary Arts: Subjugated Knowledges and the Balance of Power*, accessed June 9, 2021, http://sdrc.lib.uiowa.edu/atca/subjugated/five_12.htm; Owen Smith, "A Pilgrim's Progress," in *Alternative Traditions in the Contemporary Arts: Subjugated Knowledges and the Balance of Power*, ed. Estera Milman, accessed June 9, 2021, http://sdrc.lib.uiowa.edu/atca/subjugated/five_13.htm.

12. There are at least five different versions of this score in addition to George Maciunas's definitive design and publication. These versions are lineated differently and include different articles, and some use the word "instruction," "score," or "text" instead of "page." See Ken Friedman, *Fluxus Performance Notebook, a Special Edition of El Djardia Magazine (1990)* (Performance Research, 2002), 41; John Lely and James Saunders, *Word Events: Perspectives on Verbal Notation* (Continuum, 2012), 17; Ken Friedman, *52 Events* (Show and Tell Editions, 2002), 11; Ken Friedman and Stan Lunetta, *Five Events and One Sculpture*, 1976, flyer, offset printed, 10⅞ × 13½", https://www.monographbookwerks.com/pages/books/1064/ken-friedman-stan-lunetta/ken-friedman-five-events-and-one-sculpture; Ken Friedman, MANDATORY HAPPENING, 1993, plastic box with photocopy label, containing photocopy, overall (closed): 4 9/16 × 5⅛ × 13/16" (11.6 × 13 × 2 cm), the Gilbert and Lila Silverman Fluxus Collection Gift, the Archives, Peter Van Beveren, Rotterdam, https://www.moma.org/collection/works/135190?sov_referrer=artist&artist_id=2007&page=1.

13. Ken Friedman, Prototype for Mandatory Happening 1966/1982, plastic box with offset label, containing typewriting on paper, Gilbert and Lila Silverman Fluxus Collection Gift, Drawings and Prints, 2217.2008.a-b, https://www.moma.org/collection/works/128066.

14. Christine Hong, *A Violent Peace: Race, U.S. Militarism, and Cultures of Democratization in Cold War Asia and the Pacific* (Stanford University Press, 2020), 7.

15. Lizabeth Cohen, *A Consumers' Republic: The Politics of Mass Consumption in Postwar America* (Vintage, 2003), 193–256.

16. Ira Katznelson, *When Affirmative Action Was White: An Untold History of Racial Inequality in Twentieth-Century America* (Norton, 2006), x, 25–52; Melinda Cooper, *Family Values: Between Neoliberalism and the New Social Conservatism* (Zone, 2017), 8–33.

17. Aaron Benanav, *Automation and the Future of Work* (Verso, 2020), 22–23; Robert Brenner and Jeong Seong-jin, "Overproduction Not Financial Collapse Is the Heart of the

Crisis: The US, East Asia, and the World," *Asia-Pacific Journal: Japan Focus* 7, no. 6 (2009), https://apjjf.org/-Robert-Brenner/3043/article.html.

18. On characterizing this period of New Deal–inspired welfare policies as "affirmative action for whites," see Daniel Robert McClure, *Winter in America: A Cultural History of Neoliberalism, from the Sixties to the Reagan Revolution* (University of North Carolina Press, 2021), 8; Katznelson, *When Affirmative Action Was White*.
19. For a review of this trend across the sciences, see Elena Aronova, "Recent Trends in the Historiography of Science in the Cold War," *Historical Studies in the Natural Sciences* 47, no. 4 (September 2017): 568–77. For a thorough discussion of the trend and its effects in the humanities and social sciences, see Roderick A. Ferguson, *The Reorder of Things: The University and Its Pedagogies of Minority Difference* (University of Minnesota Press, 2012).
20. Some of these studies include Fredric Jameson, *Postmodernism, or, The Cultural Logic of Late Capitalism* (Duke University Press, 1990); Lucy R. Lippard, *Six Years: The Dematerialization of the Art Object from 1966 to 1972* (University of California Press, 1997); Harry Braverman, *Labor and Monopoly Capital: The Degradation of Work in the Twentieth Century* (Monthly Review Press, 1998); Jasper Bernes, *The Work of Art in the Age of Deindustrialization* (Stanford University Press, 2017); Lisa Duggan, *The Twilight of Equality? Neoliberalism, Cultural Politics, and the Attack on Democracy* (Beacon, 2004); Benjamin Buchloh, "Conceptual Art 1962–1969: From the Aesthetic of Administration to the Critique of Institutions," *October* 55 (December 1990): 105–43; Luc Boltanski and Eve Chiapello, *The New Spirit of Capitalism*, trans. Gregory Elliott (Verso, 2018).
21. Gayatri Chakravorty Spivak, "Can the Subaltern Speak?," in *Marxism and the Interpretation of Culture*, ed. Cary Nelson and Lawrence Grossberg (University of Illinois Press, 1988), 88.
22. Gayatri Chakravorty Spivak, "What's Left of Theory," in *An Aesthetic Education in the Era of Globalization* (Harvard University Press, 2012), 213.
23. For Spivak, this hyperexploitation includes the stripping of biodiversity, the homogenizing of discrete Indigenous cultures, subjugating rural populations (especially women), and extracting land and labor across the globe. Spivak, "What's Left of Theory," 213.
24. Benjamin Buchloh et al., "Conceptual Art and the Reception of Duchamp," *October* 70 (October 1994): 127–46. The critics in conversation include Buchloh, Rosalind Krauss, Alexander Alberro, Thierry de Duve, Martha Buskirk, and Yve-Alain Bois.
25. Buchloh et al., "Conceptual Art and the Reception of Duchamp."
26. *Kant After Duchamp* is concerned with judgments about whether or not something is art, which Thierry de Duve argues is a central question of modernist aesthetics, replacing a previous concern with the question of whether something is beautiful or not. His *Art Forum* essays of 2013–2014 trace when and how the notion that "art can be anything" became prevalent. De Duve argues that some of this paradigm began in the 1880s with the collapse of the Beaux Arts System; it was then diagnosed by Marcel Duchamp's urinal as art submission in 1917. The message was received in the art world sometime in the 1960s with an "anything goes condition" signaled by Fluxus art. In the third installment of this series of five essays, he writes, "when anything can be art, we find ourselves, as

Rosalind Krauss would say, in a 'post-medium condition.'" Thierry de Duve, *Kant After Duchamp* (MIT Press, 1996); Thierry de Duve, "Pardon My French: Theirry de Duve on the Invention of Art," *Art Forum International* 52, no. 2 (October 2013): 246–53; Thierry de Duve, "Don't Shoot the Messenger: Thierry de Duve on Duchamp Syllogism," *Art Forum International* 52, no. 3 (November 2013): 264–73; Thierry de Duve, "Why Was Modernism Born in France? Thierry de Duve on the Collapse of the Beaux-Arts System," *Art Forum International* 52, no. 5 (January 2014): 190–253; Thierry de Duve, "The Invention of Non-Art: A History," *Art Forum International* 52, no. 5 (February 2014): 192–99; Thierry de Duve, *Duchamp's Telegram: From Beaux-Arts to Art-in-General* (Reaktion /University of Chicago Press, 2023).

27. Elsewhere, de Duve argues that four artists engage and revise Karl Marx's theory of capital. For example, he argues that what Marx called labor power, Joseph Beuys calls creativity. Both are "the potential of each and every one, and, being the capacity to produce in general, it precedes the division of labor." Thierry de Duve, *Sewn in the Sweatshops of Marx: Beuys, Warhol, Klein, Duchamp*, trans. Rosalind E. Krauss (University of Chicago Press, 2012), 10–12.

28. "General, Adj. and n.," in *OED Online* (Oxford University Press), accessed June 21, 2023, https://www.oed.com/view/Entry/77489.

29. "General, Adj. and n."

30. Craig Dworkin's *No Medium* apprehends media as activities that work in concert with each other within social contexts. Craig Dworkin, *No Medium* (MIT Press, 2013), 28–33.

31. On the productivity of thinking through the "genre" of poetry (and in relation to "lyric"), see Anthony Reed, *Freedom Time: The Poetics and Politics of Black Experimental Writing* (Johns Hopkins University Press, 2014); Sonya Posmentier, *Cultivation and Catastrophe: The Lyric Ecology of Modern Black Literature* (Johns Hopkins University Press, 2017); Virginia Jackson, "Lyric," in *The Princeton Encyclopedia of Poetry and Poetics*, ed. Roland Greene et al. (Princeton University Press, 2012), 826–34; Virginia Jackson, *Dickinson's Misery: A Theory of Lyric Reading* (Princeton University Press, 2005); Gillian C. White, *Lyric Shame: The "Lyric" Subject of Contemporary American Poetry* (Harvard University Press, 2014); Jonathan Culler, *Theory of the Lyric* (Harvard University Press, 2015).

32. This articulation owes a great debt to media theory, in particular, Lisa Gitelman's explanation of the term "genre." Rather than "a question of ingredients or formal attributes," Gitelman uses the term "genre" to refer to "a mode of recognition instantiated in discourse." She contrasts this with "medium," which, in her scheme, does not signify the same ways; unlike genre, media do not necessarily carry their own logics. Gitelman's book *Paper Knowledge* studies the document, which she calls an "especially capacious genre," across different media. Lisa Gitelman, *Paper Knowledge: Toward a Media History of Documents* (Duke University Press, 2014), 2, 9. Poetry may have been thought historically to be both a genre and a medium and therefore somewhat discrete from other media, and yet here I chart a similar project to Gitelman's.

33. Nikhil Pal Singh, *Race and America's Long War* (University of California Press, 2017), 29.

34. This definition is influenced by Ruth Wilson Gilmore, Lisa Lowe, Grace Kyungwon Hong, Lisa Marie Cacho, Jodi Melamed, and Charisse Burden-Stelly. Ruth Wilson Gilmore, "Abolition Geography and the Problem of Innocence," in *Futures of Black Radicalism*, ed. Gaye Theresa Johnson and Alex Lubin (Verso, 2017), 225–26; Lisa Lowe, *The Intimacies of Four Continents* (Duke University Press, 2015), 36; Grace Kyungwon Hong, *Death Beyond Disavowal: The Impossible Politics of Difference* (University of Minnesota Press, 2015), 7; Lisa Marie Cacho, *Social Death: Racialized Rightlessness and the Criminalization of the Unprotected* (New York University Press, 2012), 33; Jodi Melamed, "Racial Capitalism," *Critical Ethnic Studies* 1, no. 1 (2015): 76–85; Charisse Burden-Stelly, "Modern U.S. Racial Capitalism: Some Theoretical Insights," *Monthly Review* (July 2020): 8–20. For historicizing the midcentury in particular, I also look to Christine Hong, who calls Cold War U.S. militarism in Asia and the Pacific "a modality of racial capitalism" that enabled a range of incommensurate political outcomes, "cognitively mapped as 'representative government' for some and 'despotism' for others." Hong, *A Violent Peace*, 6.

35. Wendy Brown, *Undoing the Demos: Neoliberalism's Stealth Revolution* (Zone, 2017), 9; David Harvey, *A Brief History of Neoliberalism* (Oxford University Press, 2007), 2.

36. Candice Amich, *Precarious Forms: Performing Utopia in the Neoliberal Americas* (Northwestern University Press, 2020), 4.

37. I appreciate Christine Hong's point that visions of the 1950s and 1960s as moneyed and cheerful fail to recognize "the potent imperialist concoction at the heart of military Keynesianism—the notion that U.S. war violence abroad stimulated universal prosperity, expanded social welfare, and democratization at home—within the lethality of Jim Crow." Hong, *A Violent Peace*, 6. On how the United States saw the Orient as a theater of "total war" making peace at home, see Sunny Xiang, *Tonal Intelligence: The Aesthetics of Asian Inscrutability During the Long Cold War* (Columbia University Press, 2020), 3–11.

38. Leigh Claire La Berge, *Wages Against Artwork: Decommodified Labor and the Claims of Socially Engaged Art* (Duke University Press, 2019).

39. Shannon Jackson, *Social Works: Performing Art, Supporting Publics* (Routledge, 2011); Helen Anne Molesworth, "Work Ethic," in *Work Ethic*, ed. Helen Anne Molesworth (Baltimore Museum of Art/Pennsylvania State University Press, 2003), 25–52; Julia Bryan-Wilson, "Occupational Realism," *TDR* 56, no. 4 (2012): 32–48.

40. On these connections, see Sophie Lewis, *Abolish the Family: A Manifesto for Care and Liberation* (Verso, 2022); Kathi Weeks, "Abolition of the Family: The Most Infamous Feminist Proposal," *Feminist Theory* 24, no. 3 (2023): 433–53; Tiffany Lethabo King, "Black 'Feminisms' and Pessimism: Abolishing Moynihan's Negro Family," *Theory & Event* 21, no. 1 (2018): 68–87.

41. These short quotations come from an artist-statement-like piece of writing, known as "To the Wesleyan People," which was first published as an insert in *The Stone* and is later widely reprinted with small changes in the 1970 edition of *Grapefruit: A Book of Instructions + Drawings*. Judson Memorial Church Archive at the Fales Library Special Collections, Box 16, Folder 52, *The Stone* script with January 23, 1966, letter; Yoko Ono, *Grapefruit: A Book of Instructions + Drawings* (Simon & Schuster, 1970).

42. Leong, *Contested Records*.

## 1. ASSIMILATING THE ARTS: POETRY AND DIFFERENCE IN YOKO ONO'S INSTRUCTIONS

1. First published as an insert in *The Stone*, this piece of writing, known as "To the Wesleyan People," is later widely reprinted with small changes in the 1970 edition of *Grapefruit: A Book of Instructions + Drawings*. Judson Memorial Church Archive at the Fales Library Special Collections, Box 16, Folder 52, *The Stone* script with January 23, 1966, letter; Yoko Ono, *Grapefruit: A Book of Instructions + Drawings* (Simon & Schuster, 1970). There are no page numbers in the 1970 edition or in the 1964 edition of *Grapefruit*. My chapter focuses on the 1964 edition (called simply *Grapefruit* without the 1970 subtitle), which is an artist book limited to five hundred copies. I am grateful to the Museum of Modern Art Artists' Book Library and to the Gilbert and Lila Silverman Fluxus Collection Archives at the Museum of Modern Art (MoMA) for allowing me to work closely with it. Yoko Ono, *Grapefruit* (Wunternam, 1964).
2. I am inspired by Jieun Rhee, who explores a phenomenon that she explains as Ono being identified as a "Japanese artist in the West and New York avant-gardist in Japan" through Ono's personal and professional history and the contexts of her performance of "Cut Piece." Jieun Rhee, "Performing the Other: Yoko Ono's 'Cut Piece,'" *Art History* 28, no. 1 (February 2005): 98–99. See also Brigid Cohen, "Limits of National History: Yoko Ono, Stefan Wolpe, and Dilemmas of Cosmopolitanism," *Musical Quarterly* 97, no. 2 (2014): 181–237; Alexandra Munroe and Jon Hendricks, eds., *Yes Yoko Ono* (Japan Society and Harry Abrams, 2000); Midori Yoshimoto, *Into Performance: Japanese Women Artists in New York* (Rutgers University Press, 2005); Barry Shank, "Abstraction and Embodiment: Yoko Ono and the Weaving of Global Musical Networks," *Journal of Popular Music Studies* 18, no. 3 (2006): 282–300.
3. See Nathan Glazer and Daniel Moynihan, *Beyond the Melting Pot, Second Edition: The Negroes, Puerto Ricans, Jews, Italians, and Irish of New York City* (1964; MIT Press, 1970).
4. United States President's Commission on Immigration and Naturalization, *Whom We Shall Welcome; Report* (U.S. Government Printing Office, 1953), http://archive.org/details/whomweshallwelcooounit.
5. Lisa Marie Cacho, *Social Death: Racialized Rightlessness and the Criminalization of the Unprotected* (New York University Press, 2012), 40–43; Joseph Jonghyun Jeon, *Racial Things, Racial Forms: Objecthood in Avant-Garde Asian American Poetry* (University of Iowa Press, 2012), 143–63.
6. Clement Greenberg, "Modernist Painting," in *Clement Greenberg: The Collected Essays and Criticism*, vol. 4, ed. John O'Brian (1965; University of Chicago Press, 1993), 85–93; Clement Greenberg, "Towards a Newer Laocoon," in *Clement Greenberg: The Collected Essays and Criticism*, vol. 1, ed. John O'Brian (1940; University of Chicago Press, 1986), 23–41; Michael Fried, "Art and Objecthood," in *Art and Objecthood: Essays and Reviews* (1967; University of Chicago Press, 1998), 148–72; Michael Fried, *Absorption and Theatricality: Painting and Beholder in the Age of Diderot* (University of California Press, 1980).
7. The term "happening" was most famously used by Allan Kaprow to indicate a long nonlinear performance. Al Hansen, *A Primer of Happenings & Time/Space Art* (Something

Else, 1965), 24. For genealogies of happenings within the Japanese and New York cultural and art historical context, see, respectively, Yoshimoto, *Into Performance*; Judith F. Rodenbeck, *Radical Prototypes: Allan Kaprow and the Invention of Happenings* (MIT Press, 2011).

8. Ono, *Grapefruit: A Book of Instructions + Drawings*.
9. Fellow Fluxus artist Dick Higgins's theory of media blending is called "intermedia," which he defines as work that falls between media; as he wrote in 1966, the happening is an example. Dick Higgins, "Intermedia," in *Intermedia, Fluxus and the Something Else Press: Selected Writings by Dick Higgins*, ed. Steve Clay and Ken Friedman (siglio, 2018), 24–30.
10. For an assessment of what he calls the "mixed bag" of Ono's personal activism and how it relates (or not) to *Grapefruit*, see Austin Allen, "'My Beautiful Never-Nevers': Yoko Ono's Poetry Revisited," *Los Angeles Review of Books*, April 4, 2022, https://lareview ofbooks.org/article/my-beautiful-never-nevers-yoko-onos-poetry-revisited/.
11. The term "racial capitalism" points to structures of capitalism that privilege certain forms of life and labor by imposing various forms of death on others. I look to Lisa Lowe, Grace Kyungwon Hong, Lisa Marie Cacho, Jodi Melamed, and Charisse Burden-Stelly for this definition. For historicizing the midcentury, I also look to Christine Hong, who calls Cold War U.S. militarism in Asia and the Pacific "a modality of racial capitalism" that enabled a range of incommensurate political outcomes, "cognitively mapped as 'representative government' for some and 'despotism' for others." Lisa Lowe, *The Intimacies of Four Continents* (Duke University Press, 2015); Grace Kyungwon Hong, *Death Beyond Disavowal: The Impossible Politics of Difference* (University of Minnesota Press, 2015); Cacho, *Social Death*; Jodi Melamed, "Racial Capitalism," *Critical Ethnic Studies* 1, no. 1 (2015): 76–85; Charisse Burden-Stelly, "Modern U.S. Racial Capitalism: Some Theoretical Insights," *Monthly Review* (July 1, 2020): 8–20; Christine Hong, *A Violent Peace: Race, U.S. Militarism, and Cultures of Democratization in Cold War Asia and the Pacific* (Stanford University Press, 2020), 6.
12. Hong, *Death Beyond Disavowal*, 1–34; Roderick A. Ferguson, *The Reorder of Things: The University and Its Pedagogies of Minority Difference* (University of Minnesota Press, 2012), 1–40.
13. Ono, *Grapefruit: A Book of Instructions + Drawings*.
14. Julia Bryan-Wilson, "Remembering Yoko Ono's 'Cut Piece,'" *Oxford Art Journal* 26, no. 1 (2003): 99–123; Kevin Concannon, "Yoko Ono's 'Cut Piece': From Text to Performance and Back Again," *PAJ: A Journal of Performance and Art* 30, no. 3 (2008): 81–93; Rhee, "Performing the Other"; Munroe and Hendricks, *Yes Yoko Ono*; Klaus Biesenbach et al., eds., *Yoko Ono: One Woman Show, 1960–1971* (Museum of Modern Art, 2015); Jane Malcolm and Sarah Dowling, eds., "Amodern 11: Body and/as Procedure (Special Issue)," *Amodern* 11 (October 2023), https://amodern.net/issues/amodern-11/.
15. Two excellent scholarly books that treat *Grapefruit* as a textual work were published very recently. See Rachel Jane Carroll, *For Pleasure: Race, Experimentalism, and Aesthetics*, (New York University Press, 2023); Sarah Dowling, *Here Is a Figure: Grounding Literary Form* (Northwestern University Press, 2024). See also the following articles: Jane Malcolm

and Sarah Dowling, "Introduction to Amodern 11: Body and/as Procedure," *Amodern* 11 (October 2023), https://amodern.net/article/amodern-11/; Jane Malcolm, "Ono Optics: Toward a Theory of the Perfectly Unreadable," *Amodern*, October 2023, https://amodern.net/article/ono-optics/; Allen, "'My Beautiful Never-Nevers'"; Fred Sasaki, "Is Yoko Ono Underappreciated as a Poet?," interview by Claire Voon, *Chicago Magazine*, May 6, 2019, https://www.chicagomag.com/Chicago-Magazine/May-2019/Revisiting-Yoko-Onos-Poetry/; Anna Ioanes, "Observations on an Event: Yoko Ono: Poetry, Painting, Music, Objects, Events, and Wish Trees," *ASAP/J* (blog), February 27, 2020, https://asapjournal.com/observations-on-an-event-yoko-ono-poetry-painting-music-objects-events-and-wish-trees-anna-ioanes/. Before this moment, most critics acknowledged the importance of *Grapefruit*, but there had not been sustained attention to the published book.

16. Most of the English-language criticism about *Grapefruit* as a textual work does not acknowledge the 1964 text and focuses instead on the 1970 edition. The later edition was "introduced by John Lennon" and it removed all Japanese language; added new sections and information that explain how each piece was first realized. It also adds more whimsical pieces (which means the whole work appears less violent), illustrations, a questionnaire, picture games, and mailing pieces. Ono, *Grapefruit: A Book of Instructions + Drawings*.

17. Lucy R. Lippard, *Six Years: The Dematerialization of the Art Object from 1966 to 1972* (University of California Press, 1997); Benjamin Buchloh, "Conceptual Art 1962–1969: From the Aesthetic of Administration to the Critique of Institutions," *October* 55 (December 1990): 105–43; John Roberts, *The Intangibilities of Form: Skill and Deskilling in Art After the Readymade* (Verso, 2007); Branden Wayne Joseph, *Beyond the Dream Syndicate: Tony Conrad and the Arts After Cage (a "Minor" History)* (Zone, 2008); Jasper Bernes, *The Work of Art in the Age of Deindustrialization* (Stanford University Press, 2017).

18. See Rhee, "Performing the Other"; Yoshimoto, *Into Performance*; Kathy O'Dell, "Fluxus Feminus," *TDR* 41, no. 1 (1997): 43–60.

19. Benjamin Buchloh et al., "Conceptual Art and the Reception of Duchamp," *October* 70 (October 1994): 141.

20. For more on this sense of poetry (lyric, in particular) as overhearing made popular by the New Critics who were inspired by John Stuart Mill's thoughts on the subject, see Virginia Jackson, *Dickinson's Misery: A Theory of Lyric Reading* (Princeton University Press, 2005), 9; Virginia Jackson and Yopie Prins, "General Introduction," in *The Lyric Theory Reader: A Critical Anthology*, ed. Virginia Jackson and Yopie Prins (Johns Hopkins University Press, 2014), 1–10.

21. Lisa Duggan, *The Twilight of Equality? Neoliberalism, Cultural Politics, and the Attack on Democracy* (Beacon, 2004), 7. See also Hong, *A Violent Peace*, for the relation between violence abroad and democratization at home.

22. The U.S. cultivated a kind of private reading within the academy that favored difficulty and aesthetic appreciation as "good" reading. Merve Emre, *Paraliterary: The Making of Bad Readers in Postwar America* (University of Chicago Press, 2017), 3.

23. For a concise summation of some recent scholarship in this area, see Andy Hines, "The Material Life of Criticism," *Public Books*, January 22, 2018, https://www.publicbooks.org/the-material-life-of-criticism/. For a large-scale evaluation of how contemporary English departments are invested in a "racial liberalism" that dictates methodology and material conditions alike, see Andy Hines, "New Criticism and the Object of American Democracy," in *Outside Literary Studies: Black Criticism and the University* (University of Chicago Press, 2022), 31–61.
24. "General, Adj. and n.," in *OED Online* (Oxford University Press), accessed June 21, 2023, https://www.oed.com/view/Entry/77489.
25. Ono, *Grapefruit*.
26. Fried, "Art and Objecthood"; Fried, *Absorption and Theatricality*.
27. The concept of modernism was codified in the 1960s by theories from Clement Greenberg, *Art and Culture: Critical Essays* (Beacon, 1965); Fried, "Art and Objecthood"; and Stanley Cavell, "Aesthetic Problems of Modern Philosophy," in *Must We Mean What We Say? A Book of Essays* (Cambridge University Press, 2002), 73–96. They all use experimentalism, or the scientific model, to explain their arguments, and the result is a privileging of visual arts over literature. Ellen Levy, *Criminal Ingenuity: Moore, Cornell, Ashbery, and the Struggle Between the Arts* (Oxford University Press, 2011), 9; Michael North, *Novelty: A History of the New* (University of Chicago Press, 2013), 173. A different but related trajectory is "experimental literature" coming from groups like the Situationist International and Fluxus; for this trajectory, experimentalism later became defined by readerly-writerly participation. First theorized in 1970 by Roland Barthes, the categories of readerly versus writerly text later become foundational for studies of experimental literature. See also Natalia Aki Cecire, *Experimental: American Literature and the Aesthetics of Knowledge* (Johns Hopkins University Press, 2019).
28. See Craig J. Saper, *Networked Art* (University of Minnesota Press, 2001).
29. For the relation between art and culture at the 1964 Olympic Games and Japan's stake in the world order, see Noriko Aso, "Sumptuous Re-Past: The 1964 Tokyo Olympics Arts Festival," *Positions: East Asia Cultures Critique* 10, no. 1 (March 1 2002): 7–38; Namiko Kunimoto, "Olympic Dissent: Art, Politics, and the Tokyo Olympic Games of 1964 and 2020," *Asia-Pacific Journal: Japan Focus* 16, no. 15 (August 2018): 5.
30. See the film *Aru wakamono tachi* (*Some young people*), dir. Chiako Nagano (1964), https://letterboxd.com/film/some-young-people/details/ released just before the Olympic Games. Nagano Chiaki and Midori Yoshimoto, "Some Young People—From Nonfiction Theater," *Review of Japanese Culture and Society* 17 (2005): 98–105; Midori Yoshimoto, "Off Museum! Performance Art That Turned the Street into 'Theatre,' Circa 1964 Tokyo," *Performance Paradigm*, no. 2 (March 2006): 102–18. See also Biesenbach et al., *Yoko Ono*, 81, 100–101.
31. These scores were first written in English for events in New York City. Some of the scores that make up *Grapefruit* were written for Ono's Chambers Street Loft series in 1960 and 1961, and others were first written for her exhibition *Paintings and Drawings* at the AG Gallery in 1961, which I will discuss in this chapter. Biesenbach et al., *Yoko Ono*, 58; Christophe Cherix, "Yoko Ono's 22 Instructions for Paintings," *Museum of Modern Art Magazine*, May 2019, https://www.moma.org/magazine/articles/61.

32. The "reverse course" began in late 1947, when the U.S. agenda in Japan embraced economic recovery foremost. At this time, leftist labor trends were halted, and tens of thousands of workers were dismissed for supposed communist sympathies during the so-called Red Purge. Eiji Takemae, *Inside GHQ: The Allied Occupation of Japan and Its Legacy*, trans. Robert Ricketts and Sebastian Swann (Continuum, 2002); John W. Dower, *Embracing Defeat: Japan in the Wake of World War II* (Norton, 2000).
33. Aso, "Sumptuous Re-Past," 8.
34. For a comparison of post–World War II Japanese scientific method and Taylorism, see William M. Tsutsui, *Manufacturing Ideology: Scientific Management in Twentieth-Century Japan* (Princeton University Press, 2001), 11, 239.
35. For example, "Stomach Piece," which reads in English, "Count the wrinkles on each other's stomach. / Put a canvas on the wall of your / bed room . . ." does not include "your bedroom" in the Japanese text. In the Japanese version of "Painting Until It Becomes Marble," white and gray are included in the colors you may ask visitors to paint over, but the English just suggests black ink. Dates, although included in English pages, are not included in the Japanese versions of scores. Translations by Yuki Obayashi, personal conversations and email, January 2022; Ono, *Grapefruit*.
36. Ono, *Grapefruit*.
37. Ono, *Grapefruit*.
38. See Kristine Stiles, "Survival Ethos and Destruction Art," *Discourse* 14, no. 2 (April 1992): 74–102; Brigid Cohen, "Ono in Opera: A Politics of Art and Action, 1960–1962," *ASAP/Journal* 3, no. 1 (February 17, 2018): 41–66.
39. Ono wrote the instructions in English, translated them into Japanese herself, and then asked Toshi Ichiyanagi to write them out in the Japanese language. As Ono herself explained, "To make the point that the instructions were not themselves graphic images, I wanted the instructions to be typed. But in those days, regular typewriters for the Japanese language were not available. Only professional printers and newspapers had typesetting machines. So I thought of the next best thing, which was to ask Toshi Ichiyangai to print out the instructions by hand." Yoko Ono, *Instruction Paintings* (Weatherhill, 1995), 5–6; Munroe and Hendricks, *Yes Yoko Ono*, 78; Biesenbach et al., *Yoko Ono*, 84.
40. Thomas Kellein, *The Dream of Fluxus: George Maciunas: An Artist's Biography* (Thames & Hudson, 2007), 98–102.
41. Ono, *Grapefruit*.
42. The Japanese language omits the subject, and this grammatical feature assists translating the scores. They are made to circulate between language as well as media; in our conversations about translating the scores, Yuki Obayashi observed that the Japanese scores in *Grapefruit* seem to have English in mind. Yuki Obayashi, personal conversation, January 2022.
43. See Jonathan Flatley, "How a Revolutionary Counter-Mood Is Made," *New Literary History* 43, no. 3 (November 2012): 503–25.
44. Wendy Brown, *Undoing the Demos: Neoliberalism's Stealth Revolution* (Zone, 2017), 39.
45. One famous example of organizing by genre is *An Anthology of Chance Operations, Concept Art, Anti Art, Indeterminacy, Plans of Action, Diagrams, Music, Dance Constructions, Improvization, Meaningless Work, Natural Disasters, Compositions, Mathematics, Essays,*

*Poetry*, ed. La Monte Young (La Monte Young and Jackson Mac Low, 1963), https://www.ubu.com/media/text/AnAnthologyOfChanceOperations.pdf. The work for it was originally compiled for a special issue of Chester Anderson's *Beatitude* that showcased East Coast writers; when the issue did not come to fruition, Young published it on its own as a book with George Maciunas's design. Each artist has a page categorizing their art, and the title plays with the complex proliferation of genre.

46. Joseph, *Beyond the Dream Syndicate*, 83.
47. Ono mentions this origin story many times, but I believe the first time she recounts it in print in relation to her art is in "To the Wesleyan People." Ono, *Grapefruit: A Book of Instructions + Drawings*.
48. Ono, *Grapefruit*.
49. Hong, *A Violent Peace*, 6.
50. Ono, *Grapefruit*.
51. "Supply," in *OED Online* (Oxford University Press), accessed April 22, 2020, http://www.oed.com/view/Entry/194666#eid19718285.
52. Audre Lorde, "Learning from the 60s," in *SOS—Calling All Black People: A Black Arts Movement Reader*, ed. John Bracey Jr, Sonia Sanchez, and James Smethurst (University of Massachusetts Press, 2014), 657.
53. Hong, *Death Beyond Disavowal*, 7.
54. Duggan, *The Twilight of Equality?*, 5.
55. Hong, *Death Beyond Disavowal*, 12.

## 2. FLUXUS SCORES AND THE BUREAUCRATIZATION OF EVERYDAY LIFE

1. Jasper Bernes, *The Work of Art in the Age of Deindustrialization* (Stanford University Press, 2017), 20. Bernes is summarizing Benjamin Buchloh's argument that conceptual art introduced the "aesthetic of administrative and legal organization and institutional validation." Benjamin Buchloh, "Conceptual Art 1962–1969: From the Aesthetic of Administration to the Critique of Institutions," *October* 55 (December 1990): 119.
2. George Brecht and George Maciunas collaborated on the look of the box. See Owen Smith, *Fluxus: The History of an Attitude* (San Diego State University Press, 1998). 107–8, for details of who designed which aspects of the box and cards, including relevant quotations from letters held in the Archiv Sohm in Stuttgart.
3. Owen Smith, whose focus is on the United States and Europe, distinguishes between "pre-Fluxus" (before 1959), "proto-Fluxus" (1959–1962) and "early Fluxus" (1962–1964). Smith, *Fluxus*.
4. Hannah Higgins puts Brecht's cards with "their deceptively simple performance structure" at the beginning of her history of Fluxus. See Hannah Higgins, *Fluxus Experience* (University of California Press, 2002), 2. Artists like Mieko Shiomi began to call their works "events" after coming into contact with Brecht and Ono's work. Sally Kawamura, "Appreciating the Incidental: Mieko Shiomi's 'Events,'" *Women & Performance: A Journal of Feminist Theory* 19, no. 3 (November 2009): 312.

# 186  2. FLUXUS SCORES AND EVERYDAY LIFE

5. Bernes, *The Work of Art in the Age of Deindustrialization*, 20.
6. Bernes, *The Work of Art in the Age of Deindustrialization*, 21.
7. See Christopher Nealon's *The Matter of Capital: Poetry in Crisis in the American Century* (Harvard University Press, 2011), which suggests a literary historical treatment of poetry that engages capital as its subject matter, making possible the work I do here.
8. Sianne Ngai, *Our Aesthetic Categories: Zany, Cute, Interesting* (Harvard University Press, 2012), 145.
9. Ngai, *Our Aesthetic Categories*, 145.
10. Ngai, *Our Aesthetic Categories*, 146.
11. Melinda Cooper, *Family Values: Between Neoliberalism and the New Social Conservatism* (Zone, 2017), 33.
12. Kenneth T. Jackson, *Crabgrass Frontier: The Suburbanization of the United States* (Oxford University Press, 1987), 7.
13. Brecht himself put it this way: the scores are a way of "ensuring that the details of everyday life, the random constellations of objects that surround us, stop going unnoticed." Ken Johnson, "George Brecht, 82, Fluxus Conceptual Artist," *New York Times*, December 15, 2008, A33.
14. Despite the clarity of the connection between *Water Yam* and *Tender Buttons*, to my knowledge, the only other critic to point it out is David Antin as he reflects on why he published several of Brecht's scores as poetry in the literary journal *some/thing*. David Antin, "The Stranger at the Door," in *Radical Coherency: Selected Essays on Art and Literature, 1966 to 2005* (University of Chicago Press, 2011), 239–58.
15. Lyn Hejinian, "Two Stein Talks," in *The Language of Inquiry* (University of California Press, 2000), 83–130; Elisabeth A. Frost, "'Replacing the Noun': Fetishism, Parody, and Gertrude Stein's Tender Buttons," in *The Feminist Avant-Garde in American Poetry* (University of Iowa Press, 2003), 3–28.
16. Although *Tender Buttons* was not disseminated widely or legally on its own in the United States until the Sun and Moon edition (1990), *Tender Buttons* had been pirated by Haskell House in New York in the 1960s, and illegal copies had been sold throughout the city. Robert A. Wilson, ed., *Gertrude Stein: A Bibliography* (Phoenix Bookshop, 1974), 3. Whether Brecht had seen this pirated copy of *Tender Buttons*, he was likely familiar with the work. He may have seen the complete *Tender Buttons* in either Random House, Modern Library, or Vintage's 1946 collections of Stein's work. By the late 1950s, Yale University Press was steadily releasing volumes of Stein's unpublished work. Stein's influence was important to Brecht's circle of companions. Something Else Press, run by Dick Higgins, a key Fluxus member and collaborator with Brecht, published several editions of early works by Stein in order to make them available in the United States. For an explanation of Stein's centrality to the press and to Fluxus artists, see Dick Higgins, "Why Gertrude Stein," in *A Dialectic of Centuries: Notes Towards a Theory of the New Arts* (Printed Editions, 1978), 121–28.
17. Natalia Aki Cecire, *Experimental: American Literature and the Aesthetics of Knowledge* (Johns Hopkins University Press, 2019), 12. For Cecire, this interest is tied historically to the Cold War.

18. Historical accounts of Fluxus trace its origins to John Cage's classes at the New School for Social Research in the late 1950s. George Maciunas, George Brecht, Jackson Mac Low, Dick Higgins, and Allan Kaprow floated in and out of these classes in 1958 and 1959; they collaborated and corresponded, and became part of a New York circle that attended and participated in performances at Yoko Ono's loft. In addition to gaining a coterie, students in that class attempted methods of writing music that relied on objects and toys rather than instruments, and they worked out ways to score music by means other than notes. Meanwhile Fluxus in Europe began with a group of artists (La Monte Young, Nam June Paik, and Emmett Williams) gravitating toward Karlheinz Stockhausen's teachings about vanguard music in Cologne. Beginning the story this way supplies a musical lineage for Fluxus, and it has oriented scholars toward understanding event scores as notation for performances. See accounts in Smith, *Fluxus*; Higgins, *Fluxus Experience*; Thomas Kellein, *The Dream of Fluxus: George Maciunas: An Artist's Biography* (Thames & Hudson, 2007); Mari Dumett, *Corporate Imaginations: Fluxus Strategies for Living* (University of California Press, 2017); Natilee Harren, *Fluxus Forms: Scores, Multiples, and the Eternal Network* (University of Chicago Press, 2020).
19. Judson Memorial Church Archive at the Fales Library Special Collections, Box 16, Folder 52, *The Stone* script with January 23, 1966, letter; Yoko Ono, *Grapefruit: A Book of Instructions + Drawings* (Simon & Schuster, 1970).
20. I am indebted to Julia Robinson's scholarship and timeline of Brecht's works and biography. George Brecht and Julia Robinson, *George Brecht: events: eine Heterospektive = a heterospective* (Walther König, 2005), 307–8. For scholarship that emphasizes Brecht's work as a research scientist and an employee at a corporation, see Mari Dumett, "George Brecht: Scoring Events," in *Corporate Imaginations: Fluxus Strategies for Living* (University of California Press, 2017), 126–69.
21. See conversation between George Brecht, Hermann Braun, Dieter Daniels, and Kasper König in Cologne, August 22, 1991, in Notebook 1 of George Brecht, *George Brecht: Notebooks*, ed. Dieter Daniels (Walther König, 1991).
22. Dumett, *Corporate Imaginations*, 174–75.
23. Fluxus work developed in New Jersey was in conversation with private research and development corporations like Bell Labs and Johnson and Johnson as well as Rutgers University and Douglass College. John Beck and Ryan Bishop, *Technocrats of the Imagination: Art, Technology, and the Military-Industrial Avant-Garde* (Duke University Press, 2020), 45, 83–84.
24. George Brecht, "Events (Assembled Notes)," in *Heterospective*, ed. Julia Robinson (Walther König, 2005), 226.
25. Brecht, "Events (Assembled Notes)," 226.
26. Brecht, *George Brecht: Notebooks*, Notebook 1.
27. Dick Higgins, "Fluxus: Theory and Reception," in *The Fluxus Reader*, ed. Ken Friedman (Academy Editions, 1998), 221.
28. Dick Higgins, *Jefferson's Birthday; Postface* (Something Else, 1964), 69.
29. Smith, *Fluxus*, 75.

30. For a comparison of Fluxus festivals and Dada performances, see Dorothée Brill, *Shock and the Senseless in Dada and Fluxus* (Dartmouth College Press, 2010).
31. Quoted in Liz Kotz, *Words to Be Looked at: Language in 1960s Art* (MIT Press, 2007), 76.
32. For a complex tracing of material and historical doors to linguistic ones in Brecht's work, see Julia Robinson, "From Abstraction to Model: George Brecht's Events and the Conceptual Turn in Art of the 1960s," *October*, no. 127 (Winter 2009): 77–108.
33. The earlier versions of dripping events can be found in Brecht's notebook from 1959. Brecht, *George Brecht: Notebooks*, Notebook 3, 35, 45. For a beautiful reading of "Drip Music (Drip Event)" see Harren, *Fluxus Forms*, 1–26.
34. Brecht, *George Brecht: Notebooks*, Notebook 3.
35. Letter from Maciunas to La Monte Young, 1962, MoMA Silverman IV.B.13.
36. See Smith, *Fluxus*, 88–89, for details of these events, including relevant quotations from letters held in the Archiv Sohm in Stuttgart. See also Kellein, *The Dream of Fluxus*, 63–75.
37. Maciunas created a chart to show who was in and who was out. "Fluxus (Its Historical Development and Relationship to Avant-Garde Movements)," 1966 [Silverman V.A.1.1], lists this information as well as the names of other members excommunicated for different reasons. Maciunas was nervous about Dick Higgins and Alison Knowles's Something Else Press as a self-promotional side project. Listed on Maciunas's chart is a section called "Competitive Attitude, Forming Rival Operations," which includes Alison Knowles, Dick Higgins, and Nam June Paik, because of the press. On Macinuas's excommunication practices for artists' work, see Kathy O'Dell, "Fluxus Feminus," *TDR* 41, no. 1 (1997): 43–60.
38. As Maciunas organized various events in Europe, he hoped to expand into the Soviet Union and Eastern Europe. A letter to the chair of the Presium in the Soviet Union from the early 1960s (the letter is undated), requested a Fluxus tour and summarized the political platform of the group as the desire to "purge the sickness of the bourgeois world ... [desire] toward concretism-realism and ... unity between concretist artists of the world and the concretist society which exists in the USSR" (quoted in Smith, *Fluxus*, 62). He later wrote to Nikita Khrushchev, secretary of the Soviet Communist Party, to share Fluxus artworks with him and explain the group's project. Brill, *Shock and the Senseless in Dada and Fluxus*, 19. For a portrait of Maciunas's communist affinities, see Emmett Williams and Noël Ann, eds., "Seeing Red," in *Mr. Fluxus: A Collective Portrait of George Maciunas, 1931–1978* (Thames and Hudson, 1998), 91–124.
39. See Julia Robinson, "Maciunas as Producer: Performative Design in the Art of the 1960s," *Grey Room*, no. 33 (2008): 56–83, for a nuanced reading of this letter.
40. See Mari Dumett, "The Great Executive Dream: George Maciunas, Adriano Olivetti, and Fluxus Incorporated," *RES: Anthropology and Aesthetics*, no. 53/54 (2008): 314–20; Cuauhtémoc Medina, "Architecture and Efficiency: George Maciunas and the Economy of Art," *Res: Anthropology and Aesthetics* 45 (March 2004): 273–84; Cuauhtémoc Medina, "The 'Kulturbolschewiken' II: Fluxus, Khrushchev, and the 'Concretist Society,'" *RES: Anthropology and Aesthetics*, no. 49/50 (2006): 231–43. Two book-length portraits of these contradictions are Emmett Williams and Noël Ann, eds., *Mr. Fluxus: A Collective Portrait of George Maciunas, 1931–1978* (Thames and Hudson, 1998); and Kellein, *The Dream of Fluxus*.

41. Medina, "Architecture and Efficiency," 283.
42. Owen Smith, "Developing a Fluxable Forum: Early Performance and Publishing," in *The Fluxus Reader*, ed. Ken Friedman (Academy Editions, 1998), 12.
43. Brecht and Robinson, *George Brecht*, 70.
44. Smith, *Fluxus*, 117–18.
45. Michelle MacCarthy, "Playing Politics with Yams: Food Security in the Trobriand Islands of Papua New Guinea," *Culture, Agriculture, Food & Environment* 34, no. 2 (December 2012): 137. See also Bronislaw Malinowski, *Argonauts of the Western Pacific* (Dutton, 1922); David Graeber, *Toward an Anthropological Theory of Value: The False Coin of Our Own Dreams* (Palgrave, 2001), 6–7, 222–47. The yams stored in houses, used as symbols of wealth, and tied to value in Trobriand cultures are not Dioscorea alata (greater yams, also known as "water yams"), but Dioscorea esculenta, commonly known as the lesser yam.
46. Malinowski, *Argonauts of the Western Pacific*, 96–97.
47. See Felix Nweke, *Yam in West Africa: Food, Money, and More* (Michigan State University Press, 2016).
48. Brecht, *George Brecht: Notebooks*, Notebook 3. See also the reproduction of handwritten scores in Higgins, *Fluxus Experience*, 146.
49. George Maciunas to La Monte Young, Letter, December 12, 1962, MoMA Silverman V.A.1.43.
50. Dolores Hayden, *Building Suburbia: Green Fields and Urban Growth, 1820–2000* (Pantheon, 2003), 147.
51. Brecht writes in his assembled notes, "Events have always been a mode of experimenting." George Brecht, "Origins of Events," in *Heterospective*, ed. Julia Robinson (Walther König, 2005), 236.
52. George Brecht, letter to George Maciunas, n.d. [ca. November/December 1962], p. 2. Archiv Schlom, quoted in Smith, *Fluxus*, 88.
53. Kotz, *Words to Be Looked at*; Anna Dezeuze, "Origins of the Fluxus Score," *Performance Research* 7, no. 3 (January 2002): 78–94.
54. Umberto Eco, *The Open Work*, trans. Anna Cancogni (Harvard University Press, 1989), 12.
55. Eco, *The Open Work*, 21.
56. Kotz, *Words to Be Looked at*, 63.
57. Cecire, *Experimental*, 189.
58. George Brecht, "Events (Assembled Notes)," unpublished manuscript (1961); George Brecht Notebook 7, March–June 1961, Silverman Collection, in Robinson, *Heterospective*, 226.
59. "Score, n.," in *OED Online* (Oxford University Press), accessed December 24, 2020, http://www.oed.com/view/Entry/173033.
60. "Score, n."
61. Natilee Harren and Mari Dumett have interpreted these marks in brilliant ways: connecting Brecht's scores to diagrams, Harren likens the bullet points to Wassily Kandinsky and John Cage's liberated points; Dumett sees reflections of the aesthetic of IBM

punch cards for beginning and ending the working day, providing a "historically specific recognition of the impossibility of being outside the bureaucratized system of regulating codes." See Harren, *Fluxus Forms*, 65, 103; Dumett, *Corporate Imaginations*, 153. Less thought has been given to reading these typographic marks as they would appear in texts at the time (as bullets).

62. Kathryn A. Neeley and Michael Alley, "The Humble History of the 'Bullet,'" *ASEE Annual Conference and Exposition, Conference Proceedings*, January 1, 2011, https://pennstate.pure.elsevier.com/en/publications/the-humble-history-of-the-bullet-2; "Bullet, n.1," in *OED Online* (Oxford University Press), accessed March 26, 2021, http://www.oed.com/view/Entry/24543.

63. John Guillory, "The Memo and Modernity," *Critical Inquiry* 31, no. 1 (September 2004): 128.

64. Brecht and Robinson, *George Brecht*, 62.

65. Craig Dworkin, *Radium of the Word: A Poetics of Materiality* (University of Chicago Press, 2020), 24–26.

66. Brecht, "Events (Assembled Notes)," 226.

67. Quoted in Brecht and Robinson, *George Brecht*, 68.

68. Henry Martin, *An Introduction to George Brecht's Book of the Tumbler on Fire* (multhipla edizioni, 1978), 111.

69. Natalia Aki Cecire, "Ways of Not Reading Gertrude Stein," *ELH* 82, no. 1 (2015): 303.

70. Sara Blair, "Home Truths: Gertrude Stein, 27 Rue de Fleurus, and the Place of the Avant-Garde," *American Literary History* 12, no. 3 (2000): 419.

71. Blair, "Home Truths," 423.

72. Juliana Spahr, *Du Bois's Telegram: Literary Resistance and State Containment* (Harvard University Press, 2018), 71.

73. Spahr, *Du Bois's Telegram*, 72.

74. Lizebeth Cohen, *A Consumers' Republic: The Politics of Mass Consumption in Postwar America* (Vintage, 2003), 127.

75. "Chair, n.1," in *OED Online* (Oxford University Press), accessed December 22, 2020, http://www.oed.com/view/Entry/30215.

76. "Chair, n.1."

77. "Chair, n.1." On Brecht's chair scores as "a caption that addresses the 'meaninglessness' that surrounds the everyday object," see Robinson, "From Abstraction to Model," 98.

78. Cohen, *A Consumers' Republic*, 13, 197.

79. Brecht, "Origin of Events," quoted in Brecht and Robinson, *George Brecht*, 236.

80. An often-quoted story about why Brecht's subsequent event scores were less elaborate: John Cage's reaction to participating in "Motor Vehicle Sundown Event" was to say, "I never felt so controlled before." Yve-Alain Bois, "On George Brecht (Review: 'George Brecht Events: A Heterospective')," *Art Forum*, April 2006, https://www.artforum.com/print/reviews/200604/george-brecht-10622.

81. On the national level, as a result of racist democratic representation, Black people "became even more significantly disadvantaged when a modern American middle class was fashioned during and after the Second World War." Ira Katznelson, *When Affirmative*

*Action Was White: An Untold History of Racial Inequality in Twentieth-Century America* (Norton, 2006), x, 15.

82. Joshua Schuster, "The Making of 'Tender Buttons': Gertrude Stein's Subjects, Objects and the Illegible," *Jacket 2*, April 21, 2011, https://jacket2.org/article/making-tender-buttons.
83. Schuster, "The Making of 'Tender Buttons.'"
84. Gertrude Stein, *Tender Buttons*, ed. Seth Perlow (City Lights, 2014), 28.
85. Karl Marx, *Capital: A Critique of Political Economy*, trans. Ben Fowkes, vol. 1 (Penguin, 1981), 128.
86. Marx, *Capital*, 1:164. This dancing table historically situates Marx's *Capital* in relation to spiritualists whose seances rattle tables, and it has been the object of analysis for arguments about temporality, potentiality, and the relations between matter and spirit. Its footnote's reference to a failed revolution in China opens a potentiality and temporal lag within the text. Amanda Armstrong, "The Wooden Brain: Organizing Untimeliness in Marx's *Capital*," *Mediations: Journal of the Marxist Literary Group* 31, no. 1 (Fall 2017): 3–26.
87. Derrida interrogates this idea of dancing headfirst as a characteristic of a specter and a crucial contradiction of capital. Jacques Derrida, *Specters of Marx: The State of the Debt, the Work of Mourning and the New International*, trans. Peggy Kamuf (Routledge, 2006), 190–92.
88. Derrida, *Specters of Marx*, 190.
89. Chris Jennings, "The Erotic Poetics of Anne Carson," *University of Toronto Quarterly* 70, no. 4 (October 2001): 91.
90. Stein, *Tender Buttons*, 51–52.
91. Marjorie Perloff suggests that the importance of pronouns and prepositions in sentences like this reveals that Stein is playing a language game. Marjorie Perloff, *Wittgenstein's Ladder: Poetic Language and the Strangeness of the Ordinary* (University of Chicago Press, 1996), 83–90.
92. Harren, *Fluxus Forms*, 161.
93. Stein, *Tender Buttons*, 63.
94. Stein, *Tender Buttons*, 64.
95. Stein, *Tender Buttons*, 76.

## 3. "I DO THIS I DO THAT": COLD WAR SPATIAL POETICS AND THE NEW YORK SCHOOL

1. The term "cut up" refers to a method invented by William Burroughs. Scholar Al Filreis explains it as "vertically cutting two texts with razors or scissors to rearrange and join them as textual strips that simultaneously mock and celebrate the state of the American language . . . thus causing meaningful confusion about the agency in radical political critique and official democratic blather." Al Filreis, "The End of Poetic Ideology, 1960." In, *The Oxford Handbook of Modern and Contemporary American Poetry*, Edited by Cary Nelson (Oxford University Press, 2012), 519. Elsewhere, Gregory Corso titled this poem "CUT UP of Eisenhower Speech & Mine Own Poem." In *Minutes to Go*, ed. Sinclair Beiles et al. (Beach Books, Texts, & Documents, 1968), 33.

2. Dwight D. Eisenhower, "Farewell Address to the Nation" January 17, 1961, https://www.archives.gov/milestone-documents/president-dwight-d-eisenhowers-farewell-address
3. Dwight D. Eisenhower, "Atoms for Peace Speech," December 8, 1953. On this speech see Christine Hong, *A Violent Peace: Race, U.S. Militarism, and Cultures of Democratization in Cold War Asia and the Pacific* (Stanford University Press, 2020), 113.
4. For a reading of obsolescence that resists normative structures in James Schuyler's poems (including this one), see Davy Knittle, "'Hints That Are Revelations': James Schuyler, Obsolescence, and the Urban Curative Imaginary," *GLQ: A Journal of Lesbian and Gay Studies* 27, no. 2 (2021): 173–200.
5. The name "I do this I do that" for New York School poetry was initiated by Frank O'Hara in a 1959 poem. After the poet gets up early, the entire day goes by because he is writing this type of poetry: "I make / myself a bourbon and commence / to write one of my 'I do this I do that'/ poems in a sketch pad / it is tomorrow." Frank O'Hara, "Getting Up Ahead of Someone (Sun)," in *The Collected Poems of Frank O'Hara*, ed. Donald Allen (University of California Press, 1995), 341. The name was so apt for the characteristic of New York School poetry that catalogued specific actions and detailed public places that critics used to describe first, second, and third "generations" or "waves" of New York School poets as an established genre. See Nick Sturm for the limitations of metaphors about generations or waves and the relation of subsequent poetry to the "personal poem," a name Eileen Myles gave to the "I do this I do that" poem. Nick Sturm, "'I've Never Liked Mimeo': Eileen Myles, Little Magazines, and the 'Umpteenth-Generation New York School,'" *Women's Studies* 51, no. 8 (November 2022): 904–24.
6. Samuel Zipp, *Manhattan Projects: The Rise and Fall of Urban Renewal in Cold War New York* (Oxford University Press, 2012); Daniel M. Abramson, *Obsolescence: An Architectural History* (University of Chicago Press, 2016); Myka Tucker-Abramson, *Novel Shocks: Urban Renewal and the Origins of Neoliberalism* (Fordham University Press, 2019); Benjamin Sitton Flowers, *Skyscraper: The Politics and Power of Building New York City in the Twentieth Century* (University of Pennsylvania Press, 2009).
7. Important accounts of the "school" as somewhat unified include Geoffrey Ward, *Statutes of Liberty: The New York School of Poets* (Macmillan, 1993); David Lehman, *The Last Avant-Garde: The Making of the New York School of Poets* (Doubleday, 1998); Terrence Diggory and Stephen Miller, eds., *The Scene of My Selves* (National Poetry Foundation, 2001); William Watkin, *In the Process of Poetry: The New York School and the Avant-Garde* (Bucknell University Press, 2001); Maggie Nelson, *Women, the New York School, and Other True Abstractions* (University of Iowa Press, 2007); Mark Silverberg, *The New York School Poets and the Neo-Avant-Garde* (Ashgate, 2010). For accounts of coterie and friendship, see Andrew Epstein, *Beautiful Enemies: Friendship and Postwar American Poetry* (Oxford University Press, 2006); Lytle Shaw, *Frank O'Hara: The Poetics of Coterie* (University of Iowa Press, 2006). For relationality in O'Hara's poetry, see Brian Glavey, "Having a Coke with You Is Even More Fun Than Ideology Critique," *PMLA* 134, no. 5 (October 2019): 996.
8. Other early anthologies to define the New York School externally include John Bernard Myers, *The Poets of the New York School* (Graduate School of Fine Arts, University of

Pennsylvania, 1969); and Ron Padgett and David Shapiro, eds., *An Anthology of New York Poets* (Vintage, 1970).

9. *Encyclopedia of the New York School Poets*, Facts on File Library of American Literature (Facts on File, 2009), 160. Quoted from Edward Field, *The Man Who Would Marry Susan Sontag and Other Intimate Portraits of the Bohemian Era* (University of Wisconsin Press, 2005), 84–85.
10. For defining and nuancing these genres as well as how they changed between generations, see Epstein, *Beautiful Enemies*; *Encyclopedia of the New York School Poets*, 186; Sturm, "'I've Never Liked Mimeo.'"
11. Christopher Sawyer-Lauçanno, "Locus Solus et Socii: Harry Matthews and John Ashbery," in *The Continual Pilgrimage: American Writers in Paris, 1944–1960* (Grove, 1992), 258.
12. Mathews letter; Kenneth Koch papers at the Berg Collection 11.10.
13. The Kenneth Koch papers Archive at the Berg Collection includes U.S. customs import statements in two increments for 1500, which appear to be the near total print runs (Koch 11.6). See also Daniel Kane, *All Poets Welcome: The Lower East Side Poetry Scene in the 1960s* (University of California Press, 2003), 156; Steven Clay and Rodney Phillips, *A Secret Location on the Lower East Side: Adventures in Writing, 1960–1980: A Sourcebook of Information* (Granary, 1998).
14. These journals were made quickly and cheaply, circulated in small bookshops (often for free), and made up a vibrant East Side culture that would also define New York School poetry, its circles, offshoots, and later generations: *Yugen* (1958–1962), *Kulchur* (1960–1966), *Fuck You, a magazine of the arts* (1962–1965), *C* (1963–1980), *Umbra* (1963–1974), and then a little later, *Angel Hair* (1966–1978). Clay and Philips call *Locus Solus* "squat and serious," which seems apt. Clay and Phillips, *A Secret Location on the Lower East Side*, 159.
15. James Schuyler, *Just the Thing: Selected Letters of James Schuyler* (Turtle Point, 2004), 129.
16. David Caute, *The Dancer Defects: The Struggle for Cultural Supremacy During the Cold War* (Oxford University Press, 2003).
17. Greg Barnhisel, *Cold War Modernists: Art, Literature, and American Cultural Diplomacy, 1946–1959* (Columbia University Press, 2015); Greg Barnhisel, "*Perspectives USA* and the Cultural Cold War: Modernism in Service of the State," *Modernism/Modernity* 14, no. 4 (2007): 729–54.
18. Sam Lebovic, "The Fulbright, History's Greatest War-Surplus Program," *BostonGlobe.com* (blog), August 11, 2013, http://www.bostonglobe.com/ideas/2013/08/10/the-fulbright-history-greatest-war-surplus-program/NiGDSEjkjLAcZcxcGowLBJ/story.html. See also Richard T. Arndt, *The First Resort of Kings: American Cultural Diplomacy in the Twentieth Century* (Potomac, 2005), 161–288.
19. Max Kozloff's 1973 article pointed out a connection between the "symbolic values" of Abstract Expressionism and the ideological circumstances of the Cold War, suggesting that the individualist "charismatic hard sell" that defined U.S. politics of the time also characterized the feeling of major Abstract Expressionist art. Max Kozloff, "American

Painting During the Cold War," *Art Forum* 11, no. 9 (May 1973): 43–54. Since then, there has been a deluge of scholarship about this issue. Art historian and Museum of Modern Art (MoMA) director Alfred Barr purported that abstraction came about autonomously as an aesthetic stage, which gave MoMA exhibitions in Europe a taint of nationalist propaganda and opened many conversations about the complicity of artists, critics, and curators with state forces. See Francis Frascina, *Pollock and After: The Critical Debate* (Harper & Row, 1985); Serge Guilbaut, *How New York Stole the Idea of Modern Art: Abstract Expressionism, Freedom, and the Cold War* (University of Chicago Press, 1983); Robert Burstow, "The Limits of Modernist Art as a 'Weapon of the Cold War': Reassessing the Unknown Patron of the Monument to the Unknown Political Prisoner," *Oxford Art Journal* 20, no. 1 (January 1997): 68–80; Frances Stonor Saunders, *The Cultural Cold War: The CIA and the World of Arts and Letters* (New Press, 2000). Anticommunist advocacy groups funded by the CIA and through foundation support operated out of Paris and throughout Europe, often involving writers and artists who created abstract art. Saunders, *The Cultural Cold War*; Andrew Rubin, *Archives of Authority: Empire, Culture, and the Cold War* (Princeton University Press, 2012); Juliana Spahr, *Du Bois's Telegram: Literary Resistance and State Containment* (Harvard University Press, 2018), 71.

20. Spahr, *Du Bois's Telegram*, 4.
21. Frank O'Hara and Bill Berkson, "From 'The Memorandums of Angelicus Fobb,'" *Locus Solus* 3–4 (Winter 1962): 101–5.
22. O'Hara and Berkson, "From 'The Memorandums of Angelicus Fobb.'"
23. John Shoptaw, *On the Outside Looking Out: John Ashbery's Poetry* (Harvard University Press, 1994), 43; Christopher Nealon, *The Matter of Capital: Poetry and Crisis in the American Century* (Harvard University Press, 2011), 73; John Ashbery, "The New Realism," *Locus Solus* 3–4 (Winter 1962): 184–90.
24. John Perreault, "Paris," *Locus Solus* 3–4 (Winter 1962): 206–7.
25. Perreault, "Paris."
26. Perreault, "Paris."
27. Lytle Shaw, "Gesture in 1960: Toward Literal Solutions," in *Frank O'Hara Now: New Essays on the New York Poet*, ed. Robert Hampson and Will Montgomery (Liverpool University Press, 2010), 42.
28. Frank O'Hara, "Adieu to Norman, Bonjour to Joan and Jean-Paul," *Locus Solus* 1 (Winter 1961): 123–25.
29. Zipp, *Manhattan Projects*, 26.
30. Digital Scholarship Lab, "Renewing Inequality," American Panorama, ed. Robert K. Nelson and Edward L. Ayers, accessed February 28, 2023, https://dsl.richmond.edu /panorama/renewal/#view=0/0/1&viz=cartogram.
31. Joshua Shannon, *The Disappearance of Objects: New York Art and the Rise of the Postmodern City* (Yale University Press, 2009), 126.
32. Knittle, "'Hints That Are Revelations.'"
33. See, for example, John Ashbery, "Idaho," *Locus Solus* 1 (Winter 1961): 55–60; Jean Boudin, "Second Story Brownstone," *Locus Solus* 3–4 (Winter 1962): 92; Musa Gaston, "Brooklyns,"

*Locus Solus* 5 (Spring 1962): 47; and the two epigraphs by Gregory Corso and Carl Morse that began this chapter.

34. Alan Filreis, *1960: The Politics and Art of the Postwar Avant-Garde* (Columbia University Press, 2021), 57–63; Epstein, *Beautiful Enemies*, 180–93; Nathaniel Mackey, "The Changing Same: Black Music in the Poetry of Amiri Baraka," in *Discrepant Engagement: Dissonance, Cross-Culturality, and Experimental Writing* (Cambridge University Press, 1993), 22–48.
35. LeRoi Jones, "Style," *Locus Solus* 3–4 (Winter 1962): 16.
36. LeRoi Jones, "The End of Man Is His Beauty," *Locus Solus* 3–4 (Winter 1962): 17–18.
37. Tucker-Abramson, *Novel Shocks*, 9.
38. LeRoi Jones, "A Long Poem for Myself," *Locus Solus* 3–4 (Winter 1962): 13–15.
39. Zipp, *Manhattan Projects*, 26.
40. Frank O'Hara, "Walking," in *The Collected Poems of Frank O'Hara*, ed. Donald Allen (University of California Press, 1995), 476–77.
41. The connection between O'Hara's poetry and the politics of Abstract Expressionism—or "action painting," a term from Harold Rosenberg—has been considered through decades of scholarship, and O'Hara's critique of and participation in commodity culture and white-collar capitalism has been written about at length. Marjoie Perloff's 1977 monograph set the tone for O'Hara scholarship that closely attended to the poems as akin to painting. Marjorie Perloff, *Frank O'Hara, Poet Among Painters* (University of Chicago Press, 1998). For writing about O'Hara's speaker as participating in market economies, see Mutlu Konuk Blasing, *Politics and Form in Postmodern Poetry: O'Hara, Bishop, Ashbery, and Merrill* (Cambridge University Press, 1995); Michael Clune, *American Literature and the Free Market, 1945–2000* (Cambridge University Press, 2009); Oren Izenberg, *Being Numerous: Poetry and the Ground of Social Life* (Princeton University Press, 2011); Susan B. Rosenbaum, *Professing Sincerity: Modern Lyric Poetry, Commercial Culture, and the Crisis in Reading* (University of Virginia Press, 2007). Scholarship that sees architecture and space as politically charged includes Shaw, "Gesture in 1960"; Robert Bennett, *Deconstructing Post-WWII New York City: The Literature, Art, Jazz, and Architecture of an Emerging Global Capital* (Routledge, 2003); Terrence Diggory, "Picturesque Urban Pastoral in Post-War New York City," in *The Built Surface Vol 2*, ed. Karen Koehler (Ashgate, 2002), 282–303.
42. Gilles Deleuze, *Kafka: Toward a Minor Literature*, trans. Dana Polan (University of Minnesota Press, 1986), 19.
43. The Lever House, built in 1952, is another model for the 1961 resolution. See the 2007 New York City Department of City Planning application for amendment to the Zoning Resolution to revise and update design and operational standards related to privately owned public plazas. New York City Department of City Planning, "In the Matter of an Application . . .," September 19, 2007, https://www.nyc.gov/assets/planning/download/pdf/about/cpc/070497.pdf. Also see New York City's history of privately owned public spaces dating back to 1961. NYC Department of City Planning, "Privately Owned Public Space History," NYC Department of City Planning, accessed July 7, 2025, https://www.nyc.gov/content/planning/pages/our-work/plans/citywide/privately-owned-public-spaces#history.

44. Marc Weiss, "Density and Intervention: New York's Planning Traditions," in *The Landscape of Modernity: Essays on New York City, 1900–1940*, ed. David Ward and Olivier Zunz (Russell Sage, 1992), 69.
45. Te-Sheng Huang and Karen A. Franck, "Let's Meet at Citicorp: Can Privately Owned Public Spaces Be Inclusive?," *Journal of Urban Design* 23, no. 4 (July 2018): 499–517.
46. Whyte began this research for the New York City Planning Commission in 1969. See William Hollingsworth Whyte, *The Social Life of Small Urban Spaces* (Conservation Foundation, 1980).
47. Frank O'Hara, "Personal Poem," in *The Collected Poems of Frank O'Hara*, ed. Donald Allen (University of California Press, 1995), 335.
48. Flowers, *Skyscraper*, 126.
49. Felicity D. Scott, "An Army of Soldiers or a Meadow," *Journal of the Society of Architectural Historians* 70, no. 3 (September 2011): 336.
50. "New Skyscraper on Park Avenue to be First Sheathed in Bronze: 38-Story House of Seagram Will Use 3,200,000 Pounds of Alloy in Outer Walls Colored for Weathering," *New York Times*, March 2, 1956.
51. "49-Star Flag Raised at Seagram Building," *New York Times*, January 14, 1959.
52. John P. Callahan, "Values Stressed for a Nuclear Age: Frost, Russell, Montagu and Others Fear Alternative at Seagram Symposium," *New York Times*, September 30, 1959.
53. Flowers, *Skyscraper*, 100.
54. Flowers, *Skyscraper*, 139.
55. Scott, "An Army of Soldiers or a Meadow," 366.
56. Michael Davidson, *Guys Like Us: Citing Masculinity in Cold War Poetics* (University of Chicago Press, 2004), 70; Diggory, "Picturesque Urban Pastoral."
57. Frank O'Hara, "Nocturne," in *The Collected Poems of Frank O'Hara*, ed. Donald Allen (University of California Press, 1995), 224–25.
58. Zipp, *Manhattan Projects*, 34.
59. Zipp, *Manhattan Projects*, 59.
60. Le Corbusier, "Architecture or Revolution," in *Towards a New Architecture*, trans. Frederick Etchells (Dover, 1986), 271.
61. Abramson, *Obsolescence*, 61.
62. Abramson, *Obsolescence*, 111.
63. Frank O'Hara, "The Lay of the Romance of the Associations," in *The Collected Poems of Frank O'Hara*, ed. Donald Allen (University of California Press, 1995), 320. In the magazine *C*, where this poem first appeared, the first stanza is underlined; in the *The Collected Poems of Frank O'Hara*, it is italicized. Either punctuation style asks us to read it paratextually to the poem.
64. The Fifth Avenue Association was one of the driving forces behind the 1916 zoning resolution, which restricts building height and density. As Marc Weiss has illustrated, the primary motivation for the resolution was the "segregation of residential uses from commerce and industry, especially the creation of exclusive districts for single family houses." The Fifth Avenue Association was in favor of the law to exclude "hordes of

factory employees" that might be brought to the Avenue from the nearby Garment District and disrupt its "exclusiveness." Weiss, "Density and Intervention," 47, 51. For the major role that the Fifth Avenue Association played in zoning and exclusivity, see Max Page, "The Heights and Depths of Urbanism: Fifth Avenue and the Creative Destruction of Manhattan," in *The American Skyscraper: Cultural Histories*, ed. Roberta Moudry (Cambridge University Press, 2005), 168.

65. Fifth Avenue Association, New York, *Fifty Years on Fifth, 1907–1957* (International Press, 1957), 36.
66. Fifth Avenue Association, *Fifty Years on Fifth*, 36.
67. James Trager, *Park Avenue: Street of Dreams* (Atheneum, 1990), 118.
68. Frequent newspaper articles cite both associations' efforts in this vein for the first half of the twentieth century. "Seeks to Abolish Taxi Whistles in Park Avenue," *New York Herald, New York Tribune*, February 15, 1926; "Wants No Skyscrapers: Fifth Avenue Section Hurt by Tall Buildings, Association Asserts," *New York Times*, July 12, 1917.
69. O'Hara, "The Lay of the Romance of the Associations."
70. Abramson, *Obsolescence*, 111.
71. Michael Warner, *Publics and Counterpublics* (Zone, 2005), 199.
72. Deborah Nelson, *Pursuing Privacy in Cold War America* (Columbia University Press, 2002), xiii. See also containment culture described as the sexualized narrative of "courtship and rivalry," sometimes in particular described as containment of "precious bodily fluids." Alan Nadel, *Containment Culture: American Narrative, Postmodernism, and the Atomic Age* (Duke University Press, 1995), 5.
73. Tucker-Abramson, *Novel Shocks*, 13.

## 4. FEMINIST PROCEDURE AND DURATIONAL CONSTRAINT: REPRODUCTION, WELFARE, AND "LOSING MYSELF"

1. Including both welfare rights and popular literature as "1970s feminism" is not a usual scholarly convention. For a varied history of 1970s popular feminism, as well as a review of scholarly literature of "standard" 1970s feminism, see Michelle Moravec and Kent K. Chang, "Feminist Bestsellers: A Digital History of 1970s Feminism," *Post45: Peer Reviewed*, April 21, 2021, https://post45.org/2021/04/feminist-bestsellers-a-digital-history-of-1970s-feminism/.
2. For changing work conditions for women in the 1960s and 1970s, see Julia Kirk Blackwelder, *Now Hiring: The Feminization of Work in the United States, 1900–1995* (Texas A&M University Press, 1997), 177–204; Claudia Dale Goldin, *Understanding the Gender Gap: An Economic History of American Women* (Oxford University Press, 1992), 119–215; Melinda Cooper, *Family Values: Between Neoliberalism and the New Social Conservatism* (Zone, 2017), 25–66.
3. *Endnotes*, "The Logic of Gender: On the Separation of Spheres and the Process of Abjection," *Endnotes*, no. 3 (September 2013), https://endnotes.org.uk/issues/3/en/endnotes-the-logic-of-gender.
4. *Endnotes*, "The Logic of Gender."

5. Although millions of Americans used birth control pills throughout the 1960s, many states still prohibited the sale of contraception or allowed it only for married women, and laws in Massachusetts and Connecticut prevented dissemination of information about it until 1972. In 1972, the Supreme Court ruling in *Eisenstadt v. Baird* prohibited states from standing in the way of distribution of birth control.
6. Sara Matthiesen, *Reproduction Reconceived: Family Making and the Limits of Choice After Roe v. Wade* (University of California Press, 2021), 4–9; Donald T. Critchlow, *Intended Consequences: Birth Control, Abortion, and the Federal Government in Modern America* (Oxford University Press, 2001), 6–7; Jennifer Mittelstadt, *From Welfare to Workfare: The Unintended Consequences of Liberal Reform, 1945–1965* (University of North Carolina Press, 2005), 5.
7. Silvia Federici, *Caliban and the Witch* (Autonomedia, 2014), 15.
8. For the emergence of body and performance art and its relationship to the feminist movement and feminist liberation, see Jayne Wark, *Radical Gestures: Feminism and Performance Art in North America* (McGill-Queen's University Press, 2006); Rebecca Schneider, *The Explicit Body in Performance* (Routledge, 1997); Amelia Jones, *Body Art /Performing the Subject* (University of Minnesota Press, 1998); Nizan Shaked, Amelia Jones, and Marsha Meskimmon, *The Synthetic Proposition: Conceptualism and the Political Referent in Contemporary Art* (Manchester University Press, 2017); Lucy R. Lippard, "The Pains and Pleasures of Rebirth: European and American Women's Body Art," in *From the Center: Feminist Essays on Women's Art* (Dutton, 1976), 121–38; Cornelia H. Butler, *From Conceptualism to Feminism: Lucy Lippard's Numbers Shows, 1969–74* (Afterall, 2012). While she does not consider feminist liberation, Kathy O'Dell's *Contract with the Skin* focuses on the relationship between the performer's body, which undergoes acts of violence, to changing "volatile political and social issues that affected the everyday lives of individuals in the early 1970s." Kathy O'Dell, *Contract with the Skin: Masochism, Performance Art, and the 1970s* (University of Minnesota Press, 1998), 12.
9. Jones, *Body Art/Performing the Subject*, 1. For a history of the term "body art," as opposed to "performance art," for example, see O'Dell, *Contract with the Skin*, 87.
10. Helen Anne Molesworth, "House Work and Art Work," *October*, no. 92 (Spring 2000): 71–97; Helen Anne Molesworth, "Cleaning Up in the 1970s: The Work of Judy Chicago, Mary Kelly and Mierle Laderman Ukeles," in *Rewriting Conceptual Art*, ed. Michael Newman and Jon Bird, Critical Views (Reaktion, 1999), 107–22.
11. Molesworth, "Cleaning Up in the 1970s," 114.
12. Mierle Laderman Ukeles, *MANIFESTO FOR MAINTENANCE ART, Proposal for an Exhibition: "CARE," 1969*, October 1969, our typewritten pages, each 8½ × 11 in., https://queensmuseum.org/wp-content/uploads/2016/04/Ukeles-Manifesto-for-Maintenance-Art-1969.pdf.
13. Karen LeCoq and Nancy Youdelman, Installation art, Womanhouse California Institute of the Arts, 1972, photo, Department of Art History Visual Resource Centre Selections, Penn State University Libraries Digital Collections, https://digital.libraries.psu.edu/digital/collection/arthist2/id/150336/.
14. For an analysis of this tension, see Andrea Brady, *Poetry and Bondage: A History and Theory of Lyric Constraint* (Cambridge University Press, 2021).

15. Joseph M. Conte, *Unending Design: The Forms of Postmodern Poetry* (Cornell University Press, 1991), 16. For other important definitions of constraint or procedurality, see Marjorie Perloff, *Radical Artifice: Writing Poetry in the Age of Media* (University of Chicago Press, 1991), 139–40; Jan Baetens and Jean-Jacques Poucel, "Introduction: The Challenge of Constraint," *Poetics Today* 30, no. 4 (December 2009): 611–34.
16. Daniel Levin Becker, *Many Subtle Channels: In Praise of Potential Literature* (Harvard University Press, 2012), 13.
17. "Oulipo" is short for *Ouvroir de littérature potentielle*. See Oulipo, *Abrégé de Littérature Potentielle* (Mille et une nuits, 2002); Harry Mathews and Alastair Brotchie, eds., *Oulipo Compendium* (Atlas, 1998); Warren F. Motte, ed., *Oulipo: A Primer of Potential Literature* (Dalkey Archive Press, 1998).
18. Conte, *Unending Design*, 41.
19. For an overview of the literature on procedure that is oriented toward "postmodern" poetry in the United States, see David Huntsperger, *Procedural Form in Postmodern American Poetry: Berrigan, Antin, Silliman, and Hejinian* (Palgrave Macmillan, 2010), 1–40.
20. Conte makes the assertion that there is not much to be gained by systematic explication or close reading in the case of procedural forms; rather, he focuses on how the composition works. Conte, *Unending Design*, 256–57. See also a focus on readership and process in Baetens and Poucel, "Introduction"; Matais Viegener and Christine Wertheim, eds., *The Noulipian Analects* (Les Figues, 2007); Peter Consenstein, *Literary Memory, Consciousness, and the Group Oulipo* (Rodopi, 2002). For the assertion that this work is viewed most importantly as a writer's device, see Johanna Drucker, "Readers, Which Brings Us to The," in *The Noulipian Analects*, ed. Matais Viegener and Christine Wertheim (Les Figues, 2007), 178–79; Johanna Drucker, "Experimental Writing (or Poetry Lab)," in *The Noulipian Analects*, ed. Matais Viegener and Christine Wertheim (Les Figues, 2007), 75.
21. Juliana Spahr and Stephanie Young, "Foulipo," in *A Megaphone: Some Enactments, Some Numbers, and Some Essays About the Continued Usefulness of Crotchless-Pants-and-a-Machine-Gun Feminism* (ChainLinks, 2011), 41.
22. Bruna Mori, "Noulipo's Oulipoed Foulipo," *Drunken Boat* (blog), 2006, http://d7.drunkenboat.com/db8/oulipo/feature-oulipo/essays/mori/noulipo.html.
23. John Parish Bowles, *Adrian Piper: Race, Gender, and Embodiment* (Duke University Press, 2011); Cherise Smith, *Enacting Others: Politics of Identity in Eleanor Antin, Nikki S. Lee, Adrian Piper, and Anna Deavere Smith* (Duke University Press, 2011).
24. On Bernadette Mayer's family background, see Bernadette Mayer, "Lives of the Poets: Bernadette Mayer by Adam Fitzgerald" (Poetry Foundation, April 2011), https://www.poetryfoundation.org/articles/69658/lives-of-the-poets-bernadette-mayer; Bernadette Mayer and Lewis Warsh, *Piece of Cake* (Station Hill, 2020). On Eleanor Antin's biography, see Eleanor Antin, *Conversations with Stalin* (Green Integer, 2013); Eleanor Antin, "Oral History Interview with Eleanor Antin, 2009 May 8–9," Archives of American Art, Smithsonian Institution, accessed October 12, 2021, https://www.aaa.si.edu/collections/interviews/oral-history-interview-eleanor-antin-15792. Adrian Piper's oral history describes her childhood in Harlem and nearby, details her family's employment and

200   4. FEMINIST PROCEDURE AND DURATIONAL CONSTRAINT

growing up, "as we said in those days 'colored.'" Oral history interview with Adrian Piper, 1990 Sept. 20, transcript, page 4, Archives of American Art, Smithsonian Institution. In 2012, Piper retired from being Black. Adrian Piper, "APRA Foundation Berlin: News," APRA Foundation Berlin: News, September 2012, http://adrianpiper.com/berlin/news.shtml#September_2012.

25. Eleanor Antin to Marcia Tucker, n.d., Eleanor Antin papers, 1953–2010, box 2, folder 26. Cited in Emily Liebert, "Roles Recast: Eleanor Antin and the 1970s" (PhD diss., Columbia University, 2013), 30.

26. Although Antin claims this was the reason for rejection, the Whitney's reason for rejection is not indicated in the correspondence. *Carving* was first shown in 1972 in an exhibition that Antin organized, Traditional Art: "Painting," "Sculpture," "Drawing," which traveled from the Orlando Gallery in Encino, California, to the Henri Gallery in Washington, DC. Liebert, "Roles Recast," 31; Antin, "Oral History Interview with Eleanor Antin."

27. Helen Anne Molesworth, ed., *Work Ethic* (Baltimore Museum of Art/Pennsylvania State University Press, 2003).

28. Shulamith Firestone, *The Dialectic of Sex: The Case for Feminist Revolution* (Bantam, 1970), 146.

29. Silvia Federici, "Wages Against Housework," in *Revolution at Point Zero: Housework, Reproduction, and Feminist Struggle* (PM Press, 2020), 11–18.

30. Eleanor Antin, *Carving: A Traditional Sculpture*, 1972, Chicago Art Institute.

31. Lisa Bloom, "Contests for Meaning in Body Politics and Feminist Conceptual Art: Revisioning the 1970s Through the Work of Eleanor Antin," in *Performing the Body/Performing the Text*, ed. Amelia Jones and Andrew Stephenson (Routledge, 1999), 153–69; Lisa Bloom, "Rewriting the Script: Eleanor Antin's Feminist Art," in *Eleanor Antin*, ed. Howard N. Fox (Los Angeles County Museum of Art, 1999), 159–90. See also Cherise Smith, *Enacting Others*, 83.

32. I quote a popular rhyming translation that is printed with the Italian on one page and the English on the other, thinking it is perhaps the edition that Antin referenced. Michelangelo Buonarroti, *Sonnets*, trans. John Addington Symonds (Scribner's, 1904), http://archive.org/details/cu31924014269975.

33. Liebert, "Roles Recast," 50.

34. Although her family were atheists, Antin says that she prayed to God when she thought she was pregnant at sixteen: "I remember desperately falling down on my knees . . . I don't remember who the father was. Maybe I didn't even know, but when I missed a period, I was terrified the way we all used to be in those days when abortions were done in back alleys with slimy amateurs and dirty knives." Her praying results in blood streaming down her legs—either her late period or a miscarriage—and she recalls the experience as when God visited her. Antin, *Conversations with Stalin*, 64–66.

35. Antin, "Oral History Interview with Eleanor Antin."

36. Antin, "Oral History Interview with Eleanor Antin."

37. Eleanor Antin, "An Autobiography of the Artist as an Autobiographer," *Los Angeles Institute of Contemporary Art* 2 (October 1974): 20.

4. FEMINIST PROCEDURE AND DURATIONAL CONSTRAINT    201

38. Antin describes her 1972 diet to Alice Butler and contrasts it to the difficulty of losing the weight for a 2017 version of *Carving*. Alice Butler, "Eleanor Antin on Art, Ageing and Grief," *Frieze* (blog), May 29, 2019, https://www.frieze.com/article/eleanor-antin-art-ageing-and-grief.
39. Howard N. Fox, "Waiting in the Wings: Desire and Destiny in the Art of Eleanor Antin," in *Eleanor Antin*, ed. Howard N. Fox (Los Angeles County Museum of Art, 1999), 59.
40. Paul McCarthy, ed., "Food for the Spirit," *High Performance* 4, no. 1 (Spring 1981): 34–39. This piece was first published in 1981 with photography from another artwork in which Piper appeared clothed. This piece and the corresponding photos were not exhibited until 1987. Adrian Piper, *Out of Order, Out of Sight, Volume I: Selected Writings in Meta-Art 1968–1992* (MIT Press, 1996), 55.
41. Adrian Piper, *Food for the Spirit* notebook, 1971 (Erben Gallery). The notebook is held by the private dealer Thomas Erben of the Thomas Erben Gallery who generously showed it to me and discussed its history.
42. Piper, *Food for the Spirit* notebook.
43. Piper, *Out of Order, Out of Sight, Volume I*, 55.
44. Piper, *Food for the Spirit* notebook.
45. This was not the sequence in which she took the photos, but she arranged them from light to dark. Thomas Erben, personal conversation, September 16, 2022. For exhibition and publication history, see the chapter "Food for the Sprit: Transcendence and Desire" (205–28) in Bowles, *Adrian Piper*.
46. Piper, *Food for the Spirit* notebook.
47. Gary Schneider was the photographer with whom Piper and Erben chose to work with Piper's negatives. Thomas Erben, conversation and e-mail, September 2022.
48. There are three full sets of fourteen signed photos owned by the Museum of Modern Art (MoMA), the Whitney, and the Serralves Museum. There are also trial proofs and artist proofs of fewer groupings of photos. For example, eleven of these are owned by the Rhode Island School of Design (RISD). Thomas Erben, personal conversation, September 16, 2022.
49. Piper, *Out of Order, Out of Sight, Volume I*, 55.
50. Laura Larson, "Food for the Spirit," *ASAP Journal Blog: B.O.S (Black One Shot)* (blog), June 18, 2020, https://asapjournal.com/b-o-s-9-2-adrian-pipers-food-for-the-spirit-laura-larson/.
51. Oral history interview with Adrian Piper, 1990 Sept. 20, transcript, page 38, Archives of American Art, Smithsonian Institution.
52. See Sandra Harvey, "Passing for Free, Passing for Sovereign: Blackness and the Formation of the Nation" (PhD diss., University of California, Santa Cruz, 2017); Smith, *Enacting Others*.
53. When asked about imperialism in Kantian writing and then a little later, "So you believe that Kant was misinterpreted rather than that racism is inherent to the Kantian position?," Piper replies, "I think that is absolutely right." Maurice Berger, "The Critique of Pure Racism: An Interview with Adrian Piper," in *Adrian Piper: A Retrospective*, ed. Maurice Berger (Fine Arts Gallery, University of Maryland, 1999), 92.

54. Adrian Piper, "Talking to Myself: The Ongoing Autobiography of an Art Object," in *Out of Order, Out of Sight, Volume I: Selected Writings in Meta-Art 1968–1992* (MIT Press, 1996), 31.
55. "The Triple Negation of Colored Women Artists," in *Next Generation: Southern Black Aesthetic*, 15–22 (Southeastern Center for Contemporary Art, 1990); Adrian Piper, *Out of Order, Out of Sight, Volume II: Selected Writings in Art Criticism 1967–1992* (MIT Press, 1996), 162.
56. Piper, "Talking to Myself," 30.
57. Piper, "Talking to Myself," 30.
58. Piper's personal chronology lists both the start of the women's consciousness-raising group and the creation of *Food for the Spirit* as events that happened in 1971. Maurice Berger, ed., *Adrian Piper: A Retrospective*, Issues in Cultural Theory 3 (Fine Arts Gallery, University of Maryland, 1999), 188.
59. In Piper's discussion with Josephine Withers, Piper explains that she was kicked out of the art world in 1970 when white males found out she was a woman and again in 1973 when white females found out that she was Black. Oral history interview with Adrian Piper, 1990 Sept. 20, transcript, pages 46–47, Archives of American Art, Smithsonian Institution.
60. Piper, *Out of Order, Out of Sight, Volume I*, 55.
61. Piper, *Out of Order, Out of Sight, Volume I*, 55.
62. Lucy R. Lippard and Adrian Piper, "Catalysis: An Interview with Adrian Piper," *Drama Review: TDR* 16, no. 1 (March 1972): 77.
63. See *Catalysis III* and *Catalysis IV* in Berger, *Adrian Piper*, 128–29.
64. Howard N. Fox, *Eleanor Antin* (Los Angeles County Museum of Art, 1999), 38–44.
65. Lippard and Piper, "Catalysis," 78.
66. Berger, *Adrian Piper*, 63.
67. Piper, "Talking to Myself," 31.
68. Piper, *Out of Order, Out of Sight, Volume I*, 55.
69. Bowles, *Adrian Piper*, 220.
70. Adrian Piper, *Escape to Berlin: A Travel Memoir/Flucht Nach Berlin: Eine Reiseerinnerung*, trans. Suzanne Schmidt (Adrian Piper Research Archive Foundation Berlin, 2018), 23–25; Thomas Chatterton Williams, "Adrian Piper's Show at MoMA Is the Largest Ever for a Living Artist. Why Hasn't She Seen It?," *New York Times*, June 27, 2018, https://www.nytimes.com/2018/06/27/magazine/adrian-pipers-self-imposed-exile-from-america-and-from-race-itself.html.
71. Williams, "Adrian Piper's Show at MoMA."
72. John Bowles claims that this note was inserted into the notebook in the 1980s; his evidence is the Apple Macintosh font that Piper used during that decade. Bowles, *Adrian Piper*, 212. In contrast, Thomas Erben argues that Piper assembled the complete notebook (including the note, which is dated July 1971) in 1971, as evidenced by its materiality. Thomas Erben, personal conversation, September 16, 2022.
73. A statement released on her website reads the following: "Dear Friends, For my 64th birthday, I have decided to change my racial and nationality designations. Henceforth,

my new racial designation will be neither black nor white but rather 6.25 percent grey, honoring my 1/16th African heritage. And my new nationality designation will be not African American but rather Anglo-German American, reflecting my preponderantly English and German ancestry. Please join me in celebrating this exciting new adventure in pointless administrative precision and futile institutional control! Adrian M.S. Piper 20 September 2012." Piper, "APRA Foundation Berlin: News."
74. Piper, *Food for the Spirit* notebook.
75. Bernadette Mayer, *Studying Hunger* (Adventures in Poetry, 1975), 7; http://eclipsearchive.org/projects/HUNGER/hunger.html.
76. For a study of procedural poetics and Oulipian influences in *o to 9* see Sophie Seita, *Provisional Avant-Gardes: Little Magazine Communities from Dada to Digital* (Stanford University Press, 2019), 56–93. Craig Dworkin's reading of *The Cave*, a 1970s collaboration by Mayer and Clark Coolidge, is instructive about procedure as well; see Craig Dworkin, *Dictionary Poetics: Toward a Radical Lexicography* (Fordham University Press, 2020), 101–28.
77. On the many possibilities and references to that poem, see Kay Gabriel and Jo Barchi, "But Everything's Outside," *Post45* (blog), July 15, 2021, https://post45.org/2021/07/but-everythings-outside/.
78. Bernadette Mayer, *Studying Hunger Journals* (Station Hill, 2011), 3.
79. Mayer, *Studying Hunger Journals*, 1.
80. Mayer, *Studying Hunger*, 71.
81. Mayer, *Studying Hunger*, 59.
82. Mayer, *Studying Hunger Journals*, 255, 351.
83. Mayer, *Studying Hunger*, 21.
84. Mayer, "Lives of the Poets."
85. Mayer, *Studying Hunger*, 29.
86. Mayer, *Studying Hunger*, 29.
87. Mayer and Warsh, *Piece of Cake*, 23.
88. Mayer and Warsh, *Piece of Cake*, 243, 318.
89. Mayer and Warsh, *Piece of Cake*, 115.
90. Mayer and Warsh, *Piece of Cake*, 116.
91. Mayer and Warsh, *Piece of Cake*, 116.
92. Mayer and Warsh, *Piece of Cake*, 102.
93. Mayer and Warsh, *Piece of Cake*, 102.
94. Mayer and Warsh, *Piece of Cake*, 104.
95. Jenny Brown, *Without Apology: The Abortion Struggle Now* (Verso, 2019), 56.
96. Rachel Benson Gold, *Lessons from Before Roe: Will Past Be Prologue?* (Guttmacher Institute, March 2003), 8, 10, quoted in Brown, *Without Apology*, 47.
97. Mayer and Warsh, *Piece of Cake*, 102, 104; Antin, "Oral History Interview with Eleanor Antin," 8–9; Adrian Piper, "Kinds of Performing Objects I Have Been (1972)," in *Out of Order, Out of Sight, Volume I: Selected Writings in Meta-Art 1968–1992* (MIT Press, 1996), 89.
98. Mayer, "Lives of the Poets."
99. Mayer and Warsh, *Piece of Cake*, 102.
100. Mayer and Warsh, *Piece of Cake*, 104.

## 204    4. FEMINIST PROCEDURE AND DURATIONAL CONSTRAINT

101. Antin, "Oral History Interview with Eleanor Antin."
102. Piper, "Kinds of Performing Objects," 89.
103. At this discotheque, Piper "danced suspended in a glass cage" at age 17. "Kinds of Performing Objects," 89.
104. Bowles, *Adrian Piper*, 27; Laura Cottingham, "The 'Autobiography' of Adrian Piper," in *Adrian Piper: A Retrospective*, ed. Maurice Berger (Fine Arts Gallery, University of Maryland, 1999), 61–75.
105. Premilla Nadasen, Jennifer Mittelstadt, and Marisa Chappell, *Welfare in the United States: A History with Documents, 1935–1996* (Routledge, 2009), 42.
106. Mittelstadt, *From Welfare to Workfare*, 1–14.
107. Nadasen, Mittelstadt, and Chappell, *Welfare in the United States*.
108. Nadasen, Mittelstadt, and Chappell, *Welfare in the United States*, 43–44.
109. Mittelstadt, *From Welfare to Workfare*, 19.
110. Nadasen, Mittelstadt, and Chappell, *Welfare in the United States*, 56.
111. Cooper, *Family Values*, 33–53.
112. Cooper, *Family Values*, 47–53.
113. Nadasen, Mittelstadt, and Chappell, *Welfare in the United States*, 3–4.
114. Linda Gordon, "Aid to Dependent Children: The Legal History," *Social Welfare History Project* (blog), January 19, 2011, https://socialwelfare.library.vcu.edu/public-welfare/aid-to-dependent-children-the-legal-history/.
115. Nadasen, Mittelstadt, and Chappell, *Welfare in the United States*, 57.
116. In the wake of the Supreme Court's ruling in *Dobbs v. Jackson Women's Health Organization* (2022), which led to abortion bans in many states, there have been renewed debates on the socialist left about the relationship between reproduction, abortion, and capitalism. See Spectre Editorial Board, "Breaking the Strategic Impasse," *Spectre Journal*, May 27, 2022, https://spectrejournal.com/breaking-the-strategic-impasse/; Emily Janakriam, "Beyond *Roe v. Wade*," *Spectre Journal*, May 18, 2022, https://spectrejournal.com/beyond-roe-v-wade/; Paul Heideman, "The Antiabortion Movement Is the Rotten Fruit of a Brutally Unequal Society," *Jacobin*, July 8, 2022, https://jacobin.com/2022/07/anti-abortion-movement-division-of-labor-patriarchy.
117. On the history of abortion arguments, see Mary Ziegler, *After Roe: The Lost History of the Abortion Debate* (Harvard University Press, 2015); Mary Ziegler, *Abortion and the Law in America: Roe v. Wade to the Present* (Cambridge University Press, 2020); Critchlow, *Intended Consequences*.
118. Piper, *Out of Order, Out of Sight, Volume I*, 55.
119. The missing day is August 7, 1972. Martina Batan to Madeleine Grynsztejn, February 28, 1996, Art Institute of Chicago, Department of Contemporary Art curatorial files, cited in Liebert, "Roles Recast," 15.
120. Eleanor Antin letter to Henrietta Ehrsam, dated July 25, 1972, Henri Gallery records, circa early 1900s, bulk 1957–1995, box 5, folder 16, Archives of American Art, Smithsonian Institution.
121. A different letter to Henrietta Ehrsam says that the photos "graphically detail the loss of 12 pounds." Eleanor Antin letter to Henrietta Ehrsam, n.d., Henri Gallery records, circa

early 1900s, bulk 1957–1995, box 5, folder 16, Archives of American Art, Smithsonian Institution.
122. I am referencing the front note in the *Food for the Spirit* notebook, which reads, "I recorded these attempts to anchor myself . . . these attempts did not succeed, so I eventually abandoned them." Piper, *Food for the Spirit* notebook.
123. Mathews and Brotchie, *Oulipo Compendium*, 126.
124. Motte, *Oulipo*, 19. For example, critics have noticed that the rules for George Perec's novel *La Vie mode d'emploi*, a quintessentially Oulipian text, breaks its procedural symmetry by naming a character Lino instead of creating an apartment with a linoleum floor, which would have followed the blueprint of the book to be one hundred chapters. Mathews and Brotchie, *Oulipo Compendium*, 126; Warren F. Motte, "Clinamen Redux," *Comparative Literature Studies* 23, no. 4 (December 1986): 275; Levin Becker, *Many Subtle Channels*, 88.
125. Cura, "Eleanor Antin in Conversation with Vincent Honore," Curamagazine.com, March 2018, accessed August 12, 2021, https://curamagazine.com/digital/eleanor-antin/.
126. Mayer, *Studying Hunger Journals*, 3.
127. Piper, *Escape to Berlin*, 55–57.
128. Piper, *Escape to Berlin*, 301.
129. Mayer, *Studying Hunger Journals*, 457.
130. Mayer, *Studying Hunger Journals*, 457.
131. Piper, *Out of Order, Out of Sight, Volume I*, 55; Antin, "An Autobiography of the Artist," 20.
132. Jane Blocker, *What the Body Cost: Desire, History, and Performance* (University of Minnesota Press, 2004), 15.

## 5. DOCUMENTAL POETRY AND THE PRIVATIZATION OF INTERPRETATION

1. This sentence contains descriptions of the following projects (in order): Mark Nowak, *Coal Mountain Elementary* (Coffee House Press, 2009); Robert Fitterman, *Holocaust Museum* (Counterpath, 2013); Vanessa Place, *Vanessa Place: Last Words*, bilingual ed. (Dis Voir, 2015); Diana Hamilton, *Okay, Okay* (Truck Books, 2012); Noah Eli Gordon, *Inbox* (BlazeVOX, 2007); Jena Osman, *Public Figures* (Wesleyan University Press, 2012); Solmaz Sharif, *LOOK* (Graywolf, 2016); Blunt Research Group, *The Work-Shy* (Wesleyan University Press, 2016); Layli Long Soldier, *WHEREAS: Poems* (Graywolf, 2017); Kenneth Goldsmith, *DAY* (The Figures, 2003).
2. Michael Leong, *Contested Records: The Turn to Documents in Contemporary North American Poetry* (University of Iowa Press, 2020), 1–36.
3. Leong, *Contested Records*, 3–4.
4. The term "conceptual writing"—which I consider as a part of "documental poetry"—was coined in 2003 for *The UbuWeb Anthology of Conceptual Writing* that included works from the 1960s to the present. In the years following, the term became much more focused and was clarified around 2008. Craig Dworkin, "A Note on Conceptualism," *Jacket 2* (blog), September 25, 2013, http://jacket2.org/article/note-conceptualism. Early

definitions of conceptual writing (during this period when it gained focus) include Kenneth Goldsmith, "Paragraphs On Conceptual Writing," *Poetry Foundation* (blog), May 15, 2007, https://www.poetryfoundation.org/harriet-books/2007/05/paragraphs-on-conceptual-writing; Vanessa Place and Robert Fitterman, *Notes on Conceptualisms* (Ugly Duckling Presse, 2009); Marjorie Perloff, *Unoriginal Genius: Poetry by Other Means in the New Century* (University of Chicago Press, 2010). In 2018, Craig Dworkin periodized conceptual writing into phases according to how it engaged with digital material. Craig Dworkin, "Poetry in the Age of Consumer-Generated Content," *Critical Inquiry* 44, no. 4 (June 2018): 674–705.

5. For more on documentary poetry and why it has been distinguished from conceptual poetry, see Mark Nowak, "Documentary Poetics," *Poetry Foundation* (blog), November 9, 2022, https://www.poetryfoundation.org/harriet-books/2010/04/documentary-poetics; Martin Earl, "Documentary Poetry and Language Surge," *Poetry Foundation* (blog), November 10, 2022, https://www.poetryfoundation.org/harriet-books/2010/04/documentary-poetry-and-language-surge.

6. On weakening state funding for universities during this period, see Christopher Newfield, "The Price of Privatization," in *The Great Mistake: How We Wrecked Public Universities and How We Can Fix Them* (Johns Hopkins University Press, 2016), 18–35. On arts and humanities research funding in particular and post-2008, see Asheesh Kapur Siddique, "Does Humanities Research Still Matter?," *Inside Higher Ed*, August 15, 2023, https://www.insidehighered.com/opinion/views/2023/08/15/does-humanities-research-matter-anymore-opinion.

7. On the rise of MFA programs and their relationship to credentialing and employment, see Melissa Korn and Andrea Fuller, "'Financially Hobbled for Life': The Elite Master's Degrees That Don't Pay Off," *Wall Street Journal*, July 8, 2021, https://www.wsj.com/articles/financially-hobbled-for-life-the-elite-masters-degrees-that-dont-pay-off-11625752773; Juliana Spahr and Stephanie Young, "The Program Era and the Mainly White Room," *Los Angeles Review of Books*, September 20, 2015, https://lareviewofbooks.org/article/the-program-era-and-the-mainly-white-room/.

8. Much documental poetry, especially work that has been classified as conceptual writing, copies texts using digital systems. See Jacob Edmond, *Make It the Same: Poetry in the Age of Global Media* (Columbia University Press, 2019), particularly "Copy Rights: Conceptual Writing, the Mongrel Coalition, and the Racial Politics of Digital Media," 151–93, for the politics of copying in and with digital information.

9. Leong, *Contested Records*; Moberley Luger, "The Conceptual Poet as Witness," *Contemporary Literature* 61, no. 4 (Winter 2020): 1–26.

10. "CREDIT by Mathew Timmons—Insert Blanc Press," accessed May 13, 2014, http://www.insertblancpress.net/products/credit-by-mathew-timmons.

11. Annie McClanahan, *Dead Pledges: Debt, Crisis, and Twenty-First-Century Culture* (Stanford University Press, 2017), 90.

12. "CREDIT by Mathew Timmons."

13. Dana Teen Lomax, *Disclosure* (Black Radish, 2011); Brian Kim Stefans, *Bank of America Online Banking* (Citoyen, 2010). For cogent analysis of these and similar projects,

## 5. POETRY AND THE PRIVATIZATION OF INTERPRETATION 207

see Paul Stephens, "Vanguard Total Index: Conceptual Writing, Information Asymmetry, and the Risk Society," *Contemporary Literature* 54, no. 4 (2013): 752–84.

14. Vanessa Place points out that this quotation comes from Wallace Stevens; accompanying the website was a corporate launch at Cage83, a nonprofit gallery; a photo shoot for breaking the ground, and a public relations event. Vanessa Place, email message to author, "Re: Questions about Inc/ Biz," December 4, 2022.

15. Juliana Spahr and Stephanie Young crunch numbers on MFA programs, racial disparity, and debt in the poetry world. Spahr and Young, "The Program Era and the Mainly White Room." On Ivy and prestigious programs in particular, see Korn and Fuller, "Financially Hobbled for Life."

16. Stephanie Young discusses this paradox. Stephanie Young, *Ursula or University* (Krupskaya, 2013), 68. Perhaps responding to these projects cataloging poets as tied to a system of debt, Troll Thread published *Money* by Maker in 2012. Free for download, it contains color images of hundred-dollar bills along with perforation lines for cutting them out. Maker, *Money* (Troll Thread, 2012), https://trollthread.tumblr.com/post/25903051525/maker-money-troll-thread-2012-purchase-color.

17. See Peggy Phelan's critique of Andrea Fraser's *Untitled* about "selling out" and Leigh Claire La Berge on art concerned with art's commodity status and the obfuscation of labor by commodity form. Leigh Claire La Berge, *Wages Against Artwork: Decommodified Labor and the Claims of Socially Engaged Art* (Duke University Press, 2019), 91–100. Vanessa Place herself nuanced this critique in an e-mail to me, in which she wrote, "The poetry Geist, at least then, was that poetry made no money, and arguably, that made it more art than art itself. But it occurred to me that poetry does quite well for itself, with professorships and prizes and honoraria, and poets were being falsely modest or modestly false to think that poetry is not 'a kind of money,' which, as you know, was one of VP, Inc's corporate mottos." Place, "Re: Questions about Inc/ Biz."

18. See Jay David Bolter and Richard Grusin for early inquiry into the purpose and process of digital remediation; Brian Reed takes this discourse to conceptual poetry experiments. Jay David Bolter and Richard Grusin, *Remediation: Understanding New Media* (MIT Press, 1999); Brian M. Reed, *Nobody's Business: Twenty-First Century Avant-Garde Poetics* (Cornell University Press, 2013).

19. "Debit, n.," in *OED Online* (Oxford University Press), accessed October 20, 2022, http://www.oed.com/view/Entry/47888.

20. Republican senators took shifts researching rules and watching Senator Wendy Davis for mistakes. Gretchen Stoeltje, director, *Shouting Down Midnight*, Documentary (2022), https://www.shoutingdownmidnight.com/.

21. A Tweet from then President Barack Obama was instrumental to the event going viral. Stoeltje, *Shouting Down Midnight*.

22. Socialist feminist philosopher Holly Lewis describes the moment this way: "Activists responded to Davis's filibuster by physically occupying the capitol building for a week. That's where the real history was made. It's very difficult for me to imagine this now because, comparatively, it's been crickets since *Roe* fell. But it was a really spirited fight. People were confident, inspired, and determined to win. When the state police told us

we couldn't bring tampons into the building, we just threw tampons everywhere to the point where they banned tampons and they searched us for tampons when we went through the metal detector. There was a festive, spirited atmosphere. It felt like we had all the momentum. Like we were bound to win." She pinpoints the dissipation of momentum after Planned Parenthood and the Democratic Party no longer backed the occupation, instead emphasizing the importance of fighting the battle in court. Camila Valle, Emily Janakriam, and Holly Lewis, "The Fight for Abortion and Reproductive Justice After *Roe*," *Spectre Journal*, September 13, 2022, https://spectrejournal.com/the-fight-for-abortion-and-reproductive-justice-after-roe/.
23. Tim Roberts, phone conversation about *Let Her Speak*, April 13, 2014.
24. Roberts, phone conversation about *Let Her Speak*.
25. Counterpath, "Publication and Readings of *Let Her Speak: Transcript of Texas State Senator Wendy Davis's June 25, 2013, Filibuster of the Texas State Senate*," accessed February 20, 2014, http://counterpathpress.org/let-her-speak-transcript-of-texas-state-sentaor-wendy-daviss-june-25-2013-filibuster-of-the-texas-state-senate.
26. Wendy Davis, *Let Her Speak: Transcript of Texas State Senator Wendy Davis's June 25, 2013, Filibuster of the Texas State Senate* (Counterpath, 2013), 30.
27. Davis, *Let Her Speak*, 1.
28. Barbara Johnson, "Apostrophe, Animation, and Abortion," *Diacritics* 16, no. 1 (1986): 29.
29. Johnson, "Apostrophe, Animation, and Abortion," 30.
30. Davis, *Let Her Speak*, 197.
31. Lauren Berlant, *Cruel Optimism* (Duke University Press, 2011), 25.
32. Berlant, *Cruel Optimism*, 25–26.
33. Berlant, *Cruel Optimism*, 252.
34. Davis, *Let Her Speak*, 157.
35. Davis, *Let Her Speak*, 159.
36. Davis, *Let Her Speak*, 160.
37. Davis, *Let Her Speak*, 162.
38. Davis, *Let Her Speak*, 172.
39. Paul Hitlin, "Research in the Crowdsourcing Age, a Case Study," *Pew Research Center: Internet, Science & Tech* (blog), July 11, 2016, https://www.pewresearch.org/internet/2016/07/11/what-is-mechanical-turk/; Jason Pontin, "Artificial Intelligence, with Help from the Humans," *New York Times*, March 25, 2007, https://www.nytimes.com/2007/03/25/business/yourmoney/25Stream.html?smid=tw-share.
40. Hitlin, "Research in the Crowdsourcing Age."
41. A 2019 *New York Times* exposé allows readers to "try their hand at Turking" to "see how much you would have made and how long it took you." After I read the article, I was told that, based on my work while reading, I could make $2.40/hour, which was more than the author of the article earned while trying his hand at working for the service. Andy Newman, "I Found Work on an Amazon Website. I Made 97 Cents an Hour," *New York Times*, November 15, 2019, sec. New York, https://www.nytimes.com/interactive/2019/11/15/nyregion/amazon-mechanical-turk.html. See also Alana Semuels,

5. POETRY AND THE PRIVATIZATION OF INTERPRETATION 209

"The Online Hell of Amazon's Mechanical Turk," *The Atlantic*, January 23, 2018, https://www.theatlantic.com/business/archive/2018/01/amazon-mechanical-turk/551192/; Mark Harris, "Amazon's Mechanical Turk Workers Protest: 'I Am a Human Being, Not an Algorithm,'" *The Guardian*, December 3, 2014, sec. Technology, https://www.theguardian.com/technology/2014/dec/03/amazon-mechanical-turk-workers-protest-jeff-bezos. The platform is now commonly used for human-subject research. For sample guidelines and issues related to research, see University of Massachusetts Amherst, "MTurk Guidance in Research Administration and Compliance Guidelines," accessed December 1, 2022, https://www.umass.edu/research/guidance/mturk-guidance.

42. "Reading @realDonaldTrump—Counterpath," accessed December 1, 2022, http://counterpathpress.org/reading-realdonaldtrump-series.
43. Lulu, "The United States Has Been Spending Billions of Dollars a Year on Illegal Immigration. This Will Not Continue. Democrats Must Give Us the Votes to Pass Strong (but Fair) Laws. If Not, We Will Be Forced to Play a Much Tougher Hand," accessed December 1, 2022, https://www.lulu.com/shop/counterpath-press/the-united-states-has-been-spending-billions-of-dollars-a-year-on-illegal-immigration-this-will-not-continue-democrats-must-give-us-the-votes-to-pass-strong-but-fair-laws-if-not-we-will-be-forced-to-play-a-much-tougher-hand/paperback/product-23861479.html.
44. Gayatri Chakravorty Spivak, *Death of a Discipline* (Columbia University Press, 2005), 52.
45. Corinne Scheiner, "Teleiopoiesis, Telepoesis, and the Practice of Comparative Literature," *Comparative Literature* 57, no. 3 (July 2005): 241.
46. Margaret Ronda, "Abortion's Poetic Figures," *Post45*, Abortion Now, Abortion Forever (June 2023), https://post45.org/2023/06/abortions-poetic-figures/.
47. Spivak, *Death of a Discipline*, 52.
48. Davis, *Let Her Speak*, 206.
49. *The Texas State Senate Video Archives*, 2013, https://senate.texas.gov/videoplayer.php?vid=17504&lang=en.
50. *The Texas State Senate Video Archives*, 12:30–40.
51. *The Texas State Senate Video Archives*, 12:31:09.
52. *The Texas State Senate Video Archives*, 12:39:49.
53. In a Hollywood version of this event, starring Sandra Bullock, apparently the early drafts of the screenplay also erased Van de Putte's contribution. Oyeniyi Doyin, "Leticia Van de Putte on 'Let Her Speak' and the True Story of the Filibuster," *Texas Monthly*, November 19, 2017, https://www.texasmonthly.com/the-daily-post/let-her-speak/; Justin Kroll, "Sandra Bullock to Star as Wendy Davis in 'Let Her Speak,'" *Variety*, November 9, 2017, https://variety.com/2017/film/news/sandra-bullock-wendy-davis-let-her-speak-1202585780/.
54. M. NourbeSe Philip and Setaey Adamu Boateng, *Zong!* (Wesleyan University Press, 2011), 200.
55. M. NourbeSe Philip, "Jammin' Still," in *Blank: Essays and Interviews* (Book*hug, 2017), 15. Philip discusses her homes and relation to them differently in earlier writings. See M. NourbeSe Philip, *Frontiers: Selected Essays and Writings on Racism and Culture, 1984–1992* (Mercury, 1992); Rachel Zucker, "Commonplace Podcast: M. NourbeSe Philip,"

210   5. POETRY AND THE PRIVATIZATION OF INTERPRETATION

Commonplace, accessed January 6, 2023, https://commonplace.today/commonplace-podcast/episode-84-m-nourbese-philip.

56. Philip, "Jammin' Still."
57. Philip, "Jammin' Still," 15.
58. In 2021, an unauthorized Italian translation of the text did not respect its authorship or its distinctive shapes, or reward the author. Philip spoke out against it, and a Change.org petition was created, urging the press to cease selling copies, remove website content, and issue an apology. Change.org, "A Public Call for the Immediate Destruction of the Unauthorized Translation of 'Zong!,'" accessed January 5, 2023, https://www.change.org/p/benway-series-a-public-call-for-the-immediate-destruction-of-the-unauthorized-translation-of-zong-as-to-aa310152-f535-4cc1-97e5-6ff856fdc593. Philip's blog post from October 2021 explains and documents the issues clearly. M. NourbeSe Philip, "Outline of Events Related to the Unauthorised Translation of *Zong!* As Told to the Author by Setaey Adamu Boateng by Renata Morresi and Benway Series Press," October 11, 2021, https://www.nourbese.com/2021/10/11/.
59. On *Zong!* and lyric form, see Anthony Reed, *Freedom Time: The Poetics and Politics of Black Experimental Writing* (Johns Hopkins University Press, 2014), 32–53; Sarah Dowling, *Translingual Poetics: Writing Personhood Under Settler Colonialism* (University of Iowa Press, 2018), 70–89; Michael Leong, "Conceptualisms in Crisis: The Fate of Late Conceptual Poetry," *Journal of Modern Literature* 41, no. 3 (2018): 109–31; Sonya Posmentier, *Cultivation and Catastrophe: The Lyric Ecology of Modern Black Literature* (Johns Hopkins University Press, 2017), 221. On the silences and gaps as philosophy in particular, see Nicole Gervasio, "The Ruth in (T)Ruth: Redactive Reading and Feminist Provocations to History in M. NourbeSe Philip's *Zong!*," *differences* 30, no. 2 (2019): 1–29.
60. Patricia Saunders, "Defending the Dead, Confronting the Archive: A Conversation with M. NourbeSe Philip," *Small Axe* 12, no. 2 (June 2008): 76.
61. Philip and Boateng, *Zong!*, 197.
62. Although Philip writes about 150 Africans killed, on the court document's account, the exact number is elided. Historian Ian Baucom cites the number of murdered African people as 132. Ian Baucom, *Specters of the Atlantic: Finance Capital, Slavery, and the Philosophy of History* (Duke University Press, 2005), 32.
63. James Walvin, *Black Ivory: Slavery in the British Empire* (Wiley-Blackwell, 2001); Baucom, *Specters of the Atlantic*, 30–32.
64. Baucom, *Specters of the Atlantic*, 7.
65. Philip and Boateng, *Zong!*, 195.
66. Philip and Boateng, *Zong!*, 206.
67. Philip and Boateng, *Zong!*, 198, 201.
68. Philip and Boateng, *Zong!*, 45.
69. Philip used scissors, glue, white out and black out techniques as well as retaining an error that her phone printer created. Philip and Boateng, *Zong!*, 193, 206.
70. Baucom, *Specters of the Atlantic*, 7.
71. Baucom, *Specters of the Atlantic*, 29.
72. Saunders, "Defending the Dead, Confronting the Archive," 76.

## CODA

1. Virginia Jackson and Meredith Martin suggest that, because of Amanda Gorman's 2021 inauguration poem performance, "poetry in public came back in style." Jackson and Martin's interest is in the immediacy of Gorman herself as medium and the process of her performance on the day, which created a specific public audience that is *against* notions of the historical white lyric. Yet, aligning with trends in contemporary scholarship that these critics previously helped seed, the lyric tradition is the public barometer. Virginia Jackson and Meredith Martin, "The Poetry of the Future," *Avidly* (blog), January 29, 2021, https://avidly.lareviewofbooks.org/2021/01/29/the-poetry-of-the-future/.
2. For studies that consider the role of institutions in lyric poetry—or "new lyric studies" and its critiques—see Virginia Jackson, "Lyric," in *The Princeton Encyclopedia of Poetry and Poetics*, ed. Roland Greene, Stephen Cushman, Clare Cavanagh et al. (Princeton University Press, 2012), 826–34; Virginia Jackson and Yopie Prins, "General Introduction," in *The Lyric Theory Reader: A Critical Anthology*, ed. Virginia Jackson and Yopie Prins (Johns Hopkins University Press, 2014), 1–10; Virginia Jackson, "Specters of the Ballad," *Nineteenth-Century Literature* 71, no. 2 (September 2016): 176–96; Virginia Jackson, *Before Modernism: Inventing American Lyric* (Princeton University Press, 2023); Dorothy Wang, *Thinking Its Presence: Form, Race, and Subjectivity in Contemporary Asian American Poetry* (Stanford University Press, 2015); Sarah Dowling, *Translingual Poetics: Writing Personhood Under Settler Colonialism* (University of Iowa Press, 2018); Kamran Javadizadeh, "The Atlantic Ocean Breaking on Our Heads: Claudia Rankine, Robert Lowell, and the Whiteness of the Lyric Subject," *PMLA* 134, no. 3 (May 2019): 475; Lytle Shaw, "Framing the Lyric," *American Literary History* 28, no. 2 (Summer 2016): 403–13; Anthony Reed, *Freedom Time: The Poetics and Politics of Black Experimental Writing* (Johns Hopkins University Press, 2014); Sonya Posmentier, *Cultivation and Catastrophe: The Lyric Ecology of Modern Black Literature* (Johns Hopkins University Press, 2017); Amy Paeth, *The American Poet Laureate: A History of U.S. Poetry and the State* (Columbia University Press, 2023).
3. Wang, *Thinking Its Presence*; Reed, *Freedom Time*; Posmentier, *Cultivation and Catastrophe*; Gillian C. White, *Lyric Shame: The "Lyric" Subject of Contemporary American Poetry* (Harvard University Press, 2014).
4. Claudia Rankine's books with subtitles "An American Lyric" clearly engage the lyric tradition by using interdisciplinary techniques of engaging public forms. Keegan Cook Finberg, "American Lyric, American Surveillance, and Claudia Rankine's *Citizen*," *Contemporary Women's Writing* 15, no. 3 (November 2021): 326–44.
5. Poet-critic Walt Hunter calls this turn to institutional studies "the emergent critical consensus, from Mark McGurl through Dan Sinykin, that institutions are the proper object of analysis for literary criticism." Walt Hunter, "American Poetry and Society," *American Literary History* 36, no. 4 (December 2024): 1146. See notes 2 and 3 for many examples of studies of institution and lyric or post-lyric. Some exceptions to the trend of using "lyric" as a definitional touchstone in studies that focus on institutions and the conditions of

poetry writing include Dowling, *Translingual Poetics*; Christopher Chen, *Literature and Race in the Democracy of Goods: Reading Contemporary Black and Asian North American Poetry* (Bloomsbury Academic, 2022); Candice Amich, *Precarious Forms: Performing Utopia in the Neoliberal Americas* (Northwestern University Press, 2020).

6. For thorough coverage of experimental writing and the positionality of its reception based on an "abstract political 'oppositionality'" and "rooted in a white poetics," see Natalia Aki Cecire, *Experimental: American Literature and the Aesthetics of Knowledge* (Johns Hopkins University Press, 2019), 34–35.

7. The term "documental" here—a portmanteau of conceptual and documentary—is from Michael Leong. The taxonomy allows me to include many types of poetry that engage with public forms, through and beyond different political commitments. Michael Leong, *Contested Records: The Turn to Documents in Contemporary North American Poetry* (University of Iowa Press, 2020), 34. Also see chapter 5 in this book, which is indebted to Leong's work.

8. Kimberly Quiogue Andrews, *The Academic Avant-Garde: Poetry and the American University* (Johns Hopkins University Press, 2023); Christopher Kempf, *Craft Class: The Writing Workshop in American Culture* (John Hopkins University Press, 2022); Paeth, *The American Poet Laureate*.

9. Andrews, *The Academic Avant-Garde*, 11, 8. Andrews discusses several poets that I would consider documental and two that I also write about in this book, Claudia Rankine and Jena Osman. Andrews intentionally separates them, however, from interdisciplinary conceptual and documentary traditions. Andrews, *The Academic Avant-Garde*, 147, 189.

10. For an argument on "the interlocking ways in which state, capital, and academy produced an adaptive hegemony where minority difference was concerned," see Roderick A. Ferguson, *The Reorder of Things: The University and Its Pedagogies of Minority Difference* (University of Minnesota Press, 2012), 6.

11. Erik Baker, "What Are You Going to Do with That? The Future of College in the Asset Economy," *Harper's Magazine*, September 2024, https://harpers.org/archive/2024/09/what-are-you-going-to-do-with-that-erik-baker-college-education/; Dennis M. Hogan and Daniel Denvir, "US Colleges and Universities Are Becoming Giant Exploitation Machines: An Interview with Dennis M. Hogan," *Jacobin*, August 2023, https://jacobin.com/2023/08/us-university-neoliberalism-exploitation-financialization-debt-jobs.

12. La Berge explains the bind: "the gradual availability of credit for students via loans would both ameliorate the difficulty of increasing tuition for individuals and exacerbate the problem collectively, as the availability of loans leads to an inflationary increase in tuition." Leigh Claire La Berge, *Wages Against Artwork: Decommodified Labor and the Claims of Socially Engaged Art* (Duke University Press, 2019), 39.

13. Mark McGurl, *The Program Era: Postwar Fiction and the Rise of Creative Writing* (Harvard University Press, 2009), 16.

14. McGurl, *The Program Era*, 401.

15. McGurl, *The Program Era*, 408.

16. Seth Perlow, *The Poem Electric: Technology and the American Lyric* (University of Minnesota Press, 2018); Paul Stephens, *The Poetics of Information Overload: From Gertrude Stein to Conceptual Writing* (University of Minnesota Press, 2015).

17. For example, Dworkin examines material realities of the production of texts by Judith Goldman and Holly Melgard, written ten years apart. Although he examines the technological, economic, and literary trends fueling each, he does not discuss each poem's relation to academia. Goldman has been fully employed within prestigious academic programs in poetics for many years; although Melgard earned a PhD from Buffalo poetics (under Goldman's direction) and ran several experimental publishing collectives, she is an adjunct at multiple New York City universities and makes her living as a freelance book designer. An article with a very different focus might use Goldman's 2001 text and Melgard's 2015 text to think about how the political economy of poetry and criticism has changed since the economic recession.

18. "Against Expression" is the name of the first major anthology of conceptual writing. Kenneth Goldsmith famously proclaimed conceptual writing "uncreative," suggesting it only replicates, copies, or appropriates other texts. Kenneth Goldsmith, *Uncreative Writing: Managing Language in the Digital Age* (Columbia University Press, 2011). For essays that characterize the debate about whether conceptual writing contains feeling, and whether that is important, see Calvin Bedient, "Against Conceptualism," *Boston Review*, July 24, 2013, http://bostonreview.net/poetry/against-conceptualism; Amy King, "Beauty and the Beastly Po-Biz, Part 1," *The Rumpus* (blog), July 15, 2013, http://therumpus.net/2013/07/beauty-and-the-beastly-po-biz-part-1/; Amy King, "Beauty and the Beastly Po-Biz, Part 2," *The Rumpus* (blog), July 16, 2013, http://therumpus.net/2013/07/beauty-and-the-beastly-po-biz-part-2/; Robert Archambeau, "Charmless and Interesting: What Conceptual Poetry Lacks and What It's Got," *Harriet: The Blog* (blog), August 2, 2013, http://www.poetryfoundation.org/harriet/2013/08/charming-and-interesting-what-conceptual-poetry-lacks-and-what-its-got/; Kent Johnson, "Notes on Safe Conceptualisms," *Lana Turner Journal Blog* (blog), April 2013, http://www.lanaturnerjournal.com/contents-current/kent-johnson-notes-on-safe-conceptualisms; Kristen Gallagher, "Why Cry? A Question for Diana Hamilton," *Jacket2* (blog), February 26, 2013, http://jacket2.org/commentary/why-cry; Susan M. Schultz, "Tinfish Editor's Blog: Conceptualism as Affect: Or, a Defense of Both at Once," *Tinfish Editor's Blog* (blog), July 27, 2013, http://tinfisheditor.blogspot.com/2013/07/conceptualism-as-affect-or-defense-of.html; Sina Queyras, "Lyric Conceptualism: A Manifesto in Progress," *Harriet: The Blog* (blog), April 2012, http://www.poetryfoundation.org/harriet/2012/04/lyric-conceptualism-a-manifesto-in-progress/.

19. Johanna Drucker, "Beyond Conceptualisms: Poetics After Critique and the End of the Individual Voice," *Poetry Project Newsletter*, no. 231 (April–May 2012): 6–9; Vanessa Place, "Poetry Is Dead, I Killed It: An Essay by Vanessa Place," *Harriet: The Blog* (blog), accessed February 20, 2014, http://www.poetryfoundation.org/harriet/2012/04/poetry-is-dead-i-killed-it/. Michael Leong has argued that the period of 2008 to 2012 brought conceptual poetry to a "thanotopetic turn" as it obsessed over its own death as well as "the saturation of images of death in social and mainstream media" that characterized

this period. Micheal Leong, "Conceptualisms in Crisis: The Fate of Late Conceptual Poetry," *Journal of Modern Literature* 41, no. 3 (2018): 111. For nuance about the term "appropriation" in conceptual writing discourse and its relation to dispossession, see Sarah Dowling, "Property, Priority, Place: Rethinking the Poetics of Appropriation," *Contemporary Literature* 60, no. 1 (Spring 2019): 98–125.

20. Craig Dworkin and Kenneth Goldsmith, eds., *Against Expression: An Anthology of Conceptual Writing* (Northwestern University Press, 2011); Caroline Bergvall, Laynie Browne, Teresa Carmody, and Vanessa Place, eds., *I'll Drown My Book: Conceptual Writing by Women* (Les Figues, 2012). I do not wish to conflate these anthologies. Les Figues is a small nonprofit press in Los Angeles that publishes experimental literature. In addition to being much larger and better funded, Northwestern, as a university press, carries a standard prestige within academia that Les Figues lacks.

21. For a thorough treatment of this work as a racist poem, and the nuance of the backlash, see Jacob Edmond, "Copy Rights: Conceptual Writing, the Mongrel Coalition, and the Racial Politics of Digital Media," in *Make It the Same: Poetry in the Age of Global Media* (Columbia University Press, 2019), 151–93; Leong, "Conceptualisms in Crisis."

22. Joshua Clover has dissected conceptual poetry's interest in the glut of digital information into several parts that amount to an accusation that work of this kind is fueled by capitalist utopian technophoria based on false promises of economic booms. He argues that works by Kenneth Goldsmith and Christian Bok, or "brand-name conceptualism," as he calls it, buy into myths of automation and even that this poetry works to mystify and conceal labor, aestheticizing the very contradictions of capitalist accumulation. Joshua Clover, "The Technical Composition of Conceptualism," *Mute* (blog), April 2, 2014, http://www.metamute.org/editorial/articles/technical-composition-conceptualism.

23. This methods crisis is also material. See Toril Moi, "Crisis in the Profession, or the Failure to Imagine the New," *American Literary History* 36, no. 4 (December 2024): 1161–82; Andy Hines, "Working Critics," *Modern Language Quarterly* 85, no. 2 (June 2024): 205–29.

24. Patricia Stuelke, *The Ruse of Repair: US Neoliberal Empire and the Turn from Critique* (Duke University Press, 2021), 9.

25. Stuelke, *The Ruse of Repair*, 15.

26. The debates about feeling contained in conceptual writing ran parallel with (and rarely touched) debates about feeling contained in literary interpretation and method. An early key moment in the scholarly discussion of affective reading practices was Eve Kosofsky Sedgwick, "Paranoid Reading and Reparative Reading, or, You're So Paranoid, You Probably Think This Essay Is About You," in *Touching Feeling: Affect, Pedagogy, Performativity* (Duke University Press, 2003), 123–54. See also Stephen Best and Sharon Marcus, "Surface Reading: An Introduction," *Representations* 108, no. 1 (November 2009): 1–21; Heather Love, "Close but Not Deep: Literary Ethics and the Descriptive Turn," *New Literary History* 41, no. 2 (2010): 371–91.

27. Stephanie Young, *Ursula or University* (Krupskaya, 2013), 68.

28. Young, *Ursula or University*, 37,39.

29. Claudia Rankine, *Citizen: An American Lyric* (Graywolf, 2014) was a finalist for the National Book Critics Circle award in the categories of criticism and poetry (it won for

poetry). There has been much excellent scholarship about it. For a scholarly take on *Citizen* in and against the lyric tradition, see Javadizadeh, "The Atlantic Ocean Breaking on Our Heads." For my own writing on *Citizen* as experimental, interdisciplinary poetry, see Finberg, "American Lyric, American Surveillance, and Claudia Rankine's Citizen."

30. Tayna Lukin Linklater, *Slow Scrape* (Center for Expanded Poetics and Anteism, 2021), 51.
31. Linklater, *Slow Scrape*, 3.
32. Kenji C. Liu, *Map of an Onion* (Inlandia Institute, 2016), 3.
33. Liu, *Map of an Onion*, 3.
34. Liu, *Map of an Onion*, 4.
35. Liu, *Map of an Onion*, 25.
36. Don Mee Choi, *DMZ Colony* (Wave, 2020), 5–6.
37. Choi, *DMZ Colony*, 99.
38. Choi, *DMZ Colony*, 123.
39. Choi, *DMZ Colony*, 6, 123.
40. Lena Chen, personal conversation on Zoom, November 12, 2024; Lena Chen, "We Lived in the Gaps Between the Stories: Performing the Radical Care Work of Abortion," *Public* 35, no. 69 (April 2024): 53–56.
41. Lena Chen, "We Lived in the Gaps Between the Stories," Lenachen.com, May 2021, https://www.lenachen.com/we-lived-in-the-gaps-between-the-stories/.
42. Chen, "We Lived in the Gaps Between the Stories," May 2021.
43. Chen, personal conversation on Zoom, November 12, 2024.
44. Chen, personal conversation on Zoom, November 12, 2024.
45. Chen, "We Lived in the Gaps Between the Stories," May 2021.
46. Here I am referencing the Stephanie Young quotation from earlier in this coda and also Stefano Harney and Fred Moten's description of the "path of the subversive intellectual in the modern university," which is "to abuse its hospitality, to spite its mission, to join its refugee colony, its gypsy encampment, to be in but not of." Stefano Harney and Fred Moten, *The Undercommons: Fugitive Planning & Black Study* (Autonomedia, 2013), 26; Young, *Ursula or University*, 39.
47. Holly Melgard, *Fetal Position* (Roof, 2021), 37.
48. Melgard, *Fetal Position*, 62–63.
49. Melgard, *Fetal Position*, 57–59.
50. Melgard, *Fetal Position*, 13.
51. Melgard, *Fetal Position*, 107.
52. Vanessa Jimenez Gabb, "You and Me, Forever," in *Basic Needs* (Rescue, 2021), 71.
53. Christina Drill, "Poems for the Final Scene in Fight Club: An Interview with Vanessa Jimenez Gabb," *Chicago Review of Books* (blog), November 19, 2021, https://chireviewofbooks.com/2021/11/19/poems-for-the-final-scene-in-fight-club-an-interview-with-vanessa-jimenez-gabb/.
54. Gabb, "You and Me, Forever," 82.
55. McGurl, *The Program Era*, 408.
56. This language is adapted from Ferguson, *The Reorder of Things*, 230–32.
57. Ferguson, *The Reorder of Things*, 232.

# BIBLIOGRAPHY

### ARCHIVAL SOURCES

#### ARCHIVES OF AMERICAN ART, SMITHSONIAN INSTITUTION

Archives of American Art, Oral History Program
The Henri Gallery records

#### ART INSTITUTE OF CHICAGO

Eleanor Antin Curatorial Files, Department of Modern and Contemporary Art

#### FALES LIBRARY AND SPECIAL COLLECTIONS, NEW YORK UNIVERSITY

Judson Memorial Church Archive
Lines Archive

#### HARVARD ART MUSEUM AND SPECIAL COLLECTIONS

Barbara and Peter Moore Fluxus Collection

#### HENRY W. AND ALBERT A. BERG COLLECTION OF ENGLISH AND AMERICAN LITERATURE, NEW YORK PUBLIC LIBRARY

Frank O'Hara collection of papers
Kenneth Koch papers

## MUSEUM OF MODERN ART ARCHIVES

Frank O'Hara papers
Gilbert and Lila Silverman Fluxus Collection Archive

## SPECIAL COLLECTIONS AT
## THE GETTY RESEARCH INSTITUTE

Jean Brown papers

## SPECIAL COLLECTIONS AT McHENRY LIBRARY,
## UNIVERSITY OF CALIFORNIA, SANTA CRUZ

Artist Books and Fluxus Archive

## SPECIAL COLLECTIONS AT THE UNIVERSITY OF MARYLAND,
## BALTIMORE COUNTY

Dick Higgins Collection

## THOMAS ERBEN GALLERY

Adrian Piper's works

## PUBLISHED SOURCES

Abramson, Daniel M. *Obsolescence: An Architectural History*. University of Chicago Press, 2016.
Allen, Austin. "'My Beautiful Never-Nevers': Yoko Ono's Poetry Revisited." *Los Angeles Review of Books*, April 4, 2022. https://lareviewofbooks.org/article/my-beautiful-never-nevers-yoko-onos-poetry-revisited/.
Allen, Donald. *The New American Poetry 1945–1960*. Grove, 1960.
Amich, Candice. *Precarious Forms: Performing Utopia in the Neoliberal Americas*. Northwestern University Press, 2020.
Andrews, Kimberly Quiogue. *The Academic Avant-Garde: Poetry and the American University*. Johns Hopkins University Press, 2023.
Antin, David. "The Stranger at the Door." In *Radical Coherency: Selected Essays on Art and Literature, 1966 to 2005*, 239–58. University of Chicago Press, 2011.
Antin, Eleanor. "An Autobiography of the Artist as an Autobiographer." *Los Angeles Institute of Contemporary Art* 2 (October 1974): 18–20.
Antin, Eleanor. *Conversations with Stalin*. Green Integer, 2013.
Antin, Eleanor. "Oral History Interview with Eleanor Antin, 2009 May 8–9." Archives of American Art, Smithsonian Institution. Accessed October 12, 2021. https://www.aaa.si.edu/collections/interviews/oral-history-interview-eleanor-antin-15792.

Archambeau, Robert. "Charmless and Interesting: What Conceptual Poetry Lacks and What It's Got." *Harriet: The Blog* (blog), August 2, 2013. http://www.poetryfoundation.org/harriet/2013/08/charming-and-interesting-what-conceptual-poetry-lacks-and-what-its-got/.
Armstrong, Amanda. "The Wooden Brain: Organizing Untimeliness in Marx's Capital." *Mediations: Journal of the Marxist Literary Group* 31, no. 1 (Fall 2017): 3–26.
Arndt, Richard T. *The First Resort of Kings: American Cultural Diplomacy in the Twentieth Century*. Potomac, 2005.
Aronova, Elena. "Recent Trends in the Historiography of Science in the Cold War." *Historical Studies in the Natural Sciences* 47, no. 4 (September 2017): 568–77.
Ashbery, John. "Idaho." *Locus Solus* 1 (Winter 1961): 55–60.
Ashbery, John. "The New Realism." *Locus Solus* 3–4 (Winter 1962): 184–90.
Aso, Noriko. "Sumptuous Re-Past: The 1964 Tokyo Olympics Arts Festival." *Positions: East Asia Cultures Critique* 10, no. 1 (March 2002): 7–38.
Baetens, Jan, and Jean-Jacques Poucel. "Introduction: The Challenge of Constraint." *Poetics Today* 30, no. 4 (December 2009): 611–34.
Baker, Erik. "What Are You Going to Do with That? The Future of College in the Asset Economy." *Harper's Magazine*, September 2024. https://harpers.org/archive/2024/09/what-are-you-going-to-do-with-that-erik-baker-college-education/.
Barnhisel, Greg. *Cold War Modernists: Art, Literature, and American Cultural Diplomacy, 1946–1959*. Columbia University Press, 2015.
Barnhisel, Greg. "*Perspectives USA* and the Cultural Cold War: Modernism in Service of the State." *Modernism/Modernity* 14, no. 4 (2007): 729–54.
Baucom, Ian. *Specters of the Atlantic: Finance Capital, Slavery, and the Philosophy of History*. Duke University Press, 2005.
Beck, John, and Ryan Bishop. *Technocrats of the Imagination: Art, Technology, and the Military-Industrial Avant-Garde*. Duke University Press, 2020.
Bedient, Calvin. "Against Conceptualism." *Boston Review*, July 24, 2013. http://bostonreview.net/poetry/against-conceptualism.
Benanav, Aaron. *Automation and the Future of Work*. Verso, 2020.
Bennett, Robert. *Deconstructing Post-WWII New York City: The Literature, Art, Jazz, and Architecture of an Emerging Global Capital*. Routledge, 2003.
Berger, Maurice, ed. *Adrian Piper: A Retrospective*. Issues in Cultural Theory 3. Fine Arts Gallery, University of Maryland, 1999.
Berger, Maurice. "The Critique of Pure Racism: An Interview with Adrian Piper." In *Adrian Piper: A Retrospective*, edited by Maurice Berger, 76–100. Fine Arts Gallery, University of Maryland, 1999.
Bergvall, Caroline, Laynie Browne, Teresa Carmody, and Vanessa Place, eds. *I'll Drown My Book: Conceptual Writing by Women*. Les Figues, 2012.
Berlant, Lauren. *Cruel Optimism*. Duke University Press, 2011.
Bernes, Jasper. *The Work of Art in the Age of Deindustrialization*. Stanford University Press, 2017.
Best, Stephen, and Sharon Marcus. "Surface Reading: An Introduction." *Representations* 108, no. 1 (November 2009): 1–21.

Biesenbach, Klaus, Christophe Cherix, Julia Bryan-Wilson et al., eds. *Yoko Ono: One Woman Show, 1960–1971*. Museum of Modern Art, 2015.

Blackwelder, Julia Kirk. *Now Hiring: The Feminization of Work in the United States, 1900–1995*. Texas A&M University Press, 1997.

Blair, Sara. "Home Truths: Gertrude Stein, 27 Rue de Fleurus, and the Place of the Avant-Garde." *American Literary History* 12, no. 3 (2000): 417–37.

Blasing, Mutlu Konuk. *Politics and Form in Postmodern Poetry: O'Hara, Bishop, Ashbery, and Merrill*. Cambridge University Press, 1995.

Blocker, Jane. *What the Body Cost: Desire, History, and Performance*. University of Minnesota Press, 2004.

Bloom, Lisa. "Contests for Meaning in Body Politics and Feminist Conceptual Art: Revisioning the 1970s Through the Work of Eleanor Antin." In *Performing the Body/Performing the Text*, edited by Amelia Jones and Andrew Stephenson, 153–69. Routledge, 1999.

Bloom, Lisa. "Rewriting the Script: Eleanor Antin's Feminist Art." In *Eleanor Antin*, edited by Howard N. Fox, 159–90. Los Angeles County Museum of Art, 1999.

Blunt Research Group. *The Work-Shy*. Wesleyan University Press, 2016.

Bois, Yve-Alain. "On George Brecht (Review: 'George Brecht Events: A Heterospective')." *Art Forum*, April 2006. https://www.artforum.com/print/reviews/200604/george-brecht-10622.

Boltanski, Luc, and Eve Chiapello. *The New Spirit of Capitalism*. Translated by Gregory Elliott. Verso, 2018.

Bolter, Jay David, and Richard Grusin. *Remediation: Understanding New Media*. MIT Press, 1999.

Boudin, Jean. "Second Story Brownstone." *Locus Solus* 3–4 (Winter 1962): 92.

Bowles, John Parish. *Adrian Piper: Race, Gender, and Embodiment*. Duke University Press, 2011.

Brady, Andrea. *Poetry and Bondage: A History and Theory of Lyric Constraint*. Cambridge University Press, 2021.

Braverman, Harry. *Labor and Monopoly Capital: The Degradation of Work in the Twentieth Century*. Monthly Review Press, 1998.

Brecht, George. "Events (Assembled Notes)." In *Heterospective*, edited by Julia Robinson, 224–26. Walther König, 2005.

Brecht, George. *Notebooks 1–3*, edited by Dieter Daniels. Walther König, 1991.

Brecht, George. *Water Yam*. Fluxus, 1963.

Brecht, George, and Julia Robinson. *George Brecht: events: eine Heterospektive = a heterospective*. Walther König, 2005.

Brenner, Robert, and Jeong Seong-jin. "Overproduction Not Financial Collapse Is the Heart of the Crisis: The US, East Asia, and the World." *Asia-Pacific Journal: Japan Focus* 7, no. 6 (2009). https://apjjf.org/-Robert-Brenner/3043/article.html.

Brill, Dorothée. *Shock and the Senseless in Dada and Fluxus*. Dartmouth College Press, 2010.

Brown, Jenny. *Without Apology: The Abortion Struggle Now*. Verso, 2019.

Brown, Wendy. *Undoing the Demos: Neoliberalism's Stealth Revolution*. Zone, 2017.

Bryan-Wilson, Julia. *Art Workers: Radical Practice in the Vietnam War Era*. University of California Press, 2009.

Bryan-Wilson, Julia. *Fray*. University of Chicago Press, 2017.

Bryan-Wilson, Julia. "Occupational Realism." *TDR* 56, no. 4 (2012): 32–48.
Bryan-Wilson, Julia. "Remembering Yoko Ono's 'Cut Piece.'" *Oxford Art Journal* 26, no. 1 (2003): 99–123.
Buchloh, Benjamin. "Conceptual Art 1962–1969: From the Aesthetic of Administration to the Critique of Institutions." *October* 55 (December 1990): 105–43.
Buchloh, Benjamin, Judith F. Rodenbeck, and Robert E. Haywood. *Experiments in the Everyday: Allan Kaprow and Robert Watts, Events, Objects, Documents*. Columbia University/Miriam and Ira D. Wallach Art Gallery, 1999.
Buchloh, Benjamin, Rosalind Krauss, Alexander Alberro, Thierry de Duve, Martha Buskirk, and Yve-Alain Bois. "Conceptual Art and the Reception of Duchamp." *October* 70 (October 1994): 127–46.
Burden-Stelly, Charisse. "Modern U.S. Racial Capitalism: Some Theoretical Insights." *Monthly Review* (July 2020): 8–20.
Burstow, Robert. "The Limits of Modernist Art as a 'Weapon of the Cold War': Reassessing the Unknown Patron of the Monument to the Unknown Political Prisoner." *Oxford Art Journal* 20, no. 1 (January 1997): 68–80.
Butler, Alice. "Eleanor Antin on Art, Ageing and Grief." *Frieze* (blog), May 29, 2019. https://www.frieze.com/article/eleanor-antin-art-ageing-and-grief.
Butler, Cornelia H. *From Conceptualism to Feminism: Lucy Lippard's Numbers Shows, 1969–74*. Afterall, 2012.
Cacho, Lisa Marie. *Social Death: Racialized Rightlessness and the Criminalization of the Unprotected*. New York University Press, 2012.
Callahan, John P. "Values Stressed for a Nuclear Age: Frost, Russell, Montagu and Others Fear Alternative at Seagram Symposium." *New York Times*, September 30, 1959.
Carroll, Rachel Jane. *For Pleasure: Race, Experimentalism, and Aesthetics*. New York University Press, 2023.
Caute, David. *The Dancer Defects: The Struggle for Cultural Supremacy During the Cold War*. Oxford University Press, 2003.
Cavell, Stanley. "Aesthetic Problems of Modern Philosophy." In *Must We Mean What We Say? A Book of Essays*, 73–96. Cambridge University Press, 2002.
Cecire, Natalia Aki. *Experimental: American Literature and the Aesthetics of Knowledge*. Johns Hopkins University Press, 2019.
Cecire, Natalia Aki. "Experimentalism by Contact." *Diacritics* 43, no. 1 (2015): 6–35.
Cecire, Natalia Aki. "Ways of Not Reading Gertrude Stein." *ELH* 82, no. 1 (2015): 281–312.
Change.org. "A Public Call for the Immediate Destruction of the Unauthorized Translation of 'Zong!'" Accessed January 5, 2023. https://www.change.org/p/benway-series-a-public-call-for-the-immediate-destruction-of-the-unauthorized-translation-of-zong-as-to-aa310152-f535-4cc1-97e5-6ff856fdc593.
Chen, Christopher. *Literature and Race in the Democracy of Goods: Reading Contemporary Black and Asian North American Poetry*. Bloomsbury Academic, 2022.
Chen, Lena. "We Lived in the Gaps Between the Stories." Lenachen.com, May 2021. https://www.lenachen.com/we-lived-in-the-gaps-between-the-stories/.

Chen, Lena. "We Lived in the Gaps Between the Stories: Performing the Radical Care Work of Abortion." *Public* 35, no. 69 (April 2024): 53–56.

Cherix, Christophe. "Yoko Ono's 22 Instructions for Paintings." *Museum of Modern Art Magazine*, May 2019. https://www.moma.org/magazine/articles/61.

Chiaki, Nagano, and Midori Yoshimoto. "Some Young People—From Nonfiction Theater." *Review of Japanese Culture and Society* 17 (2005): 98–105.

Choi, Don Mee. *DMZ Colony*. Wave, 2020.

Clay, Steven, and Rodney Phillips. *A Secret Location on the Lower East Side: Adventures in Writing, 1960–1980: A Sourcebook of Information*. Granary, 1998.

Clover, Joshua. "The Technical Composition of Conceptualism." *Mute* (blog), April 2, 2014. http://www.metamute.org/editorial/articles/technical-composition-conceptualism.

Clune, Michael. *American Literature and the Free Market, 1945–2000*. Cambridge University Press, 2009.

Cohen, Brigid. "Limits of National History: Yoko Ono, Stefan Wolpe, and Dilemmas of Cosmopolitanism." *Musical Quarterly* 97, no. 2 (2014): 181–237.

Cohen, Brigid. "Ono in Opera: A Politics of Art and Action, 1960–1962." *ASAP/Journal* 3, no. 1 (February 17, 2018): 41–66.

Cohen, Lizabeth. *A Consumers' Republic: The Politics of Mass Consumption in Postwar America*. Vintage, 2003.

Concannon, Kevin. "Yoko Ono's 'Cut Piece': From Text to Performance and Back Again." *PAJ: A Journal of Performance and Art* 30, no. 3 (2008): 81–93.

Consenstein, Peter. *Literary Memory, Consciousness, and the Group Oulipo*. Rodopi, 2002.

Conte, Joseph M. *Unending Design: The Forms of Postmodern Poetry*. Cornell University Press, 1991.

Cooper, Melinda. *Family Values: Between Neoliberalism and the New Social Conservatism*. Zone, 2017.

Corso, Gregory. "CUT UP of Eisenhower Speech & Mine Own Poem." In *Minutes to Go*, edited by Sinclair Beiles et al., 33. Beach Books, Texts, & Documents, 1968.

Corso, Gregory and Dwight Eisenhower. "Cut Up," *Locus Solus II*, (Summer 1961): 152.

Cottingham, Laura. "The 'Autobiography' of Adrian Piper." In *Adrian Piper: A Retrospective*, edited by Maurice Berger, 61–75. Fine Arts Gallery, University of Maryland, 1999.

Counterpath. "Publication and Readings of *Let Her Speak: Transcript of Texas State Senator Wendy Davis's June 25, 2013, Filibuster of the Texas State Senate*." Accessed February 20, 2014. http://counterpathpress.org/let-her-speak-transcript-of-texas-state-sentaor-wendy-daviss-june-25-2013-filibuster-of-the-texas-state-senate.

"CREDIT by Mathew Timmons—Insert Blanc Press." Accessed May 13, 2014. http://www.insertblancpress.net/products/credit-by-mathew-timmons.

Critchlow, Donald T. *Intended Consequences: Birth Control, Abortion, and the Federal Government in Modern America*. Oxford University Press, 2001.

Culler, Jonathan. *Theory of the Lyric*. Harvard University Press, 2015.

Cura. "Eleanor Antin in Conversation with Vincent Honore." Curamagazine.com, March 2018. Accessed August 12, 2021. https://curamagazine.com/digital/eleanor-antin/.

Davidson, Michael. *Guys Like Us: Citing Masculinity in Cold War Poetics*. University of Chicago Press, 2004.

Davis, Wendy. *Let Her Speak: Transcript of Texas State Senator Wendy Davis's June 25, 2013, Filibuster of the Texas State Senate*. Counterpath, 2013.
de Duve, Thierry. "Don't Shoot the Messenger: Thierry de Duve on Duchamp Syllogism." *Art Forum International* 52, no. 3 (November 2013): 264–73.
de Duve, Thierry. *Duchamp's Telegram: From Beaux-Arts to Art-in-General*. Reaktion/University of Chicago Press, 2023.
de Duve, Thierry. "The Invention of Non-Art: A History." *Art Forum International* 52, no. 5 (February 2014): 192–99.
de Duve, Thierry. *Kant After Duchamp*. MIT Press, 1996.
de Duve, Thierry. "Pardon My French: Theirry de Duve on the Invention of Art." *Art Forum International* 52, no. 2 (October 2013): 246–53.
de Duve, Thierry. *Sewn in the Sweatshops of Marx: Beuys, Warhol, Klein, Duchamp*. Translated by Rosalind E. Krauss. University of Chicago Press, 2012.
de Duve, Thierry. "Why Was Modernism Born in France? Thierry de Duve on the Collapse of the Beaux-Arts System." *Art Forum International* 52, no. 5 (January 2014): 190–235.
Deleuze, Gilles. *Kafka: Toward a Minor Literature*. Translated by Dana Polan. University of Minnesota Press, 1986.
Derrida, Jacques. *Specters of Marx: The State of the Debt, the Work of Mourning and the New International*. Translated by Peggy Kamuf. Routledge, 2006.
Dezeuze, Anna. "Origins of the Fluxus Score." *Performance Research* 7, no. 3 (January 2002): 78–94.
Diggory, Terrence. "Picturesque Urban Pastoral in Post-War New York City." In *The Built Surface Vol 2*, edited by Karen Koehler, 282–303. Ashgate, 2002.
Diggory, Terrence, and Stephen Miller, eds. *The Scene of My Selves*. National Poetry Foundation, 2001.
Dower, John W. "Preface." In *Inside GHQ: The Allied Occupation of Japan and Its Legacy*, by Eiji Takemae, translated by Robert Ricketts and Sebastian Swann, xix–xxv. Continuum, 2002.
Dower, John W. *Embracing Defeat: Japan in the Wake of World War II*. Norton, 2000.
Dowling, Sarah. *Here Is a Figure: Grounding Literary Form*. Northwestern University Press, 2024.
Dowling, Sarah. "Property, Priority, Place: Rethinking the Poetics of Appropriation." *Contemporary Literature* 60, no. 1 (Spring 2019): 98–125.
Dowling, Sarah. *Translingual Poetics: Writing Personhood Under Settler Colonialism*. University of Iowa Press, 2018.
Doyin, Oyeniyi. "Leticia Van de Putte on 'Let Her Speak' and the True Story of the Filibuster." *Texas Monthly*, November 19, 2017. https://www.texasmonthly.com/the-daily-post/let-her-speak/.
Drill, Christina. "Poems for the Final Scene in Fight Club: An Interview with Vanessa Jimenez Gabb." *Chicago Review of Books* (blog), November 19, 2021. https://chireviewofbooks.com/2021/11/19/poems-for-the-final-scene-in-fight-club-an-interview-with-vanessa-jimenez-gabb/.
Drucker, Johanna. "Beyond Conceptualisms: Poetics After Critique and the End of the Individual Voice." *Poetry Project Newsletter*, no. 231 (April–May 2012): 6–9.
Drucker, Johanna. "Experimental Writing (or Poetry Lab)." In *The Noulipian Analects*, edited by Matais Viegener and Christine Wertheim, 75. Les Figues, 2007.

Drucker, Johanna. "Readers, Which Brings Us to The." In *The Noulipian Analects*, edited by Matais Viegener and Christine Wertheim, 178–79. Les Figues, 2007.
Duggan, Lisa. *The Twilight of Equality? Neoliberalism, Cultural Politics, and the Attack on Democracy.* Beacon, 2004.
Dumett, Mari. *Corporate Imaginations: Fluxus Strategies for Living.* University of California Press, 2017.
Dumett, Mari. "George Brecht: Scoring Events." In *Corporate Imaginations: Fluxus Strategies for Living*, 126–69. University of California Press, 2017.
Dumett, Mari. "The Great Executive Dream: George Maciunas, Adriano Olivetti, and Fluxus Incorporated." *RES: Anthropology and Aesthetics*, no. 53/54 (2008): 314–20.
Dworkin, Craig. *Dictionary Poetics: Toward a Radical Lexicography.* Fordham University Press, 2020.
Dworkin, Craig. *No Medium.* MIT Press, 2013.
Dworkin, Craig. "A Note on Conceptualism." *Jacket 2* (blog), September 25, 2013. http://jacket2.org/article/note-conceptualism.
Dworkin, Craig. "Poetry in the Age of Consumer-Generated Content." *Critical Inquiry* 44, no. 4 (June 2018): 674–705.
Dworkin, Craig. *Radium of the Word: A Poetics of Materiality.* University of Chicago Press, 2020.
Dworkin, Craig, and Kenneth Goldsmith, eds. *Against Expression: An Anthology of Conceptual Writing.* Northwestern University Press, 2011.
Earl, Martin. "Documentary Poetry and Language Surge." *Poetry Foundation* (blog), November 10, 2022. https://www.poetryfoundation.org/harriet-books/2010/04/documentary-poetry-and-language-surge.
Eco, Umberto. *The Open Work.* Translated by Anna Cancogni. Harvard University Press, 1989.
Edmond, Jacob. *Make It the Same: Poetry in the Age of Global Media.* Columbia University Press, 2019.
Emre, Merve. *Paraliterary: The Making of Bad Readers in Postwar America.* University of Chicago Press, 2017.
*Encyclopedia of the New York School Poets.* Facts on File Library of American Literature. Facts on File, 2009.
*Endnotes.* "The Logic of Gender: On the Separation of Spheres and the Process of Abjection." *Endnotes*, no. 3 (September 2013). https://endnotes.org.uk/issues/3/en/endnotes-the-logic-of-gender.
Epstein, Andrew. *Beautiful Enemies: Friendship and Postwar American Poetry.* Oxford University Press, 2006.
Federici, Silvia. *Caliban and the Witch.* Autonomedia, 2014.
Federici, Silvia. "Wages Against Housework." In *Revolution at Point Zero: Housework, Reproduction, and Feminist Struggle*, 11–18. PM Press, 2020.
Ferguson, Roderick A. *The Reorder of Things: The University and Its Pedagogies of Minority Difference.* University of Minnesota Press, 2012.
Field, Edward. *The Man Who Would Marry Susan Sontag and Other Intimate Portraits of the Bohemian Era.* University of Wisconsin Press, 2005.
Fifth Avenue Association, New York. *Fifty Years on Fifth, 1907–1957.* International Press, 1957.

Filreis, Alan. *1960: The Politics and Art of the Postwar Avant-Garde*. Columbia University Press, 2021.

Filreis, Al. "The End of Poetic Ideology, 1960." In *The Oxford Handbook of Modern and Contemporary American Poetry*, edited by Cary Nelson, 507–529. Oxford University Press, 2012.

Finberg, Keegan Cook. "American Lyric, American Surveillance, and Claudia Rankine's *Citizen*." *Contemporary Women's Writing* 15, no. 3 (November 2021): 326–44.

Finberg, Keegan Cook. "Assimilating the Arts: On Poetry and Difference in Yoko Ono's *Grapefruit*." *Amodern* 11: *Body and/as Procedure*, October 2023. https://amodern.net/article/assimilating-the-arts/.

Finberg, Keegan Cook. "Frank O'Hara Rebuilds the Seagram Building: A Radical Poetry of Event." *Textual Practice* 30, no. 1 (February 2016): 113–42.

Finberg, Keegan Cook. "All the Women in the State of Texas." In "'Symposium: Repetition.' A Discussion About (Usually) Books as They Relate to a Theme of Contemporary Interest." *The Believer*, no. 115 (October/November 2017): 74–75. https://www.thebeliever.net/repetition/.

Firestone, Shulamith. *The Dialectic of Sex: The Case for Feminist Revolution*. Bantam, 1970.

Fitch, Andy. "An Interview with Craig Dworkin." *The Volta: Tremolo, Issue 4* (blog). Accessed April 3, 2015. http://www.thevolta.org/tremolo-issue4-cdworkin.html.

Fitterman, Robert. *Holocaust Museum*. Counterpath, 2013.

Flatley, Jonathan. "How a Revolutionary Counter-Mood Is Made." *New Literary History* 43, no. 3 (November 2012): 503–25.

Flowers, Benjamin Sitton. *Skyscraper: The Politics and Power of Building New York City in the Twentieth Century*. University of Pennsylvania Press, 2009.

Fox, Howard N. *Eleanor Antin*. Los Angeles County Museum of Art, 1999.

Fox, Howard N. "Waiting in the Wings: Desire and Destiny in the Art of Eleanor Antin." In *Eleanor Antin*, edited by Howard N. Fox, 15–158. Los Angeles County Museum of Art, 1999.

Frascina, Francis. *Pollock and After: The Critical Debate*. Harper & Row, 1985.

Fraser, Nancy. "Rethinking the Public Sphere: A Contribution to the Critique of Actually Existing Democracy." *Social Text*, no. 25/26 (1990): 56–80.

Fried, Michael. *Absorption and Theatricality: Painting and Beholder in the Age of Diderot*. University of California Press, 1980.

Fried, Michael. "Art and Objecthood." In *Art and Objecthood: Essays and Reviews*, 148–72. University of Chicago Press, 1998.

Friedlander, Benjamin. "Strange Fruit: O'Hara, Race, and the Color of Time." In *The Scene of My Selves*, edited by Terrence Diggory and Stephen Miller, 123–41 National Poetry Foundation, 2001.

Friedman, Ken. *52 Events*. Show and Tell Editions, 2002.

Friedman, Ken. *Fluxus Performance Notebook, a Special Edition of El Djardia Magazine (1990)*. Performance Research, 2002.

Friedman, Ken. *MANDATORY HAPPENING*. 1993. Plastic box with photocopy label, containing photocopy, overall (closed): 4 9/16 × 5 1/8 × 13/16″ (11.6 × 13 × 2 cm). The Gilbert and Lila Silverman Fluxus Collection Gift. The Archives, Peter Van Beveren, Rotterdam. https://www.moma.org/collection/works/135190?sov_referrer=artist&artist_id=2007&page=1.

Friedman, Ken, and Stan Lunetta. *Five Events and One Sculpture*. 1976. Flyer, offset printed, 10⅞ × 13½″. https://www.monographbookwerks.com/pages/books/1064/ken-friedman-stan-lunetta/ken-friedman-five-events-and-one-sculpture.

Frost, Elisabeth A. *The Feminist Avant-Garde in American Poetry*. University of Iowa Press, 2003.

Gabb, Vanessa Jimenez. "You and Me, Forever." In *Basic Needs*, 69–98. Rescue, 2021.

Gabriel, Kay, and Jo Barchi. "But Everything's Outside." *Post45* (blog), July 15, 2021. https://post45.org/2021/07/but-everythings-outside/.

Gallagher, Kristen. "Why Cry? A Question for Diana Hamilton." *Jacket2* (blog), February 26, 2013. http://jacket2.org/commentary/why-cry.

Gaston, Musa. "Brooklyns." *Locus Solus* 5 (Spring 1962): 47.

Gervasio, Nicole. "The Ruth in (T)Ruth: Redactive Reading and Feminist Provocations to History in M. NourbeSe Philip's *Zong!*." *differences* 30, no. 2 (2019): 1–29.

Gilmore, Ruth Wilson. "Abolition Geography and the Problem of Innocence." In *Futures of Black Radicalism*, edited by Gaye Theresa Johnson and Alex Lubin, 225–40. Verso, 2017.

Gitelman, Lisa. *Paper Knowledge: Toward a Media History of Documents*. Duke University Press, 2014.

Glavey, Brian. "Having a Coke with You Is Even More Fun Than Ideology Critique." *PMLA* 134, no. 5 (October 2019): 996.

Glazer, Nathan, and Daniel Moynihan. *Beyond the Melting Pot, Second Edition: The Negroes, Puerto Ricans, Jews, Italians, and Irish of New York City*. MIT Press, 1970.

Goldin, Claudia Dale. *Understanding the Gender Gap: An Economic History of American Women*. Oxford University Press, 1992.

Goldsmith, Kenneth. *DAY*. The Figures, 2003.

Goldsmith, Kenneth. "Paragraphs On Conceptual Writing." *Poetry Foundation* (blog), May 15, 2007. https://www.poetryfoundation.org/harriet-books/2007/05/paragraphs-on-conceptual-writing.

Goldsmith, Kenneth. *Uncreative Writing: Managing Language in the Digital Age*. Columbia University Press, 2011.

Gordan, Linda. "Aid to Dependent Children: The Legal History." *Social Welfare History Project* (blog), January 19, 2011. https://socialwelfare.library.vcu.edu/public-welfare/aid-to-dependent-children-the-legal-history/.

Gordon, Noah Eli. *Inbox*. BlazeVOX, 2007.

Graeber, David. *Toward an Anthropological Theory of Value: The False Coin of Our Own Dreams*. Palgrave, 2001.

Greenberg, Clement. *Art and Culture: Critical Essays*. Beacon, 1965.

Greenberg, Clement. "Avant-Garde and Kitsch." In *Clement Greenberg: The Collected Essays and Criticism*, vol. 1, edited by John O'Brian, 5–22. University of Chicago Press, 1986.

Greenberg, Clement. "Modernist Painting." In *Clement Greenberg: The Collected Essays and Criticism*, vol. 4, edited by John O'Brian, 85–93. University of Chicago Press, 1993.

Greenberg, Clement. "Towards a Newer Laocoon." In *Clement Greenberg: The Collected Essays and Criticism*, vol. 1, edited by John O'Brian, 23–41. University of Chicago Press, 1986.

Guilbaut, Serge. *How New York Stole the Idea of Modern Art: Abstract Expressionism, Freedom, and the Cold War*. University of Chicago Press, 1983.

Guillory, John. "The Memo and Modernity." *Critical Inquiry* 31, no. 1 (September 2004): 108–32.
Hamilton, Diana. *Okay, Okay*. Truck Books, 2012.
Hansen, Al. *A Primer of Happenings & Time/Space Art*. Something Else, 1965.
Harney, Stefano, and Fred Moten. *The Undercommons: Fugitive Planning & Black Study*. Autonomedia, 2013.
Harren, Natilee. *Fluxus Forms: Scores, Multiples, and the Eternal Network*. University of Chicago Press, 2020.
Harris, Mark. "Amazon's Mechanical Turk Workers Protest: 'I Am a Human Being, Not an Algorithm.'" *The Guardian*, December 3, 2014, sec. Technology. https://www.theguardian.com/technology/2014/dec/03/amazon-mechanical-turk-workers-protest-jeff-bezos.
Harvey, David. *A Brief History of Neoliberalism*. Oxford University Press, 2007.
Harvey, Sandra. "Passing for Free, Passing for Sovereign: Blackness and the Formation of the Nation." PhD diss., University of California, Santa Cruz, 2017.
Hayden, Dolores. *Building Suburbia: Green Fields and Urban Growth, 1820–2000*. Pantheon, 2003.
Heideman, Paul. "The Antiabortion Movement Is the Rotten Fruit of a Brutally Unequal Society." *Jacobin*, July 8, 2022. https://jacobin.com/2022/07/anti-abortion-movement-division-of-labor-patriarchy.
Hejinian, Lyn. "Two Stein Talks." In *The Language of Inquiry*, 83–130. University of California Press, 2000.
Higgins, Dick. "Fluxus: Theory and Reception." In *The Fluxus Reader*, edited by Ken Friedman, 217–36. Academy Editions, 1998.
Higgins, Dick. "Intermedia." In *Intermedia, Fluxus and the Something Else Press: Selected Writings by Dick Higgins*, edited by Steve Clay and Ken Friedman, 24–30. siglio, 2018.
Higgins, Dick. *Jefferson's Birthday/ Postface*. Something Else, 1964.
Higgins, Dick. "Why Gertrude Stein." In *A Dialectic of Centuries: Notes Towards a Theory of the New Arts*, 121–28. Printed Editions, 1978.
Higgins, Hannah. *Fluxus Experience*. University of California Press, 2002.
Hines, Andy. *Outside Literary Studies: Black Criticism and the University*. University of Chicago Press, 2022.
Hines, Andy. "The Material Life of Criticism." *Public Books*, January 22, 2018. https://www.publicbooks.org/the-material-life-of-criticism/.
Hines, Andy. "Working Critics." *Modern Language Quarterly* 85, no. 2 (June 2024): 205–29.
Hitlin, Paul. "Research in the Crowdsourcing Age, a Case Study." *Pew Research Center: Internet, Science & Tech* (blog), July 11, 2016. https://www.pewresearch.org/internet/2016/07/11/what-is-mechanical-turk/.
Hogan, Dennis M., and Daniel Denvir. "US Colleges and Universities Are Becoming Giant Exploitation Machines: An Interview with Dennis M. Hogan," *Jacobin*, August 2023. https://jacobin.com/2023/08/us-university-neoliberalism-exploitation-financialization-debt-jobs.
Hong, Christine. *A Violent Peace: Race, U.S. Militarism, and Cultures of Democratization in Cold War Asia and the Pacific*. Stanford University Press, 2020.
Hong, Grace Kyungwon. *Death Beyond Disavowal: The Impossible Politics of Difference*. University of Minnesota Press, 2015.
Huang, Te-Sheng, and Karen A. Franck. "Let's Meet at Citicorp: Can Privately Owned Public Spaces Be Inclusive?" *Journal of Urban Design* 23, no. 4 (July 2018): 499–517.

Hunter, Walt. "American Poetry and Society." *American Literary History* 36, no. 4 (December 2024): 1142–48.
Huntsperger, David. *Procedural Form in Postmodern American Poetry: Berrigan, Antin, Silliman, and Hejinian*. Palgrave Macmillan, 2010.
Ioanes, Anna. "Observations on an Event: Yoko Ono: Poetry, Painting, Music, Objects, Events, and Wish Trees." *ASAP/J* (blog), February 27, 2020. https://asapjournal.com/observations-on-an-event-yoko-ono-poetry-painting-music-objects-events-and-wish-trees-anna-ioanes/.
Izenberg, Oren. *Being Numerous: Poetry and the Ground of Social Life*. Princeton University Press, 2011.
Jackson, Kenneth T. *Crabgrass Frontier: The Suburbanization of the United States*. Oxford University Press, 1987.
Jackson, Shannon. *Social Works: Performing Art, Supporting Publics*. Routledge, 2011.
Jackson, Virginia. *Before Modernism: Inventing American Lyric*. Princeton University Press, 2023.
Jackson, Virginia. *Dickinson's Misery: A Theory of Lyric Reading*. Princeton University Press, 2005.
Jackson, Virginia. "Lyric." In *The Princeton Encyclopedia of Poetry and Poetics*, edited by Roland Greene, Stephen Cushman, Clare Cavanagh et al., 826–34. Princeton University Press, 2012.
Jackson, Virginia. "Specters of the Ballad." *Nineteenth-Century Literature* 71, no. 2 (September 2016): 176–96.
Jackson, Virginia, and Meredith Martin. "The Poetry of the Future." *Avidly* (blog), January 29, 2021. https://avidly.lareviewofbooks.org/2021/01/29/the-poetry-of-the-future/.
Jackson, Virginia, and Yopie Prins. "General Introduction." In *The Lyric Theory Reader: A Critical Anthology*, edited by Virginia Jackson and Yopie Prins, 1–10. Johns Hopkins University Press, 2014.
Jameson, Fredric. *Postmodernism, or, The Cultural Logic of Late Capitalism*. Duke University Press, 1990.
Janakriam, Emily. "Beyond *Roe v. Wade*." *Spectre Journal*, May 18, 2022. https://spectrejournal.com/beyond-roe-v-wade/.
Javadizadeh, Kamran. "The Atlantic Ocean Breaking on Our Heads: Claudia Rankine, Robert Lowell, and the Whiteness of the Lyric Subject." *PMLA* 134, no. 3 (May 2019): 475.
Jennings, Chris. "The Erotic Poetics of Anne Carson." *University of Toronto Quarterly* 70, no. 4 (October 2001): 923–36.
Jeon, Joseph Jonghyun. *Racial Things, Racial Forms: Objecthood in Avant-Garde Asian American Poetry*. University of Iowa Press, 2012.
Johnson, Barbara. "Apostrophe, Animation, and Abortion." *Diacritics* 16, no. 1 (1986): 29–47.
Johnson, Kent. "Notes on Safe Conceptualisms." *Lana Turner Journal Blog* (blog), April 2013. http://www.lanaturnerjournal.com/contents-current/kent-johnson-notes-on-safe-conceptualisms.
Jones, Amelia. *Body Art/Performing the Subject*. University of Minnesota Press, 1998.
Jones, LeRoi (Amiri Baraka). "The End of Man Is His Beauty." *Locus Solus* 3–4 (Winter 1962): 17–18.
Jones, LeRoi (Amiri Baraka). "A Long Poem for Myself." *Locus Solus* 3–4 (Winter 1962): 13–15.

Jones, LeRoi (Amiri Baraka). "Style." *Locus Solus* 3–4 (Winter 1962): 16.
Joseph, Branden Wayne. *Beyond the Dream Syndicate: Tony Conrad and the Arts After Cage (a "Minor" History)*. Zone, 2008.
Kane, Daniel. *All Poets Welcome: The Lower East Side Poetry Scene in the 1960s*. University of California Press, 2003.
Katznelson, Ira. *When Affirmative Action Was White: An Untold History of Racial Inequality in Twentieth-Century America*. Norton, 2006.
Kawamura, Sally. "Appreciating the Incidental: Mieko Shiomi's 'Events.'" *Women & Performance: A Journal of Feminist Theory* 19, no. 3 (November 2009): 311–36.
Kellein, Thomas. *The Dream of Fluxus: George Maciunas: An Artist's Biography*. Thames & Hudson, 2007.
Kempf, Christopher. *Craft Class: The Writing Workshop in American Culture*. John Hopkins University Press, 2022.
King, Amy. "Beauty and the Beastly Po-Biz, Part 1." *The Rumpus* (blog), July 15, 2013. http://therumpus.net/2013/07/beauty-and-the-beastly-po-biz-part-1/.
King, Amy. "Beauty and the Beastly Po-Biz, Part 2." *The Rumpus* (blog), July 16, 2013. http://therumpus.net/2013/07/beauty-and-the-beastly-po-biz-part-2/.
King, Tiffany Lethabo. "Black 'Feminisms' and Pessimism: Abolishing Moynihan's Negro Family." *Theory & Event* 21, no. 1 (2018): 68–87.
Knittle, Davy. "'Hints That Are Revelations': James Schuyler, Obsolescence, and the Urban Curative Imaginary." *GLQ: A Journal of Lesbian and Gay Studies* 27, no. 2 (2021): 173–200.
Korn, Melissa, and Andrea Fuller. "'Financially Hobbled for Life': The Elite Master's Degrees That Don't Pay Off." *Wall Street Journal*, July 8, 2021. https://www.wsj.com/articles/financially-hobbled-for-life-the-elite-masters-degrees-that-dont-pay-off-11625752773.
Kotz, Liz. *Words to Be Looked at: Language in 1960s Art*. MIT Press, 2007.
Kozloff, Max. "American Painting During the Cold War." *Art Forum* 11, no. 9 (May 1973): 43–54.
Kramnick, Jonathan, and Anahid Nersessian. "Form and Explanation." *Critical Inquiry* 43, no. 3 (March 2017): 650–69.
Kroll, Justin. "Sandra Bullock to Star as Wendy Davis in 'Let Her Speak.'" *Variety*, November 9, 2017. https://variety.com/2017/film/news/sandra-bullock-wendy-davis-let-her-speak-1202585780/.
La Berge, Leigh Claire. *Wages Against Artwork: Decommodified Labor and the Claims of Socially Engaged Art*. Duke University Press, 2019.
Larson, Laura. "Food for the Spirit." *ASAP Journal Blog: B.O.S (Black One Shot)* (blog), June 18, 2020. https://asapjournal.com/b-0-s-9-2-adrian-pipers-food-for-the-spirit-laura-larson/.
Le Corbusier. "Architecture or Revolution." In *Towards a New Architecture*, translated by Frederick Etchells, 267–89. Dover, 1986.
Lebovic, Sam. "The Fulbright, History's Greatest War-Surplus Program." *BostonGlobe.com* (blog), August 11, 2013. http://www.bostonglobe.com/ideas/2013/08/10/the-fulbright-history-greatest-war-surplus-program/NiGDSEjkjLAcZcxcGowLBJ/story.html.
Lehman, David. *The Last Avant-Garde: The Making of the New York School of Poets*. Doubleday, 1998.
Lely, John, and James Saunders. *Word Events: Perspectives on Verbal Notation*. Continuum, 2012.

Leong, Michael. "Conceptualisms in Crisis: The Fate of Late Conceptual Poetry." *Journal of Modern Literature* 41, no. 3 (2018): 109–31.

Leong, Michael. *Contested Records: The Turn to Documents in Contemporary North American Poetry*. University of Iowa Press, 2020.

Levin Becker, Daniel. *Many Subtle Channels: In Praise of Potential Literature*. Harvard University Press, 2012.

Levy, Ellen. *Criminal Ingenuity: Moore, Cornell, Ashbery, and the Struggle Between the Arts*. Oxford University Press, 2011.

Lewis, Sophie. *Abolish the Family: A Manifesto for Care and Liberation*. Verso, 2022.

Liebert, Emily. "Roles Recast: Eleanor Antin and the 1970s." PhD diss., Columbia University, 2013.

Linklater, Tayna Lukin. *Slow Scrape*. Center for Expanded Poetics and Anteism, 2021.

Lippard, Lucy R. "The Pains and Pleasures of Rebirth: European and American Women's Body Art." In *From the Center: Feminist Essays on Women's Art*, 121–38. Dutton, 1976.

Lippard, Lucy R. *Six Years: The Dematerialization of the Art Object from 1966 to 1972*. University of California Press, 1997.

Lippard, Lucy R., and Adrian Piper. "Catalysis: An Interview with Adrian Piper." *Drama Review: TDR* 16, no. 1 (March 1972): 76–78.

Liu, Kenji C. *Map of an Onion*. Inlandia Institute, 2016.

*Locus Solus* I–V, 1961–1962.

Lomax, Dana Teen. *Disclosure*. Black Radish, 2011.

Lorde, Audre. "Learning from the 60s." In *SOS—Calling All Black People: A Black Arts Movement Reader*, edited by John Bracey Jr, Sonia Sanchez, and James Smethurst, 656–62. University of Massachusetts Press, 2014.

Love, Heather. "Close but Not Deep: Literary Ethics and the Descriptive Turn." *New Literary History* 41, no. 2 (2010): 371–91.

Lowe, Lisa. *The Intimacies of Four Continents*. Duke University Press, 2015.

Luger, Moberley. "The Conceptual Poet as Witness." *Contemporary Literature* 61, no. 4 (Winter 2020): 1–26.

Lulu. "The United States Has Been Spending Billions of Dollars a Year on Illegal Immigration. This Will Not Continue. Democrats Must Give Us the Votes to Pass Strong (but Fair) Laws. If Not, We Will Be Forced to Play a Much Tougher Hand." Accessed December 1, 2022. https://www.lulu.com/shop/counterpath-press/the-united-states-has-been-spending-billions-of-dollars-a-year-on-illegal-immigration-this-will-not-continue-democrats-must-give-us-the-votes-to-pass-strong-but-fair-laws-if-not-we-will-be-forced-to-play-a-much-tougher-hand/paperback/product-23861479.html.

MacCarthy, Michelle. "Playing Politics with Yams: Food Security in the Trobriand Islands of Papua New Guinea." *Culture, Agriculture, Food & Environment* 34, no. 2 (December 2012): 136–47.

Mackey, Nathaniel. "The Changing Same: Black Music in the Poetry of Amiri Baraka." In *Discrepant Engagement: Dissonance, Cross-Culturality, and Experimental Writing*, 22–48. Cambridge University Press, 1993.

Maker. *Money.* Troll Thread, 2012. https://trollthread.tumblr.com/post/25903051525/maker-money-troll-thread-2012-purchase-color.
Malcolm, Jane. "Ono Optics: Toward a Theory of the Perfectly Unreadable." *Amodern*, October 2023. https://amodern.net/article/ono-optics/.
Malcolm, Jane, and Sarah Dowling, eds. "*Amodern* 11: Body and/as Procedure (Special Issue)." *Amodern* 11 (October 2023). https://amodern.net/issues/amodern-11/.
Malcolm, Jane, and Sarah Dowling. "Introduction to *Amodern* 11: Body and/as Procedure." *Amodern* 11 (October 2023). https://amodern.net/article/amodern-11/.
Malinowski, Bronislaw. *Argonauts of the Western Pacific.* Dutton, 1922.
Martin, Henry. *An Introduction to George Brecht's Book of the Tumbler on Fire.* multhipla edizioni, 1978.
Marx, Karl. *Capital: A Critique of Political Economy.* Translated by Ben Fowkes. Vol. 1. Penguin, 1981.
Mathews, Harry, and Alastair Brotchie, eds. *Oulipo Compendium.* Atlas, 1998.
Matthiesen, Sara. *Reproduction Reconceived: Family Making and the Limits of Choice After* Roe v. Wade. University of California Press, 2021.
Mayer, Bernadette. "Lives of the Poets: Bernadette Mayer by Adam Fitzgerald." Poetry Foundation, April 2011. https://www.poetryfoundation.org/. https://www.poetryfoundation.org/articles/69658/lives-of-the-poets-bernadette-mayer.
Mayer, Bernadette. *Memory.* Siglio, 2020.
Mayer, Bernadette. *Studying Hunger.* Adventures in Poetry, 1975. http://eclipsearchive.org/projects/HUNGER/hunger.html.
Mayer, Bernadette. *Studying Hunger Journals.* Station Hill, 2011.
Mayer, Bernadette, and Lewis Warsh. *Piece of Cake.* Station Hill, 2020.
McCarthy, Paul, ed. "Food for the Spirit." *High Performance* 4, no. 1 (Spring 1981): 34–39.
McClanahan, Annie. *Dead Pledges: Debt, Crisis, and Twenty-First-Century Culture.* Stanford University Press, 2017.
McClure, Daniel Robert. *Winter in America: A Cultural History of Neoliberalism, from the Sixties to the Reagan Revolution.* University of North Carolina Press, 2021.
McGurl, Mark. *The Program Era: Postwar Fiction and the Rise of Creative Writing.* Harvard University Press, 2009.
Medina, Cuauhtémoc. "Architecture and Efficiency: George Maciunas and the Economy of Art." *Res: Anthropology and Aesthetics* 45 (March 2004): 273–84.
Medina, Cuauhtémoc. "The 'Kulturbolschewiken' II: Fluxus, Khrushchev, and the 'Concretist Society.'" *RES: Anthropology and Aesthetics*, no. 49/50 (2006): 231–43.
Melamed, Jodi. "Racial Capitalism." *Critical Ethnic Studies* 1, no. 1 (2015): 76–85.
Melgard, Holly. *Fetal Position.* Roof, 2021.
Michelangelo Buonarroti. *Sonnets.* Translated by John Addington Symonds. Scribner's, 1904. http://archive.org/details/cu31924014269975.
Milman, Estera, ed. "Ken Friedman: Art[Net]Worker Extra-Ordinaire." In *Alternative Traditions in the Contemporary Arts: Subjugated Knowledges and the Balance of Power.* Accessed June 9, 2021. http://sdrc.lib.uiowa.edu/atca/subjugated/five_12.htm.

Mittelstadt, Jennifer. *From Welfare to Workfare: The Unintended Consequences of Liberal Reform, 1945–1965*. University of North Carolina Press, 2005.

Moi, Toril. "Crisis in the Profession, or the Failure to Imagine the New." *American Literary History* 36, no. 4 (December 2024): 1161–82.

Molesworth, Helen Anne. "Cleaning Up in the 1970s: The Work of Judy Chicago, Mary Kelly and Mierle Laderman Ukeles." In *Rewriting Conceptual Art*, edited by Michael Newman and Jon Bird, 107–22. Critical Views. Reaktion, 1999.

Molesworth, Helen Anne. "House Work and Art Work." *October*, no. 92 (Spring 2000): 71–97.

Molesworth, Helen Anne. "Work Ethic." In *Work Ethic*, edited by Helen Anne Molesworth, 25–52. Baltimore Museum of Art/Pennsylvania State University Press, 2003.

Moravec, Michelle, and Kent K. Chang. "Feminist Bestsellers: A Digital History of 1970s Feminism." *Post45: Peer Reviewed*, April 21, 2021. https://post45.org/2021/04/feminist-bestsellers-a-digital-history-of-1970s-feminism/.

Mori, Bruna. "Noulipo's Oulipoed Foulipo." *Drunken Boat* (blog), 2006. http://d7.drunkenboat.com/db8/oulipo/feature-oulipo/essays/mori/noulipo.html.

Motte, Warren F. "Clinamen Redux." *Comparative Literature Studies* 23, no. 4 (December 1986): 263–81.

Motte, Warren F., ed. *Oulipo: A Primer of Potential Literature*. Dalkey Archive Press, 1998.

Munroe, Alexandra, and Jon Hendricks, eds. *Yes Yoko Ono*. Japan Society and Harry Abrams, 2000.

Myers, John Bernard. *The Poets of the New York School*. Graduate School of Fine Arts, University of Pennsylvania, 1969.

Nadasen, Premilla, Jennifer Mittelstadt, and Marisa Chappell. *Welfare in the United States: A History with Documents, 1935–1996*. Routledge, 2009.

Nadel, Alan. *Containment Culture: American Narrative, Postmodernism, and the Atomic Age*. Duke University Press, 1995.

Namiko Kunimoto. "Olympic Dissent: Art, Politics, and the Tokyo Olympic Games of 1964 and 2020." *Asia-Pacific Journal: Japan Focus* 16, no. 15 (August 2018). https://apjjf.org/2018/15/kunimoto, 5–5.

Nealon, Christopher. *The Matter of Capital: Poetry and Crisis in the American Century*. Harvard University Press, 2011.

Neeley, Kathryn A., and Michael Alley. "The Humble History of the 'Bullet.'" *ASEE Annual Conference and Exposition, Conference Proceedings*, January 1, 2011. https://pennstate.pure.elsevier.com/en/publications/the-humble-history-of-the-bullet-2.

Nelson, Deborah. *Pursuing Privacy in Cold War America*. Columbia University Press, 2002.

Nelson, Maggie. *Women, the New York School, and Other True Abstractions*. University of Iowa Press, 2007.

New York City Department of City Planning. "In the Matter of an Application . . ." September 19, 2007. https://www.nyc.gov/assets/planning/download/pdf/about/cpc/070497.pdf.

Newfield, Christopher. "The Price of Privatization." In *The Great Mistake: How We Wrecked Public Universities and How We Can Fix Them*, 18–35. Johns Hopkins University Press, 2016.

Newman, Andy. "I Found Work on an Amazon Website. I Made 97 Cents an Hour." *New York Times*, November 15, 2019, sec. New York. https://www.nytimes.com/interactive/2019/11/15/nyregion/amazon-mechanical-turk.html.

Ngai, Sianne. *Our Aesthetic Categories: Zany, Cute, Interesting*. Harvard University Press, 2012.

North, Michael. *Novelty: A History of the New*. University of Chicago Press, 2013.

Nowak, Mark. *Coal Mountain Elementary*. Coffee House Press, 2009.

Nowak, Mark. "Documentary Poetics." *Poetry Foundation* (blog), November 9, 2022. https://www.poetryfoundation.org/harriet-books/2010/04/documentary-poetics.

Nweke, Felix. *Yam in West Africa: Food, Money, and More*. Michigan State University Press, 2016.

NYC Department of City Planning. "Privately Owned Public Space History." Accessed July 7, 2025, https://www.nyc.gov/content/planning/pages/our-work/plans/citywide/privately-owned-public-spaces#history.

O'Dell, Kathy. *Contract with the Skin: Masochism, Performance Art, and the 1970s*. University of Minnesota Press, 1998.

O'Dell, Kathy. "Fluxus Feminus." *TDR* 41, no. 1 (1997): 43–60.

O'Hara, Frank. "Adieu to Norman, Bonjour to Joan and Jean-Paul." *Locus Solus* 1 (Winter 1961): 123–25.

O'Hara, Frank. "Getting Up Ahead of Someone (Sun)." In *The Collected Poems of Frank O'Hara*, edited by Donald Allen, 341. University of California Press, 1995.

O'Hara, Frank. "The Lay of the Romance of the Associations." In *The Collected Poems of Frank O'Hara*, edited by Donald Allen, 320. University of California Press, 1995.

O'Hara, Frank. "Nocturne." In *The Collected Poems of Frank O'Hara*, edited by Donald Allen, 224–25. University of California Press, 1995.

O'Hara, Frank. "Personal Poem." In *The Collected Poems of Frank O'Hara*, edited by Donald Allen, 335. University of California Press, 1995.

O'Hara, Frank. "Walking." In *The Collected Poems of Frank O'Hara*, edited by Donald Allen, 476–77. University of California Press, 1995.

O'Hara, Frank, and Bill Berkson. "From 'The Memorandums of Angelicus Fobb.'" *Locus Solus* 3–4 (Winter 1962): 101–5.

Ono, Yoko. *Grapefruit*. Wunternam, 1964.

Ono, Yoko. *Grapefruit: A Book of Instructions + Drawings*. Simon & Schuster, 1970.

Ono, Yoko. *Instruction Paintings*. Weatherhill, 1995.

Ono, Yoko. "Summer of 1961." In *Fluxus Scores and Instructions: The Transformative Years: "Make a Salad": Selections from the Gilbert and Lila Silverman Fluxus Collection, Detroit*, edited by Jon Hendricks, Marianne Bech, and Media Farzin, 38–40. Gilbert and Lila Silverman Fluxus Collection/Museum of Contemporary Art, 2008.

Ono, Yoko. "Untitled [to the Wesleyan People]." *The Stone*, 1966.

Osman, Jena. *Public Figures*. Wesleyan University Press, 2012.

Oulipo. *Abrégé de Littérature Potentielle*. Mille et une nuits, 2002.

Padgett, Ron, and David Shapiro, eds. *An Anthology of New York Poets*. Vintage, 1970.

Paeth, Amy. *The American Poet Laureate: A History of U.S. Poetry and the State*. Columbia University Press, 2023.

Page, Max. "The Heights and Depths of Urbanism: Fifth Avenue and the Creative Destruction of Manhattan." In *The American Skyscraper: Cultural Histories*, edited by Roberta Moudry, 165–84. Cambridge University Press, 2005. Perez, Craig Santos. *From Unincorporated Territory [Åmot]*. Omnidawn, 2023.

Perloff, Marjorie. *Frank O'Hara, Poet Among Painters*. University of Chicago Press, 1998.

Perloff, Marjorie. *Radical Artifice: Writing Poetry in the Age of Media*. University of Chicago Press, 1991.

Perloff, Marjorie. *Unoriginal Genius: Poetry by Other Means in the New Century*. University of Chicago Press, 2010.

Perloff, Marjorie. *Wittgenstein's Ladder: Poetic Language and the Strangeness of the Ordinary*. University of Chicago Press, 1996.

Perlow, Seth. *The Poem Electric: Technology and the American Lyric*. University of Minnesota Press, 2018.

Perreault, John. "Paris." *Locus Solus* 3–4 (Winter 1962): 206–7.

Philip, M. NourbeSe. *Frontiers: Selected Essays and Writings on Racism and Culture, 1984–1992*. Mercury, 1992.

Philip, M. NourbeSe. "Jammin' Still." In *Blank: Essays and Interviews*, 13–24. Book*hug, 2017.

Philip, M. NourbeSe. "Outline of Events Related to the Unauthorised Translation of *Zong!* As Told to the Author by Setaey Adamu Boateng by Renata Morresi and Benway Series Press." October 11, 2021. https://www.nourbese.com/2021/10/11/.

Philip, M. NourbeSe, and Setaey Adamu Boateng. *Zong!* Wesleyan University Press, 2011.

Piper, Adrian. "APRA Foundation Berlin: News." APRA Foundation Berlin: News, September 2012. http://adrianpiper.com/berlin/news.shtml#September_2012.

Piper, Adrian. *Escape to Berlin: A Travel Memoir/Flucht Nach Berlin: Eine Reiseerinnerung*. Translated by Suzanne Schmidt. Adrian Piper Research Archive Foundation Berlin, 2018.

Piper, Adrian. "Kinds of Performing Objects I Have Been (1972)." In *Out of Order, Out of Sight, Volume I: Selected Writings in Meta-Art 1968–1992*, 89–90. MIT Press, 1996.

Piper, Adrian. *Out of Order, Out of Sight, Volume I: Selected Writings in Meta-Art 1968–1992*. MIT Press, 1996.

Piper, Adrian. *Out of Order, Out of Sight, Volume II: Selected Writings in Art Criticism 1967–1992*. MIT Press, 1996.

Piper, Adrian. "Talking to Myself: The Ongoing Autobiography of an Art Object." In *Out of Order, Out of Sight, Volume I: Selected Writings in Meta-Art 1968–1992*, 29–54. MIT Press, 1996.

Place, Vanessa. "Poetry Is Dead, I Killed It: An Essay by Vanessa Place." *Harriet: The Blog* (blog). Accessed February 20, 2014. http://www.poetryfoundation.org/harriet/2012/04/poetry-is-dead-i-killed-it/.

Place, Vanessa. *Vanessa Place: Last Words*. Bilingual ed. Dis Voir, 2015.

Place, Vanessa, and Robert Fitterman. *Notes on Conceptualisms*. Ugly Duckling Presse, 2009.

Pontin, Jason. "Artificial Intelligence, with Help from the Humans." *New York Times*, March 25, 2007. https://www.nytimes.com/2007/03/25/business/yourmoney/25Stream.html?smid=tw-share.

Posmentier, Sonya. *Cultivation and Catastrophe: The Lyric Ecology of Modern Black Literature*. Johns Hopkins University Press, 2017.

Queyras, Sina. "Lyric Conceptualism: A Manifesto in Progress." *Harriet: The Blog* (blog), April 2012. http://www.poetryfoundation.org/harriet/2012/04/lyric-conceptualism-a-manifesto-in-progress/.
Rankine, Claudia, *Citizen: An American Lyric*. Graywolf, 2014.
"Reading @realDonaldTrump—Counterpath." Accessed December 1, 2022. http://counterpathpress.org/reading-realdonaldtrump-series.
Reed, Anthony. *Freedom Time: The Poetics and Politics of Black Experimental Writing*. Johns Hopkins University Press, 2014.
Reed, Brian M. *Nobody's Business: Twenty-First Century Avant-Garde Poetics*. Cornell University Press, 2013.
Rhee, Jieun. "Performing the Other: Yoko Ono's 'Cut Piece'." *Art History* 28, no. 1 (February 2005): 96–118.
Roberts, John. *The Intangibilities of Form: Skill and Deskilling in Art After the Readymade*. Verso, 2007.
Robinson, Julia. "From Abstraction to Model: George Brecht's Events and the Conceptual Turn in Art of the 1960s." *October*, no. 127 (Winter 2009): 77–108.
Robinson, Julia. "Maciunas as Producer: Performative Design in the Art of the 1960s." *Grey Room*, no. 33 (2008): 56–83.
Rodenbeck, Judith F. *Radical Prototypes: Allan Kaprow and the Invention of Happenings*. MIT Press, 2011.
Ronda, Margaret. "Abortion's Poetic Figures." *Post45*, Abortion Now, Abortion Forever (June 2023). https://post45.org/2023/06/abortions-poetic-figures/.
Rosenbaum, Susan B. *Professing Sincerity: Modern Lyric Poetry, Commercial Culture, and the Crisis in Reading*. University of Virginia Press, 2007.
Rubin, Andrew. *Archives of Authority: Empire, Culture, and the Cold War*. Princeton University Press, 2012.
Saper, Craig J. *Networked Art*. University of Minnesota Press, 2001.
Sasaki, Fred. "Is Yoko Ono Underappreciated as a Poet?" Interview by Claire Voon. *Chicago Magazine*, May 6, 2019. https://www.chicagomag.com/Chicago-Magazine/May-2019/Revisiting-Yoko-Onos-Poetry/.
Saunders, Frances Stonor. *The Cultural Cold War: The CIA and the World of Arts and Letters*. New Press, 2000.
Saunders, Patricia. "Defending the Dead, Confronting the Archive: A Conversation with M. NourbeSe Philip." *Small Axe* 12, no. 2 (June 2008): 63–79.
Sawyer-Lauçanno, Christopher. "*Locus Solus et Socii*: Harry Matthews and John Ashbery." In *The Continual Pilgrimage: American Writers in Paris, 1944–1960*, 233–61. Grove, 1992.
Scheiner, Corinne. "Teleiopoiesis, Telepoesis, and the Practice of Comparative Literature." *Comparative Literature* 57, no. 3 (July 2005): 239–45.
Schneider, Rebecca. *The Explicit Body in Performance*. Routledge, 1997.
Schultz, Susan M. "Tinfish Editor's Blog: Conceptualism as Affect: Or, a Defense of Both at Once." *Tinfish Editor's Blog* (blog), July 27, 2013. http://tinfisheditor.blogspot.com/2013/07/conceptualism-as-affect-or-defense-of.html.
Schuster, Joshua. "The Making of 'Tender Buttons': Gertrude Stein's Subjects, Objects and the Illegible." *Jacket 2*, April 21, 2011. https://jacket2.org/article/making-tender-buttons.

Schuyler, James. *Just the Thing: Selected Letters of James Schuyler*. Turtle Point, 2004.
Scott, Felicity D. "An Army of Soldiers or a Meadow." *Journal of the Society of Architectural Historians* 70, no. 3 (September 2011): 330–53.
Sedgwick, Eve Kosofsky. "Paranoid Reading and Reparative Reading, or, You're So Paranoid, You Probably Think This Essay Is About You." In *Touching Feeling: Affect, Pedagogy, Performativity*, 123–54. Duke University Press, 2003.
Seita, Sophie. *Provisional Avant-Gardes: Little Magazine Communities from Dada to Digital*. Stanford University Press, 2019.
Semuels, Alana. "The Online Hell of Amazon's Mechanical Turk." *The Atlantic*, January 23, 2018. https://www.theatlantic.com/business/archive/2018/01/amazon-mechanical-turk/551192/.
Shaked, Nizan, Amelia Jones, and Marsha Meskimmon. *The Synthetic Proposition: Conceptualism and the Political Referent in Contemporary Art*. Manchester University Press, 2017.
Shank, Barry. "Abstraction and Embodiment: Yoko Ono and the Weaving of Global Musical Networks." *Journal of Popular Music Studies* 18, no. 3 (2006): 282–300.
Shannon, Joshua. *The Disappearance of Objects: New York Art and the Rise of the Postmodern City*. Yale University Press, 2009.
Sharif, Solmaz. *LOOK*. Graywolf, 2016.
Shaw, Lytle. "Framing the Lyric." *American Literary History* 28, no. 2 (Summer 2016): 403–13.
Shaw, Lytle. *Frank O'Hara: The Poetics of Coterie*. University of Iowa Press, 2006.
Shaw, Lytle. "Gesture in 1960: Toward Literal Solutions." In *Frank O'Hara Now: New Essays on the New York Poet*, edited by Robert Hampson and Will Montgomery, 29–48. Liverpool University Press, 2010.
Shoptaw, John. *On the Outside Looking Out: John Ashbery's Poetry*. Harvard University Press, 1994.
Siddique, Asheesh Kapur. "Does Humanities Research Still Matter?" *Inside Higher Ed*, August 15, 2023. https://www.insidehighered.com/opinion/views/2023/08/15/does-humanities-research-matter-anymore-opinion.
Silverberg, Mark. *The New York School Poets and the Neo-Avant-Garde*. Ashgate, 2010.
Singh, Nikhil Pal. *Race and America's Long War*. University of California Press, 2017.
Smith, Cherise. *Enacting Others: Politics of Identity in Eleanor Antin, Nikki S. Lee, Adrian Piper, and Anna Deavere Smith*. Duke University Press, 2011.
Smith, Owen. "Developing a Fluxable Forum: Early Performance and Publishing." In *The Fluxus Reader*, edited by Ken Friedman, 3–21. Academy Editions, 1998.
Smith, Owen. *Fluxus: The History of an Attitude*. San Diego State University Press, 1998.
Smith, Owen. "A Pilgrim's Progress." In *Alternative Traditions in the Contemporary Arts: Subjugated Knowledges and the Balance of Power*, ed. Estera Milman. Accessed June 9, 2021. http://sdrc.lib.uiowa.edu/atca/subjugated/five_13.htm.
Soldier, Layli Long. *WHEREAS: Poems*. Graywolf, 2017.
Spahr, Juliana. *Du Bois's Telegram: Literary Resistance and State Containment*. Harvard University Press, 2018.
Spahr, Juliana, and Stephanie Young. "Foulipo." In *A Megaphone: Some Enactments, Some Numbers, and Some Essays About the Continued Usefulness of Crotchless-Pants-and-a-Machine-Gun Feminism*, 31–42. ChainLinks, 2011.

Spahr, Juliana, and Stephanie Young. "The Program Era and the Mainly White Room." *Los Angeles Review of Books*, September 20, 2015. https://lareviewofbooks.org/article/the-program-era-and-the-mainly-white-room/.
Spectre Editorial Board. "Breaking the Strategic Impasse." *Spectre Journal*, May 27, 2022. https://spectrejournal.com/breaking-the-strategic-impasse/.
Spivak, Gayatri Chakravorty. "Can the Subaltern Speak?" In *Marxism and the Interpretation of Culture*, edited by Cary Nelson and Lawrence Grossberg, 271–313. University of Illinois Press, 1988.
Spivak, Gayatri Chakravorty. *Death of a Discipline*. Columbia University Press, 2005.
Spivak, Gayatri Chakravorty. "What's Left of Theory." In *An Aesthetic Education in the Era of Globalization*, 191–217. Harvard University Press, 2012.
Stefans, Brian Kim. *Bank of America Online Banking*. Citoyen, 2010.
Stein, Gertrude. *Tender Buttons*, edited by Seth Perlow. City Lights, 2014.
Stephens, Paul. *The Poetics of Information Overload: From Gertrude Stein to Conceptual Writing*. University of Minnesota Press, 2015.
Stephens, Paul. "Vanguard Total Index: Conceptual Writing, Information Asymmetry, and the Risk Society." *Contemporary Literature* 54, no. 4 (2013): 752–84.
Stiles, Kristine. "Survival Ethos and Destruction Art." *Discourse* 14, no. 2 (April 1992): 74–102.
Stoeltje, Gretchen, dir. *Shouting Down Midnight*. 2022. MSNBC. https://www.shoutingdownmidnight.com/. Documentary film.
Stuelke, Patricia. *The Ruse of Repair: US Neoliberal Empire and the Turn from Critique*. Duke University Press, 2021.
Sturm, Nick. "'I've Never Liked Mimeo': Eileen Myles, Little Magazines, and the 'Umpteenth-Generation New York School.'" *Women's Studies* 51, no. 8 (November 2022): 904–24.
Takemae, Eiji. *Inside GHQ: The Allied Occupation of Japan and Its Legacy*. Translated by Robert Ricketts and Sebastian Swann. Continuum, 2002.
Trager, James. *Park Avenue: Street of Dreams*. Atheneum, 1990.
Tsutsui, William M. *Manufacturing Ideology: Scientific Management in Twentieth-Century Japan*. Princeton University Press, 2001.
Tucker-Abramson, Myka. *Novel Shocks: Urban Renewal and the Origins of Neoliberalism*. Fordham University Press, 2019.
Ukeles, Mierle Laderman. *MANIFESTO FOR MAINTENANCE ART, Proposal for an Exhibition: "CARE,"* 1969. October 1969. Four typewritten pages, each 8½ × 11 in. https://queensmuseum.org/wp-content/uploads/2016/04/Ukeles-Manifesto-for-Maintenance-Art-1969.pdf.
United States President's Commission on Immigration and Naturalization. *Whom We Shall Welcome; Report*. U.S. Government Printing Office, 1953. http://archive.org/details/whomweshallwelcooounit.
University of Massachusetts Amherst. "MTurk Guidance in Research Administration and Compliance Guidelines." Accessed December 1, 2022. https://www.umass.edu/research/guidance/mturk-guidance.
Valle, Camila, Emily Janakriam, and Holly Lewis. "The Fight for Abortion and Reproductive Justice After *Roe*." *Spectre Journal*, September 13, 2022. https://spectrejournal.com/the-fight-for-abortion-and-reproductive-justice-after-roe/.

Viegener, Matais, and Christine Wertheim, eds. *The Noulipian Analects*. Les Figues, 2007.
Walvin, James. *Black Ivory: Slavery in the British Empire*. Wiley-Blackwell, 2001.
Wang, Dorothy. *Thinking Its Presence: Form, Race, and Subjectivity in Contemporary Asian American Poetry*. Stanford University Press, 2015.
Ward, Geoffrey. *Statutes of Liberty: The New York School of Poets*. Macmillan, 1993.
Wark, Jayne. *Radical Gestures: Feminism and Performance Art in North America*. McGill-Queen's University Press, 2006.
Warner, Michael. *Publics and Counterpublics*. Zone, 2005.
Watkin, William. *In the Process of Poetry: The New York School and the Avant-Garde*. Bucknell University Press, 2001.
Weeks, Kathi. "Abolition of the Family: The Most Infamous Feminist Proposal." *Feminist Theory* 24, no. 3 (2023): 433–53.
Weeks, Kathi. *The Problem with Work: Feminism, Marxism, Antiwork Politics, and Postwork Imaginaries*. Duke University Press, 2011.
Weiss, Marc. "Density and Intervention: New York's Planning Traditions." In *The Landscape of Modernity: Essays on New York City, 1900–1940*, edited by David Ward and Olivier Zunz, 46–75. Russell Sage, 1992.
White, Gillian C. *Lyric Shame: The "Lyric" Subject of Contemporary American Poetry*. Harvard University Press, 2014.
Whyte, William Hollingsworth. *The Social Life of Small Urban Spaces*. Conservation Foundation, 1980.
Williams, Emmett, and Noël Ann, eds. *Mr. Fluxus: A Collective Portrait of George Maciunas, 1931–1978*. Thames and Hudson, 1998.
Williams, Thomas Chatterton. "Adrian Piper's Show at MoMA Is the Largest Ever for a Living Artist. Why Hasn't She Seen It?" *New York Times*, June 27, 2018. https://www.nytimes.com/2018/06/27/magazine/adrian-pipers-self-imposed-exile-from-america-and-from-race-itself.html.
Wilson, Robert A., ed. *Gertrude Stein: A Bibliography*. Phoenix Bookshop, 1974.
Xiang, Sunny. *Tonal Intelligence: The Aesthetics of Asian Inscrutability During the Long Cold War*. Columbia University Press, 2020.
Yoshimoto, Midori. *Into Performance: Japanese Women Artists in New York*. Rutgers University Press, 2005.
Yoshimoto, Midori. "Off Museum! Performance Art That Turned the Street into 'Theatre,' Circa 1964 Tokyo." *Performance Paradigm*, no. 2 (March 2006): 102–18.
Young, La Monte, ed. *An Anthology of Chance Operations*. La Monte Young and Jackson Mac Low, 1963. https://www.ubu.com/media/text/AnAnthologyOfChanceOperations.pdf.
Young, Stephanie. *Ursula or University*. Krupskaya, 2013.
Ziegler, Mary. *Abortion and the Law in America: Roe v. Wade to the Present*. Cambridge University Press, 2020.
Ziegler, Mary. *After Roe: The Lost History of the Abortion Debate*. Harvard University Press, 2015.
Zipp, Samuel. *Manhattan Projects: The Rise and Fall of Urban Renewal in Cold War New York*. Oxford University Press, 2012.
Zucker, Rachel. "Commonplace Podcast: M. NourbeSe Philip." Commonplace. Accessed January 6, 2023. https://commonplace.today/commonplace-podcast/episode-84-m-nourbese-philip.

# INDEX

abortion, 11–15, 17–18, 95–96, 115, 117–22, 129, 135–45; and access, 105, 135; criminalization of, 11–12, 95, 117–22, 135–37, 162–63, 204n114; *Dobbs v. Jackson Women's Health Organization*, 137–37, 162, 204n114; normalization of, 120; as a poetic figure, 142–43; *Roe v. Wade*, 13, 101, 119–20; Senate Bill 5 (SB5), 135–36; *Shout Your Abortion* (PM Press), 137–38. *See also* contraception; Counterpath Press; Davis, Wendy; unwanted pregnancy

Abramowitz, Harold, 143. *See also* CREDIT (Timmons)

Abramson, Daniel: on obsolescence, 88–89. *See also* obsolescence; preservationism

Abstract Expressionism, 75, 77, 193n19, 195n41

abstraction, 8–9, 14, 63–65; and anticommunism, 193n19; in Baraka's works, 78–79; and Brecht's "Table" events, 61; and labor, 12; monetizing of, 134–35; and poetry, 12; vs. realism, 74

academia: and alienation, 166–67; and debt, 13, 19, 128, 130, 133–34, 153–55, 158, 167, 207n15, 212n12; and disinvestment, 2, 158; and labor, 154–55, 164–65; and poetry, 14–15, 128, 151–68, 213n17. *See also* documental poetry; MFA programs; university

access, 10; and abortion, 105, 135; and the MFA, 158; and plazas, 83, 195n43; and "the public," 26;. *See also* privatization

Acconci, Vito: and *o to 9* magazine, 110, 114

accumulation: and patriotism, 56–57

administrative aesthetics, 13, 41–43, 145, 147, 150. *See also* Fluxus

AG Gallery, 32, 51, 183n31. *See also* Maciunas, George

Allen, Austin, 181n10. *See also* Ono, Yoko

Allen, Donald: *The New American Poetry: 1945–1960*, 71, 74. *See also* New York School

Americanization, 15; of Japan, 30–31; and Ono, 21, 23, 30–31. *See also* Ono, Yoko

Amich, Candice: on neoliberalism, 11. *See also* neoliberalism

Andrews, Kimberly: on the academic avant-garde, 153, 212n9. *See also* academia; conceptual writing/poetry

Antin, David, 105, 123; on *Water Yam* and *Tender Buttons*, 186n14. *See also Tender Buttons* (Stein); *Water Yam* (Brecht)

Antin, Eleanor, 11, 14, 17, 28, 100, 111–12, 119, 200n32, 200n34; *Carving: A Traditional Sculpture*, 101–6, 110, 113, 115, 121–24, 200n26, 201n38, 204n119; on conceptual artists, 105–6; *Domestic Peace*, 111–12; *Eight Temptations*, 106; *4 Transactions*, 111–12; and unwanted pregnancy, 105, 119, 200n34

apology, 160, 164, 210n58

apostrophe, 138–39, 142. *See also Let Her Speak* (Counterpath)

appropriation: and the avant-garde, 50, 126, 146, 156, 158, 213n19. *See also* conceptual writing/poetry; Fluxus; plagiarism

architecture: and obsolescence, 79, 86–89; and privatization, 12–14, 70, 81–83, 195nn43–44. *See also* Seagram Building; UN building

Ashbery, John, 70–73, 75–76, 78; "New Realism," 76. *See also Locus Solus* (journal); New York School

Aso, Noriko: on the arts fest at Tokyo Olympics, 30

assimilation, 6, 20–38, 78. *See also* immigration; Ono, Yoko

associations, neighborhood, 69, 89–93, 196n65, 197n69; romance of, 90–91

authorship: and body art, 99; collective, 47–48, 53

autonomy: and abortion, 13, 119, 140; in Antin's *Carving*, 106; artistic, 22, 24; protection of, 92. *See also* abortion

Baraka, Amiri (LeRoi Jones), 13, 28, 78–80; and abstraction, 78–79; "The End of Man Is His Beauty," 79; "A Long Poem for Myself," 67, 69, 71, 79–80; "Style," 78–79

Barr, Alfred: on abstraction in art, 193n19. *See also* abstraction

Barthes, Roland, 183n27. *See also* reading

Baucom, Ian: on slavery and finance, 148–49, 210n62. *See also Zong!* (Philip and Boateng)

Beau Geste (press), 29

beauty: and labor, 104; and procedure, 98, 104; and social acceptability, 96. *See also Carving: A Traditional Sculpture* (Antin)

Becker, Daniel Levin, 99. *See also* Oulipo

Benedikt, Michael: and *Locus Solus*, 73. *See also Locus Solus* (journal); New York School

Berkson, Bill: "From the Memorandums of Angelicus Fobb" (with O'Hara), 75–76; and *Locus Solus*, 73, 75–76. *See also Locus Solus* (journal)

Berlant, Lauren: on apostrophe, 139. *See also* apostrophe

Bernes, Jasper: on 1960s artists and administrative aesthetics, 41–42, 185n1. *See also* administrative aesthetics

Beuys, Joseph, 178n27

Bezos, Jeff, 141. *See also* Mechanical Turk

birds: as accompaniment, 25; defecation of, 87–88; flight of (as time-telling), 64–65

Blair, Sarah: on the domestic space of Stein's texts, 55–56. *See also* Stein, Gertrude

Blocker, Jane: on "the body in general," 125. *See also* body, the

"Blood Piece" (Ono), 27, 33, 37, 152. *See also* Ono, Yoko

Bloom, Lisa: on Antin's *Carving*, 104–5. *See also Carving: A Traditional Sculpture* (Antin)

Blunt Research Group: *The Work-Shy*, 159–60

Boateng, Setaey Adamu, 146–47. *See also Zong!* (Philip and Boateng)

body, the: body art, 14, 95–125, 198n8; "The Body of Michael Brown" (Goldsmith), 156–57, 214n21; body supplies, 35–37; and censorship, 17; as commodity, 104; constructed bodies, 96; as currency, 147–49; as food, 114–15; drag of, 112; and gender, 97; in general, 125; limitations of, 104, 111; and neoliberalism, 11; and poetry, 11, 14, 23; and purity, 125; violation of, 112

Bok, Christian, 214n22. *See also* conceptual writing/poetry

Boudin, Jean, 78. *See also Locus Solus* (journal)
Bowers, Andrea: *Wall of Letters*, 162
Bowes, Ed: and Mayer, 118. *See also* Mayer, Bernadette; unwanted pregnancy
Bowles, John: on *Food for the Spirit*, 112, 202n72. *See also Food for the Spirit* (Piper)
Brecht, George, 13, 28, 45, 53, 93, 185n2, 185n4, 186n13, 186n16, 187n18, 189n51; "Chair Event," 56–57, 190n77; "Dresser," 46–47; "Drip Music (Drip Event)," 46–47; and enumeration, 54, 64; "Exit," 45–46, 65; as inventor, 46; "Motor Vehicle Sundown (Event)," 58, 190n80; "No Vacancy," 65; "Origin of Events," 46; research of, 45, 52, 158, 187n23; "Stool," 62–64; "Table," 59–60, 64; "Two Clocks," 64–65; "Two Definitions," 63–64; "2 Umbrellas," 64; *Water Yam*, 16, 41–44, 50–66, 186n14; "Word Event," 39–40; and the Yam Festival, 49–50. *See also* Fluxus; commodities; suburbanization
Brown, Michael, 160; "The Body of Michael Brown" (Goldsmith), 156–57, 214n21
Brown, Wendy, 11; on increased marketization, 37
Bryan-Wilson, Julia: on occupational realism, 12
Buchloh, Benjamin, 41–42, 185n1. *See also* administrative aesthetics
Bullock, Sandra: and the film version of *Let Her Speak*, 209n53. *See also Let Her Speak* (Counterpath)
Burden-Stelly, Charisse, 181n11. *See also* racial capitalism
bureaucratization, 12, 39–66; and white supremacy, 145. *See also* Fluxus
Burroughs, William S.: and the cut up, 191n1

Cabaret Voltaire, 46. *See also* Dada
Cacho, Lisa Marie, 181n11. *See also* racial capitalism
Cage, John, 189n61; on Brecht's "Motor Vehicle Sundown Event," 190n80; and Fluxus, 187n18. *See also* Fluxus

Cardew, Cornelius, 46. *See also* Fluxus
*Carving: A Traditional Sculpture* (Antin), 101–6, 110, 113, 115, 121–24, 200n26, 201n38, 204n119; reperformance of, 123. *See also* Antin, Eleanor
Caute, David: on the Cold War, 74
Cecire, Natalia, 186n17; on experimental writing, 212n6; on Stein's poetics, 55; on the white recovery project, 44
Cha, Theresa Hak Kyung, 161
chance-based artwork, 45, 106; *An Anthology of Change Operations* (Young), 184n45
change: of labor practices, 23, 26, 30–31, 38, 43, 56; and the work of Bernadette Mayer, 10, 113, 115–16, 124. *See also Carving: A Traditional Sculpture* (Antin); Mayer, Bernadette
Chappell, Marisa, 121. *See also* welfare
Chen, Lena, 19, 28, 159, 163; *We Lived the Gaps Between Stories*, 162–63
Chicago, Judy, 97–98
Choi, Don Mee, 163; *DMZ Colony*, 159, 161
Clay, Steven: on *Locus Solus*, 193n13. *See also Locus Solus* (journal)
Clover, Joshua: on conceptual writing, 156, 214n22. *See also* conceptual writing/poetry
code, 113–15. *See also Studying Hunger* (Mayer)
Cohen, Lizabeth: on the "consumers' republic" of the 1950s, 56–58
Cold War: and Abstract Expressionism, 75; and interdisciplinarity, 7; spatial poetics of the, 67–94
collage, 18, 152, 163
Collingwood, Luke: and the slave ship *Zong*, 147–48. *See also Zong!* (Philip and Boateng)
commodity: administration of (vs. production of), 8; body as, 104; commodification, 93; decommodification, 12–13, 158, 207n17; resistance to commodification, 33; yams as, 50

complicity, 116
conceptual art, 42, 105–6, 185n1
conceptual writing/poetry, 14, 130, 133–34, 153, 156–57, 205n4, 206n8, 213nn18–19, 214n22, 214n26; and politics, 127; and the refusal of expression, 156–57
constraint, 17–18, 152; durational, 95–125; and food, 95–125; and freedom, 99; as resistance, 17; state, 119–25; and writing, 98–100
containment, 92–93, 197n73
Conte, Joseph: on procedural form, 99, 199n20
contraception, 96, 198n5. *See also* abortion
Cooper, Melinda: on Nixon's family assistance plan, 121. *See also* welfare
Corso, Gregory, 78; "Cut Up," 67–68, 191n1. *See also Locus Solus* (journal)
Counterpath Press: *Let Her Speak*, 13, 15, 129, 135–45, 147, 150; *Reading @ realDonaldTrump*, 141–42. *See also* abortion; Davis, Wendy
CREDIT (Timmons), 15, 18, 23–24, 129–35, 147–48, 150, 165. *See also* Timmons, Mathew
crowdsourcing, 135–41. *See also Let Her Speak* (Counterpath); Mechanical Turk
"Cut Up" (Corso), 67–68, 191n1. *See also* Corso, Gregory

Dada: vs. Fluxus, 46, 48. *See also* Fluxus
Daniels, Dieter, 45
Davidson, Michael: on O'Hara's work, 86. *See also* O'Hara, Frank
Davis, Angela, 166
Davis, Wendy, 15, 18, 135–45, 207n20, 207n22, 209n53. *See also* abortion; *Let Her Speak* (Counterpath)
death: abortion (illegal) and, 119; and art/poetry, 27, 38; feeding of, 105; premature, 78; and racial capitalism, 11
debt: and documental poetry, 165; and education, 13, 19, 128, 130, 133–34, 153–55, 158, 167, 207n15, 212n12. *See also* academia; MFA programs; university
de Duve, Thierry: on art(ists) in general, 9, 25–26; on Marx and Beuys, 178n27; on modernist aesthetics, 177n26
Deleuze, Gilles, 82
democracy: hope of, 91–93
Derrida, Jacques: on capital, 191n87; on Marx's table, 61; on teleiopoesis, 142. *See also* Marx, Karl; teleiopoesis
destruction art, 32. *See also* Ono, Yoko
Dewhurst, David, 138–39, 143–44. *See also* abortion: criminalization of
Dezeuze, Anna: on *Water Yam*, 52. *See also Water Yam* (Brecht)
diet, 5, 10, 14, 102–6, 201n38; grapefruit, 106. *See also Carving: A Traditional Sculpture* (Antin); hunger
difference: information as, 42; and Ono, 15–16, 20–38; and strength, 36; and typicality, 61. *See also* Ono, Yoko
disinvestment, 8; in education, 2, 158
displacement, 68, 78, 88–90. 93. *See also* urban renewal
disrobing, 100, 102–3, 109; of language, 100. *See also* Antin, Eleanor; Piper, Adrian
*Dobbs v. Jackson*, 13, 137, 162, 204n114
documental poetry, 2, 14, 17–19, 126–50, 152–59, 165, 175n3, 205n4, 206n8, 212n7. *See also* academia
"Drip Music (Drip Event)" (Brecht), 46–47. *See also* Brecht, George
Duchamp, Marcel, 9, 45, 177n26
Duggan, Lisa: on the political categories of public and private, 37. *See also* privatization
Dumett, Mari, 189n61
durational artwork: and constraint, 95–125; for Ono, 22, 24–25, 27, 33, 35, 44, 184n35. *See also* temporality
Dworkin, Craig: on conceptual writing, 205n4; on formatting and poetic form, 54; on media, 178n30; on poetry in the

twentieth and twenty-first centuries, 4, 156, 213n17

Eco, Umberto: on open works, 52. *See also* open works
Ehrsam, Henrietta, 122
Eisenhower, Dwight, 67–68
Eisenhower, Milton S., 85
Elmslie, Kenward: and *Locus Solus*, 73. *See also Locus Solus* (journal)
Endnotes Collective: on women and labor, 96
Erben, Thomas: on the *Food for the Spirit* notebook, 202n72. *See also Food for the Spirit* (Piper)
exploitation, 8, 177n23; Fair Labor Standards Act, 142; and Mechanical Turk, 141–42, 208n41
Export, Valie, 100
eye: cinder caught in the, 80–81; of the other, 61, 143; reflecting, 87; static of the, 80; third, 35

failure, 14, 18; and academia, 163; in *Carving*, 122, 125; in *Food for the Spirit*, 112, 121–23, 125; to obtain an abortion, 115; and procedural poetry, 123; of *Studying Hunger*, 114, 121–23, 125; to vote (due to filibuster/protest), 144. *See also Carving: A Traditional Sculpture* (Antin); *Food for the Spirit* (Piper); *Let Her Speak* (Counterpath); *Studying Hunger* (Mayer)
Federici, Silvia: on power relations and women's bodies, 97
feminism, 14, 17, 197n1; and body art, 95–125, 198n8
Ferguson, Roderick: on interdisciplinarity in academia, 167–68. *See also* interdisciplinarity
Field, Edward: and O'Hara, 71. *See also* O'Hara, Frank
fire: in Ono's work, 22, 24, 32, 44–45. *See also* Ono, Yoko

Firestone, Shulamith: on dieting, 104. *See also* diet
Fitterman, Robert, 127. *See also* conceptual writing/poetry
Flowers, Benjamin: on the Seagram Building, 85. *See also* Seagram Building
Fluxus, 13–16, 28–29, 39–66, 69, 82, 94, 111, 152, 154, 158, 176n11, 183n27, 185nn2–4, 186n7, 187n18, 187n23, 188nn37–38; boxes, 5, 41, 51–52, 63–64, 185n2; and Communism, 48–49, 188n38; vs. Dada, 46, 48; and genre, 34, 37, 41; and happenings, 5, 20, 22, 24; and instructions, 23, 39–40, 46, 69; and intermedia, 22, 181n9; and iterability, 39–40, 45–46, 54; and labor, 48; and music, 187n18; performance festivals, 45–47, 49–50, 188n38; and unrealizability, 27, 32–33, 35
*Food for the Spirit* (Piper), 101–2, 107–13, 122–24, 201nn40–41, 201n45, 201nn47–48, 202n58, 202n72, 205n120. *See also* Piper, Adrian
form: vs. format, 43, 54–55; and political life, 176n10; public, 4–5
foulipo, 100–101. *See also* Oulipo
fountain: for O'Hara, 81, 84; for Stein, 65
Fraser, Nancy: on the phrase "the public sphere," 4
Fried, Michael: on interdisciplinary artwork, 22. *See also* interdisciplinarity
Friedman, Ken: "Mandatory Happening," 5, 45; and Something Else Press, 176n11. *See also* happenings; Something Else Press
Frost, Robert, 85

Gabb, Vanessa Jiminez, 19, 28, 159; *Basic Needs*, 159, 164–68
gender, 10, 17; and the body, 97; as constructed, 106; and labor, 96, 116–25; and Ono, 24, 37; and privatization, 14
genre, 10; and Fluxus, 24–25, 34, 37, 41; vs. medium, 178n32

Gitelman, Lisa: on genre, 178n32. *See also* genre
Goldman, Emma, 166
Goldman, Judith, 213n17
Goldsmith, Kenneth, 127, 214n22; "The Body of Michael Brown," 156–57; on conceptual writing, 213n18. *See also* conceptual writing/poetry
Gordon, Noah Eli, 175n5
Gorman, Amanda, 211n1
*Grapefruit* (Ono), 15, 23–38, 39–41, 179n41, 180n1, 181n9, 181n15, 182n16, 183n31, 184n35, 184n42; as bilingual, 25, 31, 34–35, 182n16, 184n35, 184n42; and genre, 24–25; 1964 edition, 24–25, 31, 180n1, 182n16; as political text, 28. *See also* Ono, Yoko
Greenberg, Clement, 183n27; on interdisciplinary artwork, 22. *See also* interdisciplinarity
*Gregson v. Gilbert*, 147–48; and abolition, 148. *See also Zong!* (Philip and Boateng)
Guest, Barbara, 71, 73. *See also* New York School
Guillory, John: on memos and formatting, 53–54
Guston, Musa, 78. *See also Locus Solus* (journal)

Hamilton, Diana, 175n5
happenings, 180n7; "Mandatory Happening" (Friedman), 5–6, 45; for Ono, 20, 22, 24. *See also* Friedman, Ken; Ono, Yoko
Harney, Stefano, 163, 215n46
Harren, Natilee: on Brecht's scores, 189n61; on Fluxboxes, 63–64. *See also* Fluxus
Hart-Celler Act, 21. *See also* immigration
Harvey, David, 11
Hayden, Dolores: on "sitcom suburbs," 52
Helal, Marwa: *Invasive Species*, 159
Higgins, Dick: "Danger Music 2," 46; and Fluxus, 45–46, 48–49, 186n16, 187n18, 188n37; and intermedia, 181n9. *See also* Fluxus; Something Else Press

Higgins, Hannah: on Fluxus, 185n4. *See also* Fluxus
Hines, Andy, 183n23
Hong, Christine: on the 1950s and 1960s, 35, 179n37; on racial capitalism, 179n34, 181n11; on racial profiling, 6
Hong, Grace Kyungwon: on difference, 37–37; on racial capitalism, 38, 181n11. *See also* difference; racial capitalism
Housing Act of 1954, 68. *See also* urban renewal
Hughes, Langston, 127
hunger, 11, 14, 35; fasting, 95–96, 101, 107–13, 124; and filibustering, 135–36, 140; food-assistance programs, 12–13, 96, 101–2, 117; "regular," 114; as resistance, 17; *Studying Hunger* (Mayer), 101–2, 113–19. *See also* diet; welfare
Hunter, Walt: on the emergent critical consensus, 211n5

identity: collective (for Fluxus), 45, 47–50; and the feminist body, 112; layers of, 160; national, 77; relational (for the New York School), 72
immigration, 12–15; and assimilation, 21. *See also* assimilation
impossibility: and Ono's work, 27, 32–33, 35. *See also* Ono, Yoko
Insert Press, 130, 132–34. *See also CREDIT* (Timmons)
instructions, 3, 5–6, 10–11, 15–16, 20–38, 54, 69, 93, 111. *See also* Brecht, George; Fluxus; Ono, Yoko; Maciunas, George
interdisciplinarity, 1–11, 16, 22, 49, 167–68, 176n10; and generality, 7–10, 25–26; and politics, 11, 36, 40
interiors, domestic, 55–60, 65; and taste, 56. *See also Tender Buttons* (Stein)
International Style, 85, 87. *See also* architecture
isolation, 20, 22, 24, 107. *See also* Ono, Yoko; Piper, Adrian

Jackson, Kenneth T.: on the privatization of American life, 43. *See also* privatization
Jackson, Shannon: on occupational realism, 12
Jackson, Virginia, 211nn1–2: on Amanda Gorman's 2021 inauguration poem performance, 211n1; on new lyric studies, 211n2
Jacobs, Jane: *The Death and Life of Great American Cities*, 88
Jim Crow, 35, 179n37
Johnson, Barbara: on apostrophe, 138. *See also* apostrophe
Johnson, Philip: and the Seagram Building, 81. *See also* Seagram Building
Jones, Amelia: on body art, 97, 99. *See also* body, the
Jones, LeRoi. *See* Baraka, Amiri
Joseph, Branden: on generic nominalism in Fluxus, 34. *See also* genre; Fluxus

Kaizen, 30–31
Kallman, Chester, 74
Kandinsky, Wassily, 189n61
Kant, Immanuel: *Critique of Pure Reason*, 101, 107–8, 110. *See also Food for the Spirit* (Piper)
Kaprow, Allan, 45, 180n7, 187n18. *See also* happenings; Fluxus
Katznelson, Ira: on race and class around World War II, 190n81
Kellein, Thomas: on Fluxus and unrealizability, 32–33. *See also* Fluxus; impossibility
Kelly, Mary, 97–98; *Post-Partum Document*, 98
Knittle, Davy: on Schuyler's "December," 78. *See also* Schuyler, James; urban renewal
Knowles, Allison: and Fluxus, 45–46, 188n37. *See also* Fluxus
Koch, Kenneth, 13, 71–73, 193n13; and *Locus Solus*, 70. *See also Locus Solus* (journal); New York School
Kosugi, Takehisa, 46. *See also* Fluxus

Kotz, Liz, on *Water Yam*, 52–53. *See also Water Yam* (Brecht)
Kozloff, Max: on Abstract Expressionism, 193n19. *See also* Abstract Expressionism
Kramnick, Jonathan: on form, 176n10
Krauss, Rosalind, 42, 44, 177n26
Kubota, Shigeko, 46, 98. *See also* Fluxus

La Berge, Leigh Claire: on conceptual writing, 156; on decommodification, 12, 158, 207n17; on MFA programs and debt, 154–55, 212n12
labor. *See* work
Lambert, Phyllis, 81: and the Seagram Building, 81–83. *See also* Seagram Building
Larson, Laura: on *Food for the Spirit*, 110; *See also Food for the Spirit* (Piper)
Lax, Robert, 78. *See also Locus Solus* (journal)
lean production, 30
Lebovic, Sam: on the Fulbright, 75
Le Corbusier: and the UN building, 88. *See also* UN building
legibility: and the avant-garde, 28, 43
Lennon, John: and Ono's *Grapefruit*, 182n16. *See also Grapefruit* (Ono)
Leong, Michael, 18; on conceptual writing, 130, 213n19; documental poetry, 127–28, 175n3, 212n7. *See also* documental poetry
Les Figues (press), 214n20
*Let Her Speak* (Counterpath), 13, 15, 129, 135–45, 147, 150; film version, 209n53. *See also* abortion; Counterpath Press
Lewis, Holly: on Davis's filibuster, 207n22. *See also* Davis, Wendy
linguistic turn, 8
Linklater, Tanya Lukin: *Slow Scrape*, 159
Lippard, Lucy, 42, 112
lists, 10, 13–14, 57, 166; and bullets, 13, 53, 59, 63–64, 69; to-do, 16, 69. *See also* Fluxus
Liu, Kenji: *Map of an Onion*, 159–61; *Monsters I Have Been*, 159

*Locus Solus* (journal), 16, 67–68, 70–80, 94, 193n14; as bilingual, 74–76
Lomax, Dana Teen, 133
Long Soldier, Layli: *WHEREAS*, 159–60
Lorde, Audre: on coalition-building in Black communities, 36
loss: and connectivity, 69; of mind/self (for Piper), 107, 111–13, 122–24
Lowe, Lisa, 181n11. *See also* racial capitalism
Luger, Moberley: on conceptual writing. *See also* conceptual writing/poetry
lyric: lay, 90; new lyric studies, 211n2; theory, 18, 151–52, 155; tradition, 70, 182n20, 211nn4–5

MacArthur, Douglas: and labor changes in post-war Japan, 30
Maciunas, George, 5, 29, 32–33, 46–49, 176n12, 184n45, 185n2, 187n18, 188nn37–38; and *Water Yam* (Brecht), 41, 50–51. *See also* Fluxus
Mac Low, Jackson, 48, 187n18. *See also* Fluxus
Magritte, René, 60
mail art, 29, 41, 50. *See also* Fluxus
"Mandatory Happening" (Friedman), 5, 45. *See also* Friedman, Ken
Martin, Meredith: on Amanda Gorman's 2021 inauguration poem performance, 211n1
Marx, Karl, 178n27; *Capital*, 60–61
Mathews, Harry; and *Locus Solus*, 70, 73; and Oulipo, 73. *See also Locus Solus* (journal); Oulipo
Mayer, Bernadette, 10–11, 14, 17, 28, 101, 111, 119; and attention, 113–15, 124; *Memory*, 113–14, 123; *Piece of Cake* (with Warsh), 116–17, 119; *Poetry*, 114; on poetry, 10; *Story*, 114; *Studying Hunger*, 101–2, 113–19, 122; *Studying Hunger Journals*, 115, 119, 123–24; and unwanted pregnancy, 117–19; and *o to 9* (magazine), 110, 114. *See also* Warsh, Lewis
Mayer, Rosemary, 111, 118

McClanahan, Annie: on Timmons's *CREDIT*, 132. *See also CREDIT* (Timmons)
McGurl, Mark, 211n5; on the program era, 133, 155, 163, 167. *See also* academia; MFA programs
Mechanical Turk, 129, 141–42, 144–45, 208n41; and exploitation, 141–42, 208n41. *See also Let Her Speak* (Counterpath)
Medina, Cuauhtémoc, on the discourse of Fluxus, 48. *See also* Fluxus
Melamed, Jodi, 181n11; on "racial liberalism," 79. *See also* racial capitalism
melancholy: queerness and, 78, 87; space, 88–89; violence, 71
Melgard, Holly, 19, 28, 159, 213n17; *Fetal Position*, 159, 164–65. *See also* academia
Mercury Press, 146. *See also Zong!* (Philip and Boateng)
MFA programs, 19, 128, 130, 133–34, 141, 152–55, 158, 163. *See also* debt
Michelangelo Buonarroti, 104–5, 200n32. *See also* sculpture
Mies van der Rohe, Ludwig: and the Seagram Building, 81–83. *See also* Seagram Building
Mittelstadt, Jennifer: on welfare, 120–21. *See also* welfare
Mohammed, Kasey Silem, 175n5
Molesworth, Helen Anne: on feminine/body art, 97–99; on occupational realism, 12
Morse, Carl, 78; "Anchor Demolition: East 82nd Street," 68–69. *See also Locus Solus* (journal)
Moses, Robert, 70, 77. *See also* urban renewal
Moten, Fred, 163, 215n46
multiplicity: of score realization, 32–33, 39–40, 45–46, 54. *See also* Fluxus; Ono, Yoko
Muybridge, Eadweard, 102
Myers, Holly: on *CREDIT*, 134. *See also CREDIT* (Timmons)
Myers, John Bernard, 192n8. *See also* New York School
Myles, Eileen, 192n5. *See also* O'Hara, Frank

Nadasen, Premilla, 121. *See also* welfare
Nakayasu, Sawako, 134. *See also* CREDIT (Timmons)
nationalism: and the Cold War, 70, 75, 83–86, 92. *See also* Seagram Building
Nealon, Christopher: on poetry and capital, 186n7
Nelson, Cary: on the cut up, 191n1
Nelson, Deborah: on Cold War rhetoric, 92
neoliberalism, 11, 14, 31, 36–37, 127; and the body, 11; and the public, 34
Nersessian, Anahid: on form, 176n10
New York School, 13–14, 16, 66–94, 192n5, 192nn7–8, 193n14; and collaboration, 74–76; and friendship, 71–73
Ngai, Sianne: on the administrative aesthetic, 42; on difference and typicality, 61. *See also* administrative aesthetics
Niemeyer, Oscar: and the UN building, 88. *See also* UN building
noise, 87; advocacy against, 89–90
Nowak, Mark: and documentary poetry, 127

Obama, Barack, 160, 207n21
Obayashi, Yuki, 184n42. *See also Grapefruit* (Ono)
obsolescence, 68, 76, 78–79, 82, 86–89. *See also* New York School; temporality
Occupy Movement, 2–3, 83. *See also* protest
O'Dell, Kathy: on performance art, 198n8
offer, credit, 103–33; as obligation, 131, 133. *See also* CREDIT (Timmons)
O'Grady, Lorraine, 98
O'Hara, Frank, 13–14, 16–17, 23–24, 28, 70–73, 195n41, 192n5, 195n41; "Adieu to Norman, Bonjour to Joan and Jean-Paul," 77; "The Day That Lady Died," 72; "From the Memorandums of Angelicus Fobb" (with Berkson), 75–76; "The Lay of the Romance of the Associations," 89–93, 196n64; *Lunch Poems*, 82, 84; and MoMA, 75, 77, 84; "Nocturne," 86–88;

152; "Personal Poem," 84–86; "Walking," 80–94
Ono, Yoko, 11, 13, 15, 20–38, 93, 181n9, 185n47, 187n18; "Blood Piece," 27, 33, 37, 152; and community, 32–34; "Cough Piece," 33; "Cut Piece," 180n2; and difference, 15–16, 20–38; and gender, 24, 37; *Grapefruit*, 15, 23–38, 39–41, 179n41, 180n1, 181n9, 182n16, 183n31, 184n35, 184n42; "Laugh Piece," 33; "Lighting Piece," 25, 44; *Paintings and Drawings* (exhibition), 32, 183n31; "Painting to Be Stepped on," 32; "Painting Until It Becomes Marble," 184n35; on poetry, 10; "Secret Piece," 25; "Smoke Painting," 32; "Stomach Piece," 184n35; "Supply Goods Store Piece," 35–37; "Touch Poem VI," 38; "Tunafish Sandwich Piece," 35, 37
open works, 52–53
optical character recognition (OCR), 129, 134. *See also* CREDIT (Timmons)
ordinariness, 55–56, 61, 65
Osman, Jena, 127, 212n9; *Public Figures*, 2–3, 5–6
Oulipo, 73, 98–100, 106, 123, 199n17, 205n122; N+7 procedure, 98. *See also* constraint

Padgett, Ron, 192n8. *See also* New York School
Page, Robin, 46. *See also* Fluxus
Paik, Nam June, 48–49, 187n18, 188n37. *See also* Fluxus
paronomasia, 27, 57, 64, 90
Patterson, Ben, 46, 50. *See also* Fluxus
Perec, George: *La Vie mode d'emploi*, 205n122. *See also* Oulipo
Perloff, Marjorie, 191n91, 195n41. *See also* O'Hara, Frank; Stein, Gertrude
Perlow, Seth: on experimental writing, 156
Perrault, John: "Paris," 76–77. *See also Locus Solus* (journal)
Perry, Rick: and Senate Bill 5 (SB5), 136. *See also Let Her Speak* (Counterpath)

Philip, M. NourbeSe, 15, 28, 145; on poetry, 10; on unauthorized translations of *Zong!*, 210n58; *Zong!*, 18, 128–30, 146–50, 210n58, 210n62, 210n69

Phillips, Rodney: on *Locus Solus*, 193n13. See also *Locus Solus* (journal)

pink: -collar logic, 16, 69; feet, 68; granite, 85; running shoes, 136; shadows, 87

Piper, Adrian, 11, 14, 17, 23–24, 28, 119, 202nn58–59; *Catalysis* series, 111–12; *Food for the Spirit*, 101–2, 107–13, 122–24, 201nn40–41, 201n45, 201nn47–48, 202n58, 202n72, 205n120; on Kant, 201n53; retirement from being Black, 113, 199n24, 202n73; "The Triple Negation of Colored Women Artists," 110

Place, Vanessa, 127, 133–34, 207n14; on poetry and money, 207n17. See also conceptual writing/poetry

plagiarism: and documental poetry, 126. See also appropriation; documental poetry

poetry: and abstraction, 12; as capacious/voracious, 4, 9, 13; and capital, 186n7; conceptual, 14, 127, 130, 133–34, 153, 156–57, 205n4, 206n8, 213nn18–19, 214n22, 214n26; as currency, 133, 207n16; documental, 2, 14, 17–19, 126–50, 152–59, 165, 175n3, 205n4, 206n8, 212n7; in general, 2, 10, 23–29, 70, 82, 95, 101, 124–25, 151; intermedial, 15, 22; and money, 207n17; nonrepresentational, 64; occasional/personal, 72, 192n5; and overhearing, 26, 182n20; participatory, 82, 94; procedural, 14, 95–125; and publicness, 3; and resistance, 14–15; and solitude, 151

prepositions, enigmatic, 62–64, 191n91

preservationism, 88–92

privatization, 3–4, 6–7, 12–14; of American life, 43; of architectural spaces, 12–14, 70, 81–83, 195nn43–44; of education, 13; and gender, 14; of interpretation, 126–50; and poetry, 3, 18, 128

procedural poetry, 14, 95–125

procedural reading, 28, 33

prosopopoeia, 61

protest: and Mechanical Turk, 141; Occupy Movement, 2–3, 83; Standing Rock, 1; student, 2. See also *Carving: A Traditional Sculpture* (Antin); Davis, Wendy; *Let Her Speak* (Counterpath); Mechanical Turk

public good: abortion and the, 13; neoliberalism vs. the, 34; poetry and the, 18

purity: and the body, 125; *Critique of Pure Reason*, 101, 107–8, 10; pure media, 15, 22, 27, 36, 38; and use value, 155, 167

queerness: and architecture, 82, 92–93; and melancholy, 78, 87; and the New York School / *Locus Solus*, 71, 75–76. See also *Locus Solus* (journal); New York School

racial capitalism, 11–13, 15–16, 35, 37–38, 40, 43, 71, 129, 179n34, 181n11

racial liberalism, 79

Rankine, Claudia, 212n9; *Citizen: An American Lyric*, 159, 211n4, 214n29; *Just Us: An American Conversation*, 159

reading: and action/participation, 33, 52–55, 62, 65, 70; affective, 214n26; close, 199n20; ethical, 157; as "event," 5; and event scores, 39, 45, 69; as expansive process, 28; good, 26, 182n22; imperative, 41; modernist, 26, 28; and Ono's work, 22–23, 26–29; vs. performance, 16; procedural, 28, 33; and public/private, 26; and resistance, 15; surface, 157; and teleiopoesis, 142

Red Purge, 184n32

reflection: and the city, 81; of the eyes, 87; and sense of self, 107, 124

repair, 19, 149, 157. See also *Zong!* (Philip and Boateng)

repetition: of architectural style, 87; and labor, 55; in *Tender Buttons* (Stein), 55

resistance: to assimilation, 31; to colonialism, 56; to commodification, 33; constraint/

hunger as, 17; to efficiency, 34; to ordinality, 31, 52; reading and, 15; to self-promotion, 48, 188n37
Reverdy, Pierre, 77
Rhee, Jieun: on Ono, 180n2. *See also* Ono, Yoko
Roberts, Tim: and Counterpath's *Let Her Speak*, 136–37. *See also Let Her Speak* (Counterpath)
Robinson, Julia, 187n20, 190n77. *See also* Brecht, George
*Roe v. Wade*, 13, 101, 119–20, 162, 207n22. *See also* abortion
Ronda, Margaret: on abortion as a poetic figure, 142–43. *See also* abortion
Roussel, Raymond, 73
Rubinfine, David: and Meyer's *Studying Hunger*, 114–15, 117. *See also Studying Hunger* (Mayer)
Rukeyser, Muriel, 127
Russell, Bertrand, 85

satisfaction, 6, 48, 50, 103–4
Schmit, Tomas, 49. *See also* Fluxus
Schneemann, Carolee, 48. *See also* Fluxus
Schneider, Gary: and *Food for the Spirit*, 201n47. *See also Food for the Spirit* (Piper)
Schuster, Joshua: on Stein's *Tender Buttons*, 58–59. *See also Tender Buttons* (Stein)
Schuyler, James: "December," 67–69, 78; and *Locus Solus*, 70; on *Locus Solus*, 74; and the New York School, 71, 73–74. *See also Locus Solus* (journal)
Scott, Felicity: on the on the Seagram Building, 85. *See also* Seagram Building
sculpture, 102–5. *See also Carving: A Traditional Sculpture* (Antin)
Seagram Building, 17, 80–94. *See also* O'Hara, Frank
Sealy, Nicole: *The Ferguson Report: An Erasure*, 159–60
self: -effacement, 32; -expression, 155; knowledge, 111; loss of, 107, 111–13;

122–24; -promotion, 48; -publishing, 29; -sufficiency, 76; -violation, 112
Shannon, Joshua: on urban renewal, 78. *See also* urban renewal
Shapiro, David, 192n8. *See also* New York School
Sharif, Solmaz, 163; *LOOK*, 159–60
shaving: armpit hair (in Perrault's "Paris"), 76; heads (in Higgins's "Danger Music 2"), 46
Shaw, Lytle: on O'Hara's "Adieu," 77. *See also* O'Hara, Frank
Sherman, Cindy, 98
Shiomi, Mieko, 46, 185n4. *See also* Fluxus
*Shout Your Abortion* (PM Press), 137–38. *See also* abortion
Sinykin, Dan, 211n5
Situationist International, 183n27
slenderizing, 100, 105–6. *See also Carving: A Traditional Sculpture* (Antin); diet
Smith, Cherise: on Antin's *Carving*, 104–5. *See also Carving: A Traditional Sculpture* (Antin)
Smith, Owen: on Fluxus, 49, 185n3. *See also* Fluxus
Social Security Act, 120. *See also* welfare
Something Else Press, 29, 176n11, 186n16, 188n37. *See also* Higgins, Dick
Sorrentino, Gilbert, 99
Spahr, Juliana: on Cold War cultural fields, 75; on foulipo, 100; on MFA programs, 207n15; on Stein's description of household objects, 56. *See also* foulipo; ordinariness; Stein, Gertrude
Spivak, Gayatri Chakravorty, 177n23; on teleiopoesis, 142–43; on Western abstraction, 8. *See also* abstraction
Standing Rock, 1. *See also* protest
Stefans, Brian Kim, 133
Stein, Gertrude, 191n91; *Tender Buttons*, 43–44, 54–66, 186n14, 186n16
Stephens, Paul: on experimental writing, 156
Stockhausen, Karlheinz, 187n18

*Studying Hunger* (Mayer), 101–2, 113–19, 122. See also Mayer, Bernadette
Stuelke, Patricia: on the turn to affect in the humanities, 157
Sturm, Nick, 192n5
suburbanization, 12–13, 16, 40, 43, 52, 56, 58, 69, 78, 93
"Supply Goods Store Piece" (Ono), 35–37. See also Ono, Yoko
surveillance, 3; and documentary poetry, 126; and welfare, 102, 117–18, 120–21. See also documentary poetry; welfare

tables, 55–62; dancing, 61, 66, 191n86; as event, 61. See also *Tender Buttons* (Stein)
teleiopoesis, 142–43
temporality: durational artwork, 22, 24–25, 27, 33, 35, 44, 95–125, 184n35; and Kant's *Critique*, 110; one's own "now," 6, 45, 54; and poetry, 14, 78; "scrape of time" (Linklater), 159; "Two Clocks" (Brecht), 64–65
*Tender Buttons* (Stein), 43–44, 54–66, 186n14, 186n16. See also Stein, Gertrude
*Things Fall Apart* (Achebe): and yam festivals, 50. See also yams
Timmons, Mathew, 28; *CREDIT*, 15, 18, 23–24, 129–35, 147–48, 150, 165
Tokyo Olympics (1964), 29–30
Troll Thread, 134, 207n16. See also conceptual writing/poetry
Tucker-Abramson, Myka: on containment and Cold War ideology, 93; on urban renewal in NYC, 79. See also urban renewal

Ukeles, Mierle Laderman, 97–98, 100; "I Make Maintenance Art One Hour Every Day," 98
UN building, 87–88
Uncle Sam, 5–6
university, 215n46; state disinvestment in, 2. See also academia

unwanted pregnancy: and Antin, 105, 119, 200n34; and Mayer, 117–19. See also abortion; contraception; Antin, Eleanor; Mayer, Bernadette
urban planning, 68–69, 72, 81–82, 89, 91. See also displacement
urban renewal, 11–13, 68–70, 77–81, 89; Housing Act of 1954, 68; and the UN building, 88

Van de Putte, Leticia, 144. See also *Let Her Speak* (Counterpath)
violence: global, 6; homophobic, 76; melancholy, 71; in New York City, 77, 91–92; state, 2, 6, 27, 44, 129
Vostell, Wolf: and Fluxus, 46, 49. See also Fluxus

Wages Against Housework (campaign), 104, 121
"Walking" (O'Hara), 80–94. See also O'Hara, Frank
Warner, Michael: on "criminal intimacy," 92
Warsh, Lewis, 116–20; *Piece of Cake*, 116–17, 119; and the welfare system, 118, 120. See also Mayer, Bernadette; welfare
water, city, 92–93
*Water Yam* (Brecht), 16, 41–44, 50–66, 186n14; and participation, 52–55, 62. See also Brecht, George; Fluxus; yams
Watts, Robert, 45–46; and the Yam Festival, 49–50. See also Fluxus
Weeks, Kathi: on "public" categories like work, 4
Weingart, Paul, 50. See also Watts, Robert; yams
welfare, 6–8, 11–15, 17, 95–96, 101–2, 197n1; Aid to Families with Dependent Children, 120–21; criminalization of, 11–12, 122; crisis in, 13, 120; National Welfare Rights Organization, 121; Social Security Act, 120; as stigmatized, 96; and surveillance, 102, 117–18, 120–21

Wheatley, Phillis, 146
white flight, 12. *See also* suburbanization
whiteness, 61; and body art, 97; of chairs, 56–58; of the city's will, 67, 69, 71, 80; and Greek/Renaissance art, 104; as social construction, 58; of stools, 62; of tables, 60, 66; of teeth, 76; as wrong, 65
white supremacy, 8, 43, 78–79, 145, 150; and bureaucracy, 145
Whyte, William H.: on the Seagram Plaza, 83. *See also* Seagram Building
Wilke, Hannah, 98
Williams, Emmett, 48, 187n18. *See also* Fluxus
*Womanhouse*, "Leah's Room," 98. *See also* beauty
women's liberation movement, 96, 101, 110–11, 121–22
"Word Event" (Brecht), 39–40. *See also* Brecht, George
word of mouth: and Ono's work, 32–33. *See also* Ono, Yoko
work, 4; and art, 12–13, 15; change of labor practices, 23, 26, 30–31, 38, 43, 56; and generality, 26; gig, 8, 13, 165; and infrastructure, 52; and poetry, 7; white-collar, 8, 12, 16, 39, 41, 43, 48–49, 52, 56, 69, 84; Works Progress Administration (WPA), 127
Wunternam (press), 29. *See also Grapefruit* (Ono)

yams, 49–50, 189n45. *See also Water Yam* (Brecht)
Young, La Monte, 47, 187n18; *An Anthology of Change Operations*, 184n45
Young, Stephanie: on foulipo, 100; on MFA programs, 207n15, 215n46; on poetry and publicness, 3; on poets in the Bay Area in 2011, 158, 163. *See also* foulipo; MFA programs

*0 to 9* (magazine), 110, 114. *See also* Acconci, Vito; Mayer, Bernadette; Piper, Adrian
Zipp, Samuel: on NYC during the Cold War, 77–78, 80; on the UN building, 88. *See also* Cold War
*Zong!* (Philip and Boateng), 18, 128–30, 146–50, 210n58, 210n62, 210n69; unauthorized translations of, 210n58
zoning: and the Fifth Avenue Association, 196n65; incentive, 82–83, 195n43; and race, 6. *See also* architecture

GPSR Authorized Representative: Easy Access System Europe, Mustamäe tee 50, 10621 Tallinn, Estonia, gpsr.requests@easproject.com

www.ingramcontent.com/pod-product-compliance
Lightning Source LLC
Chambersburg PA
CBHW022047290426
44109CB00014B/1009